LANGUAGE AND LITER W9-ACH-752

Dorothy S. Strickland and Celia Genishi
EDITORS

The Complete Theory-to-Practice
Handbook of Adult Literacy:
Curriculum Design and Teaching Approaches

*Rena Soifer, Martha E. Irwin, Barbara M. Crumrine, Emo Honzaki,
Blair K. Simmons, and Deborah L. Young*

Literacy for a Diverse Society:
Perspectives, Practices, and Policies

Elfrieda H. Hiebert (Editor)

The Child's Developing Sense of Theme:
Responses to Literature

Susan S. Lehr

The Child's Developing Sense of Theme

Responses to Literature

Susan S. Lehr

Teachers College, Columbia University
New York and London

To my children —
Kristin and Matthew

Published by Teachers College Press, 1234 Amsterdam Avenue
New York, NY 10027

Library of Congress Cataloging-in-Publication Data

Lehr, Susan S.
    The child's developing sense of theme : responses to literature /
Susan S. Lehr.
        p.   cm. — (Language and literacy series ; #3)
    Includes bibliographical references and index.
    ISBN 0-8077-3106-4 (cloth : alk. paper). — ISBN 0-8077-3105-6
(alk. paper)
    1. Reading (Preschool) — United States — Language experience
approach.   2. Reading (Elementary) — United States — Language
experience approach.   3. Children — United States — Books and reading.
I. Title.   II. Series: Language and literacy series (New York, N.Y.)
; v. 3.
LB1181.33.L44   1991   91-30121
372.4′1 — dc20   CIP

Printed on acid-free paper

Manufactured in the United States of America

98 97 96 95 94 93 92 91   8 7 6 5 4 3 2 1

Contents

Foreword   vii

Introduction   ix

1. CHILDREN AND THE CONSTRUCTION OF MEANING   **1**

What Is Theme?   2

What Is a Child's Concept of Story?   5

A Constructivist View of Reading   10

The Building Blocks of Meaning   16

How Children Use the Structure of Stories to Build Meaning   20

2. THEME: THE CHILD'S PERSPECTIVE   **32**

A Child's Exposure to Literature   34

Design of the First Study   36

Identifying and Generating Themes in a Literature Setting   43

Characteristics of a Child's Developing Sense of Theme   46

Children's Responses to Realistic Fiction and Folktales   54

Comments   67

Implications   69

3. A PRESCHOOL CHILD'S DEVELOPING SENSE OF THEME   **70**

Design of the Second Study   71

Preschool Attitudes Toward Books and Reading   75

Early Development of Theme: A Study of One Child's Response   78

Can Four-Year-Old Children Identify Themes?   89

Comments   91

4. ILLUSTRATIONS, DRAWING, AND WRITING: THE LINK BETWEEN ART AND LANGUAGE   **93**

Importance of the Reading Context to Children's Responses   95

Constructing Meaning by Drawing and Writing   97

**5. CLASSROOM PROFILES: EXPLORING THEMES IN THE
     CLASSROOM   133**
    Encouraging Active Thinkers and Lifelong Readers   134
    Classroom Profile: *Thunder Cake*   135
    Book Discussions and Comparison Charts   138
    Classroom Profile: *The Three Little Pigs*   139
    Classroom Profile: *The Fisherman and His Wife*   146
    Classroom Profile: *Rapunzel*   149
    Asking the Right Questions   153
    Classroom Profile: *My Friend Jacob*   154
    Classroom Profile: *How Much Is a Million?*   157
    Classroom Profile: *The Whipping Boy*   159
    Classroom Profile: Response Journals   161
    Conclusion   164

Appendix A: Folktales for Comparison Charts   169
Appendix B: Response Guides   173
References   185
Children's Literature Bibliography   193
Index   197
About the Author   204

Foreword

Adults frequently choose books for children because the story seems to carry a particular message — be yourself, be wary of strangers, save the earth, plan ahead. Yet when we talk about that story with children, and especially with young children, we often find that the message they want to talk about is not the one for which the story was chosen. Are they not listening attentively? Are they not good readers? Are they just too young to understand?

Susan Lehr says no on all counts. Her research on sense of theme with children across age levels indicates that children have good reason for constructing meanings that are different from adults. She cautions that adults must listen carefully to understand how children use language to express their view of the world and of stories. "I am no longer looking for my adult answer," she says, "my adult point of view. . . . I am giving credence to the child's verbalization." As her insightful commentary shows, she is very good at listening between the lines.

This book is welcome on my shelf for many reasons. The research on which it is based ventures into territory that has not been well explored. Although we have heard a great deal about children as makers of meaning, we have not heard much about what meanings they make. Lehr's analysis helps to fill that gap. The role of various aspects of development in children's response is an area that has already received research attention; but this work, in looking at the intersection of age, story selection, and familiarity with literature, provides a new perspective on what children *can* do. In particular, Lehr's discussions of story themes with four-year-olds are a contribution to our understanding of how children begin to formulate meaning in the larger sense. Finally, at a time when visual literacy is so important but so widely ignored, it is gratifying to see the inclusion of a chapter that deals with illustration as part of the reading context and children's art as a form of response.

"It is not sufficient," the author says, "to conduct research and leave it for others to decipher." This is a book that speaks to practitioners as well as to scholars. A chapter on "Classroom Profiles" provides rich detail on the exploration of particular themes in real teaching situations. Appendices also provide suggestions for classroom practice in both primary and middle grades.

The tone of the writing is consistently engaging, sometimes conversational. The most memorable voices, however, are those of children. Their words are quoted, repeated, and examined in new ways. The end result is that we can begin to listen with real attention to what children say about stories, and to hear what they mean.

Janet Hickman
The Ohio State University

Introduction

Can children talk about themes in books? Are children viable meaning makers when they encounter print? Very few studies have shown that children as young as 5 are capable of responding to themes in books. Studies of themes in literature are generally done at the junior high and high school levels.

Basal readers and accompanying workbooks in the elementary classroom have traditionally stressed finding the main idea of short paragraphs or phrases in an attempt to simplify the process and lead children toward meaning building at concrete levels, or they have included comprehension questions that are literal. Inference questions and even those that are interpretative usually have answers that suggest a static view of the text.

Yet parents of 5-year-old children or even of 3-year-old children accustomed to hearing stories read aloud will often say, "Of course my child understands the story. Of course my child talks about what the story means." At least this has been my experience with parents and teachers around the country at conferences and workshops. They are sometimes appalled that researchers and proponents of child development would suggest otherwise. The same parents and teachers know the level of thinking of which their young children are capable, and many believe that the elementary school should challenge them further and take their critical thinking seriously.

This book is based upon my own experiences teaching in the classroom, my own research working with young children, and my own experiences as a parent. As a parent, educator, and researcher, I agree with the many parents and teachers I have met who suggest that youngsters are prolific meaning builders. Linguists write about the amazing ability of young children to learn language. Children are indeed "meaning makers," as Gordon Wells (1986) has so aptly put it. They do not learn language in a vacuum, void of critical thinking. It would be presumptuous of us as adults to assume that children do not understand the stories that they read or hear at young ages simply because their perspectives of meaning may be different from ours. Yet researchers and child psychologists have done exactly that. Piaget (1926/1960) has suggested that the child below the age of 7 or 8 is incapable of developing critical thought. Building on his work, Applebee (1978) has suggested that the critical responses of children to stories do not reach analytical levels of thought before a child is 12. The ability to generalize information gleaned from stories is the last hurdle to be jumped and does not occur until the age of 16.

In research with preschool and elementary age students, I have found that children are busy exploring theme with narratives. Individually and in groups children do talk about what they know, think, and perceive in the books they hear and read. Children offer their views and their responses to what they hear. In my work with children, I have learned to listen as children explain what they mean, what they think or feel about a particular story, a particular character, or the actions of a character. Given time to think, time to speak, and open-ended questions about the text, many children will offer their views of meaning in narrative. Listening is a key factor in this process. Children need time to formulate their thoughts, and they need the freedom to speak openly without fear of being labeled wrong.

This was driven home when several fourth-grade boys in one of my studies kept pestering me with the questions: "Was I right? Did I get it right? Was that the right answer?" This preoccupation with being right, that is, matching the teacher's notion of correct, or a published answer key's notion of correct, is a constricting and learned behavior. I did not find this attitude as prevalent among younger students.

We as educators must take part of the blame for teaching children not to think on their own. It is in large part because of our programming that children like the fourth-grade boys mentioned above view learning as a process of identifying the right answer. Filling in the blanks throughout elementary school nurtures the view of learning as a finite process that is rote in nature and at the lowest levels of Bloom's taxonomy, the recitation of facts. Critical-thinking skills are more complex than that simplistic view toward learning, and at the same time a child's developing sense of theme is based on the ability to think in abstract terms. Children who are expected to be risk takers will offer their constructs of meaning without fear of being wrong. Being wrong won't matter, if children are expected to support their views with clear, logical thinking.

I have also learned in my research and experience with learners that children interactively construct meaning with others, so that oral discussion is a critical piece in developing a sense of theme. Furthermore, providing books of a high quality is essential in this process. In a study of the responses of third-grade children to nonfiction and fiction, I found that those listening to well-written picture books were able to talk about meaning in the stories as they related the events in the lives of characters to the events of their own lives. They also constructed thematic meaning in relation to what others had to say about the book. The interactive nature of reading books is powerful, as Hepler (1982) found in her study with sixth graders.

In this book I discuss the child's sense of theme in relation to critical thinking, the use of well-written literature, and the reading process. Specifically, the child's concept of story is discussed at length as it relates to comprehension. Understanding how readers read is critical in building an understanding of how children develop a sense of theme. The child's perspective of meaning is the central focus of my research with children, and I discuss at length what children have to say in response to books shared both individually and in group sessions.

In the last chapter I discuss practical classroom application. It is not sufficient to conduct research and leave it for others to decipher. Research that exists without practical application is of little value to the classroom teacher; therefore, the final chapter moves from theory toward practice.

1

Children and the Construction of Meaning

The story of *The Three Bears* is familiar to most teachers and children and is about a young girl who enters the home of the three bears without permission. While inside she literally tears their home apart with her thoughtlessness and has the gall to fall asleep after her efforts.

This brief synopsis of a common fairy tale is considered a summary of the story. At a literal level it can be viewed as a rendering of the story's main idea in concrete terms with elements of the plot interspersed throughout. You'll notice that my interpretation of this common fairy tale is not static. I have deliberately chosen words that reflect my own personal view of the story. Although this summary matches the literal content of the text, my remarks contain elements that involve a transaction between the reader and the text, in effect, a highly personalized account.

I have labeled Goldilocks as thoughtless. Culturally we do not think of curly-headed little girls as breaking into a home and wreaking havoc. The original form of this story, credited to a handwritten version by Eleanor Mure in 1831, had a wicked old woman visiting the three bears (Huck, Hepler, & Hickman, 1987). One could more easily credit this wicked old woman with attributes of thoughtlessness and gall, given our cultural framework and the fairy tales of wicked witches in which we are immersed from our youngest years. One can clearly see the meaning that I, the reader, bring to the text and the background knowledge I possess that impacts on what I have to say about the story. Does knowing the origins of this story affect the meaning I construct? Does that knowledge make me a harsher critic of Goldilocks than is perhaps warranted?

1

Is my reaction to the destruction of the bears' property culturally derived?

WHAT IS THEME?

Meaning building is a complex process. My notion of how to interpret this fairy tale began long ago when I first heard it as a 3-year-old child. How many times did I hear this story? Who were the tellers? Did they use a book? Did they speak from memory? How did they react to the acts of Goldilocks? Did a parent talk about the inappropriateness of entering another's home without permission?

As a young child I learned how to listen, how to respond, whether it would be appropriate or acceptable to side with Goldilocks or the smallest of the three bears. What code of ethics was I seeing and hearing about as a young child? Did someone admonish Goldilocks for her acts during the reading or telling? Were the bears applauded or chastised? Values are conveyed as children listen to the stories of their culture. Readers interpret while children learn at tacit levels.

At what point did I own my first version of this story in a book form? At what point did I first tell this story? How many times have I read this story to my own children? or to children in the first-grade classroom? or to preschool children? How many times have I referred to this story in the course of my lifetime?

From a thematic viewpoint *The Three Bears* can be characterized as a story about the perils of disobedience or the complete lack of regard in which some hold the property of others. These statements of theme do not include specific elements of plot and are more abstract in nature than the summary or main idea statement above. Different interpretations are possible, but couched in abstract terms they become thematic statements about the story. Thus the word *theme* in this sense is used to identify a statement about the story that steps back from the literal interpretation; however, even a plot summary contains thematic elements, words that suggest a particular stance toward meaning, toward the structuring of text.

The concept of theme is that of an abstraction that can link stories and ideas in general terms. Therefore, *The Three Bears* can be related to other stories that share the same central idea without including specific elements of plot. The term *theme* has been identified by Lukens (1982) in the following manner. "Theme in literature is the idea that holds the story together, such as a comment about either society, human nature, or the human condition. It is the main idea or central meaning of a piece of writing" (p. 101). In this case *main idea* and *central meaning* are used synonymously. However, Huck, Hepler, & Hickman (1987) write that "the theme of a book reveals the author's purpose in writing the story," and that "most well written books may be read for several layers of meaning—plot, theme or metaphor. . . . Theme provides a dimension to the story that goes beyond the action of the plot" (p. 8). Lukens (1982) suggests that when we ask of a story, "What does it all mean?" we begin to touch on the central core of theme.

Meaning is not achieved in a vacuum, nor does it magically appear one day. Understanding text is an ongoing process. The manner in which I talk about *The Three Bears* now is based on a lifetime of experience with this and other narratives, so those early encounters are perhaps crucial in forming a sense of theme. Narratives become a part of us. We hear stories from our earliest moments as young children. Hardy (1977) suggests that narrative is a primary act of the mind. We "story." We listen to stories. We tell stories. We do not outgrow story telling. She suggests that narrative is a basic way of organizing human experience.

Children listen to stories from their youngest moments. A father tells his wife about the difficulties he encountered running from the office to the market to the baby-sitter's. This is narrative. Our children are immersed in stories from birth. Although the 2-year-old Piagetian child is egocentric and bases his or her thinking on direct experience and the immediate, this child is nonetheless building narrative links between what is heard, what is seen, and what is perceived, what was, what is, and what will be, and the child takes a stance toward narrative.

Narrative in all of its varied forms is necessarily a part of this assimilation. Certain oral cultures value story telling and encourage children first learning to speak to become storytellers (Heath, 1983). In fact, the children in these cultures are rewarded intrinsically and extrinsically for how well they tell stories, young male storytellers more so than young female storytellers.

So we must view the child as a meaning maker with narrative as an important function of language, because the process of learning language cannot be separated from the stories that children hear and are learning to tell. And when that 3-year-old hears her father telling about his hectic day and responds with, "Daddy had a bad day and is sleepy," hasn't that child begun to develop a sense of theme? Isn't that statement, in effect, a tidy summary of the narrative that the child just heard, and doesn't it contain thematic elements?

When we read books we may, over time, forget the details of plot, but what often remains firmly fixed in mind is the notion of theme.

"Oh, that book was about a boy who escaped from his village so that he could be free from these giants that were controlling the minds of his people." A plot summary to be sure, but also a bit more. The thread of the science fiction novel is here; the central meaning that Christopher intended to impart to his readers in *The White Mountains* is still fixed in the mind of this child. Mind control, freedom, and escape. Themes can remain firmly rooted in our minds long after the details of a story are forgotten.

Schema theory suggests that we link broad concepts and store information hierarchically in our brains, but that storage and retrieval system is highly selective and is unique to each individual. Personal experiences, value systems, and background information, all impact on how one reads, interprets, and remembers textual information. In reference to *The White Mountains*, one may remember different facets of the text and cue in on a different thematic interpretation. The book was characterized by an adult as being about a rebel group in the mountains who seeks young boys and girls with spirit enough to say no to the tripods and leave their homes permanently to fight against tyranny. You can see the overlap of ideas, and at the same time you can see the distinct differences in the two interpretations. What is important to one reader is not mentioned by another. This suggests a view of meaning that is fluid. Identifying themes or important ideas is not a finite task.

Each reader brings meaning to the act of reading. This meaning includes certain biases. Notice that the second interpretation of *The White Mountains* includes males and females. The futuristic book, however, is about males who escape from the tripods. Were females indeed encouraged to join the rebels, or did this reader merely bring a particular bias to his or her reading? Meaning building is a selective process. We remember what is important to us and we see, in a sense, what we want to see or what we are capable of seeing. This latitude in accepting the reader's thematic response is critical in understanding how young readers interpret what they read. The result is a transaction that occurs between the reader and text within a context. This transaction, according to Rosenblatt (1938/1976), focuses upon the generative role of the reader. She views the reading act as an interaction between the text, which is an encoding of the author's intended meaning, and the reader, who brings his or her own interpretation to the experience.

Spiro (1977) found that when there is an apparent conflict between text and a reader's understanding of that text, the reader will make the text meaningful by adding information if necessary. This suggests that reading is an active process (Blachowicz, 1977) where the reader constructs meaning that coincides with his or her personal knowledge base.

In other words, regardless of the author's intentions, a reader will bring personal meaning to the text, especially when the meaning in the text is not clear or does not mesh with his or her understanding of the world. The adult responding to *The White Mountains* brought a nonsexist view into her interpretation, suggesting her value system rather than an accurate rendering of the all male cast of characters. Readers do this constantly.

In my work with second-grade children (Lehr, 1988a) I found that reading a nontraditional folktale where the princess did not live happily ever after caused some children to alter the events of the story during the retelling to mesh with their notion of a traditional fairy tale with a happy ending. In an illustration at the end of Zwerger's retelling of *The Swineherd*, the princess is shown sitting alone and crying, and the text supports this ending. Nonetheless, three children said that the princess lived happily ever after at the end of the story. Why? Should I conclude that they did not listen as I read the story or did not see the illustration? Not necessarily. Another plausible answer is that the children were familiar with a particular story pattern for fairy tales—not many end in this manner—and that the children instantiated a familiar frame when later asked about the ending of the story. The ending they chose was more satisfying and meshed with their picture of a princess living happily ever after.

Memory is selective. One remembers what one expects to remember and integrates what one knows with what is presented. If this is the case, how is it that the child builds a concept of story? And if these three second-grade children were attending as I read this fairy tale and still changed the ending completely, what is the process of developing a sense of story? Does this negate an author's intentions? If the reader actively constructs meaning, am I saying that the text must take a back seat? A consideration of the child's sense of story and its relation to the child's sense of theme will be helpful in exploring the reader's construction of meaning with regard to the text.

WHAT IS A CHILD'S CONCEPT OF STORY?

Developmentally the child moves from responding with concrete answers, up a scale of abstraction, toward an ability to make generalizations about the stories he or she hears. This process has not generally been taken into consideration in measuring children's thematic responses. Applebee's (1973) groundbreaking work describing the preschool child's sense of story suggests that the young child has difficulty generating a story framework with a clear thematic focal point, or center. Authoring a story with a theme or moral or identifying the theme of a story is the last of the stages that Applebee identifies. He parallels this to Vygotsky's notion of "true concept" (Applebee, 1978), and the example he cites is that of a child aged 5 years 8 months. The implication is that the younger child has great difficulty generating such a narrative, and that a child's narratives prior to this stage of development lack true theme.

The notion that a child's "earliest interpretation seems to be that a story is something that happened in the past, a history rather than a fictional construct" (Applebee, 1973, p. 116) leads one to question how the young child represents story in memory and whether a child can actually pull out meaning before he or she is able to ascertain fact from fiction. White's (1954) diary of her daughter supplies no evidence that a child questions the truth of a story before the age of 4. How then do young children represent story in memory, and what meanings do they attach to the varied forms of literature to which they are exposed? As the child matures, how does this representation of meaning alter? That the child actively constructs meaning in early experiences with stories demonstrates that the process is more than just a function of memory (Cochran-Smith, 1984; Paley, 1981; Paris, 1975). A child may remember the details of a story and may even be able to retell it in a sequential fashion, but can the young child define the overarching concept of meaning that fluent readers construct?

Vygotsky (1978) argued, on the basis of his experiments with young children, that before children form concepts they use pseudoconcepts, which on the surface are similar to concepts but are actually based on perceptions. Blocks of one color may be grouped together not because the child can abstract the concept of red or yellow, but because the child concretely perceives that the blocks comprise a set. As Baumann (1981) and Baker and Stein (1981) have suggested, the child may be unable to generate theme or a main idea—or, as in this case, the concept that blocks belong together because they occupy the same color set—but he or she may well be able to identify the concept or idea.

In research with 4-year-old children (Lehr, 1990), I found this to be the case. Although the children did not specifically state the theme of *Titch* by Pat Hutchins, they were able to identify statements of theme applicable to the book when they heard them. This suggests that the 4-year-old children in this particular study understood the overarching meaning in the story and could identify it but were merely unable to put it into words themselves.

When Applebee (1978) asked children to discuss a story they knew at some length, he found that the typical response from 50% of the 6-year-olds was a retelling of the story, complete with title, formal opening and closing lines, and dialogue. Twenty-seven percent of the 6-year-old children interviewed would not respond to the question because they were worried that they might answer incorrectly. He concluded that 6-year-old children do not typically summarize stories but rather represent the story concretely "with little or no reorganization of events into superordinate categories" (p. 93).

This type of response coincides with Piaget's (1926/1960) preoperational stage of development (2 to 7 years of age) and Flavell's (1963) notion of "an isomorphic step-by-step mental replica of concrete actions and events" (p. 158). Children of this age typically focus on action when recalling a story (Stein & Glenn, 1978). Applebee (1978) argues, on the basis of children's own oral stories, that there is "little or no reorganization of events into superordinate categories or more general schematizations; the child has great difficulty in integrating individual elements from the story into any sort of general framework" (p. 93). He states that it is not until concrete operational stages (7 to 11 years of age) that the child can form symbolic representations that involve hierarchies of categories and subcategories. He also found that preadolescent children were unable to verbalize themes for familiar stories, common sayings, and fables. Since he did not read the stories to the children, but relied on their knowledge of the stories, it is difficult to argue that they were unable to verbalize themes.

When I specifically asked kindergarten children in individual interviews to retell the story of *The Carrot Seed* or *Titch* several days after I read it aloud to a small group of children, I received this type of response from 5-year-old children:

He put a seed in and the mother and dad said it wouldn't grow and the brother and sister said it wouldn't grow and it turned into a big carrot and it did grow. (Peter, age 5:8, *The Carrot Seed*)

A boy planted a plant and his mother and dad said, "It won't grow. It won't grow." But he thought it would and he was right. So . . . so he ate it all. The end. (Katie, age 5:5, *The Carrot Seed*)

It was about a little boy that always did little things, that only got little things. And his brother and sister got big things, but when they grew the plant, he got the biggest and they got the littlest thing. (Mary, age 5:6, *Titch*)

> Ever since he was little and everything that he had was little and then when he planted a seed he got a big plant. (Andy, age 5:11, *Titch*)

> A boy planted a carrot seed. But his mother said it wouldn't grow and his father said it wouldn't grow and his brother said that it wouldn't grow. And he watered it each day. And finally it grew. (Elizabeth, age 5, *The Carrot Seed*)

Even the older children in Applebee's study gave lengthy summaries of common fairy tales when asked to discuss stories they knew. Compare these responses with the answers of the 5-year-old children quoted above, and perhaps it was the question itself that prompted the lengthy answers, not the child's "difficulty in integrating individual elements from the story into any sort of general framework" (Applebee, 1978, p. 93). The kindergarten children responding to *Titch* and *The Carrot Seed* were able to relate the story in a brief form and at the same time convey the overall plot. Andy was able to step back from the story and talk about Titch in general terms. "Ever since he was little . . . " suggests a stance removed from the concrete. The superordinate idea is the concept that everything Titch had was little. Notice the use of the past tense as Andy distances himself from the immediacy of the story. Andy is speaking in general terms about Titch's life, and in one sentence he is able to capture Titch's dilemma and show how, in the end, balance was achieved.

Elizabeth is much more concrete, yet succinct. She has re-created the plot of the story with brevity. Mary collapses the individual events of the story under the broader categories of having and doing little things and big things. In addition, Mary balances the scales of justice by reversing the positions of the siblings, as does Katie by stating that the main character was right.

Thus their concept of story is such that by the age of 5, children are able to collapse the events of a story down to its sparest parts and relate the main events. This indicates that the 5-year-old child can integrate narrative information with a thematic center and relate that information verbally.

Using a Piagetian perspective, Applebee (1978) discusses the egocentrism of the child in terms of his or her inability to communicate effectively based on the needs of the listener. Thus he argues that the child will not necessarily justify a chain of reasoning or be aware of contradictory conclusions. Applebee talks about the child's syncretistic linking of memorable incidents in the story rather than conceptualizing the story as a whole. One example shows a 6-year-old child responding to *Little Red Riding Hood* unfavorably. "Why didn't you like it?" "He eats the grandma" (p. 99). Piaget refers to this as centration, focusing attention on a single detail and neglecting other important aspects. Nonetheless, the child may be focusing on the violent nature of the wolf in an extremely concrete manner without being able to articulate this directly. Use of the word "he" rather than "the wolf" demonstrates the child's unclear use of reference. In essence, violence is a clear focus of this fairy tale and the child has identified the theme implicitly but does not generate a thematic statement.

The same is true of Joe's (age 5:10) answer, when he responds negatively to *The Three Little Pigs* with "they get all eaten up" (Applebee, 1978, p. 99). He too has captured the core of danger central to the story — going out into the world and attempting to make a life for oneself. Both children key in on the downside of going out into the world unprepared. Joe, like many other 5-year-old children, may realize at a tacit level that he would not survive, just as two of the pigs did not survive. The children have not missed the central idea that holds the stories together; rather at a tacit level they have identified the negative effects of being caught off guard.

The same type of responses to *The Three Little Pigs* and *The Gingerbread Boy* occurred with kindergarten children I studied. Thirteen of the twenty children I interviewed referred to the fact that "they all get eaten." In fact, the language varied little and the books were linked thematically by most of the 5-year-old children because the two pigs and the gingerbread boy all get eaten up. This preoccupation with getting eaten up is not haphazard but is closely related to the child's developmental level. Perhaps a child's perspective would necessarily stress the unreadiness of going out into the world and leaving the nurturing environment of the home. The child's construction of meaning would be that of fear — fear of leaving home, fear of the unknown, fear of striking out alone and taking care of self — in short, fear of being swallowed up by the unknown. This understanding of the child's perspective is crucial in learning how children construct meaning.

Traditionally, comprehension of story and thematic content have been viewed as static components, comprised of acquired comprehension skills that could be isolated and tested. The notion that interpreting a story was negotiable or subject to the reader's own worldview and perspective were not thought to be valid assumptions to make about the reading process. Rosenblatt's breakthrough book, *Literature as Exploration*, published in 1938, challenged traditional notions regarding text but was not widely accepted prior to the late 1970s. Thus the research of the 70s and early 80s continued to reflect this text-centered perspective and did not make allowances for the child's own unique view, even when the child's observations were solidly based on the print itself. A child who is preoccupied with getting eaten up is just not ready to go out and build a house of brick and outwit a wolf. This is not to say that the child is not ready to begin hearing those success stories as preparation for later building. It would also be erroneous to suggest that this same child is incapable of constructing meaning with narratives. Rather one must consider the child's perspective of meaning and not make assumptions based on adult perspectives.

The following review of related literature and research examines a theoretical framework upon which the child's meaning structures are built. From this base research done in the area of theme is explored. Selected studies are examined that suggest the importance of the child's ability to identify theme in passages read.

A CONSTRUCTIVIST VIEW OF READING

The child's attempts to become a meaning maker during reading can be considered from a variety of perspectives. The prevalent view throughout the 1960s and first half of the 1970s was a "bottom up" view of reading, which maintained that the knowledge the reader wished to gain was textually based and that all the reader had to do was to unlock the meaning by breaking the phonetic code. This model of reading, in a sense, suggests that the author never lets go and that the reader is a passive participant during the reading process and must attempt to find the meaning that the author locked into the text at the point of composition. The reader actively decodes and searches for the author's intended meaning but does not actively construct meaning beyond those confines.

A phonetic approach has automaticity as the goal of reading instruction. Flash-card drills at the letter and word level indicate whether the student can decode appropriately. Slower decoders are remediated for further isolated drills, whereas faster decoders are given more challenging reading material and become, ultimately, better readers (Stanovich, 1986). In my visits to numerous classrooms I have watched teachers give direct instruction to groups of first-grade children for the first 6 weeks of school that involved reading isolated words or sounds from charts and flash cards with no thought of having the children read before they were ready. Meanwhile the faster readers were galloping through basals and picture books and were encouraged to read everything in sight. It is little wonder that such huge gaps occurred over time between the two groups.

The bottom-up model was rigorously challenged in the early 1970s by the "top down" view of reading, which minimized the role of print and put the onus on the reader and the focus on meaning. This view has gained momentum during the last decade, even as it has come under fire. Suddenly, it is the reader who is central to unlocking meaning during the reading process. What the reader already knows and brings to the act of reading determines meaning. As Smith (1988) writes:

> Meaning can take priority over the identification of individual words in two ways, both for fluent readers and for beginners. In the first case, the meaning of a sequence of words facilitates the identification of individual words with relatively less visual information. In the second case, written words can be understood without being identified precisely. Usually both aspects of meaning identification occur simultaneously; we comprehend text using far less visual information than would be required to identify the individual words, and without the necessity of identifying individual words. Both aspects of meaning identification are, in fact, reflections of the same underlying process—the use of minimal visual information to make decisions specific to implicit questions (or predictions) about meaning on the part of the reader. . . . What is different about comprehension is that readers bring to the text implicit questions about meaning rather than about letters or words. . . . Meaning does not reside in surface structure. The meaning that readers comprehend from text is always relative to what they already know and to what they want to know. (p. 152)

Tierney and Pearson (1983) have extended this view by introducing a composing model of reading that explores the reading/writing connection. They conclude that "what drives reading and writing is . . . the desire to make sense of what is happening, to make things cohere" (p. 572). They view both reading and writing as creative composing acts. Current research has taken the reading/writing connection into account and also the role of well-written texts.

Well-Written Texts

Why is it crucial to provide well-written texts or open learning contexts for children in a balanced reading and writing program? Studies like DeFord's (1981) show the strong influence of a reading program on the child's writing, but the teacher's attitude toward the reading process also is central to how children learn to read and write (Goodman, Goodman, & Hood, 1988). DeFord found that the type of reading program affects the writing of first-grade children. The following three samples of writing, taken from her study, indicate the type of reading program that children experienced in three different first-grade classrooms.

- I had a gag. I had a dad. I had a cat. (phonics)
- Bill can run. Jill can run. Jeff can run. I can run. (basal)
- Iran is fighting us. 19 bombers went down. 14 fighters. We only have 3 bombers down 6 fighters. we have droped 9 bombs over iran the hostages have been ther to long. Now we head twards them It's like a game of checers. (whole language)

As evidenced above by the child who is learning about the conflict in Iran, the focus is on content, not skills, using skills to talk about world events rather than to create text that is as meaningless as the models provided. Therefore, the curriculum is dictated by teaching content. It is worth mentioning that the writing of the third child indicates a wealth of rich experiences, a depth of background knowledge, and the ability to think critically about world events. Can anyone doubt that this 6-year-old child will be able to sort out the conventional spelling for *dropped*, *there*, and *checkers* or supply a missing capital letter?

Stanovich (1980) gave support to both the top-down and bottom-up models of reading with his interactive-compensatory model in individual differences in the development of reading fluency, which suggested that how one interacts with text and how well one decodes text both impact on the reading process. This means that the text has some integrity on its own, but that the reader also brings meaning to the act of reading. There are times when readers race through text and times when they pause to decode at the word level. Poor readers are said to be more reliant on context than fluent readers, much the way emergent readers are reliant on context (Biemiller, 1970). The difference is that fluent readers move on to an automaticity that is not reliant on context, whereas struggling readers are locked into earlier strategies.

Sheer Volume

Stanovich (1986) is also a proponent of the Matthew Effect in reading (Merton, 1968; Walberg, Strykowski, Rovai, & Hung, 1984; Walberg & Tsai, 1983). "For unto every one that hath shall be given, and he shall have abundance: but from him that hath not shall be taken away even that which he hath" (Matthew 25:29). If the act of reading is the "major mechanism leading to vocabulary growth—which in turn will enable more efficient reading" (Stanovich, 1986, p. 380), then the actual amount of material read causes individual differences in the development of reading. In classrooms, as already described, the rich get richer and the poor get poorer. Those who read a lot in turn become better readers. Those who read less, over time, become developmentally less able readers. This must necessarily impact on the child's ability to construct meaning.

Nagy and Anderson (1985) have studied the amount of text that children read on the average in school. The amount of words read for middle-grade children ranges from 100,000 words a year for the lowest groups to 1,000,000 for average readers. The most fluent readers range from 10,000,000 to 50,000,000 words a year. This is certainly an imprecise kind of study to undertake, but if the researchers have estimated the proportions correctly, the readers at the bottom of the scale are reading a fraction of a percent of what the most active readers consume. The amount of new vocabulary being learned by the more active readers is considerable, and their access to meaning structures and new ideas is far richer.

In working with the child's developing sense of theme (Lehr, 1988b), I found that the children with a higher exposure to literature were able to discuss themes for books at more abstract and generalized levels of meaning than were their less well-read counterparts. This supports the theory that the rich get richer and the poor get poorer. This exposure to new vocabulary and a wide variety of reading material must also have an impact on the child's ability to think critically about what is read.

Reading Is a Transaction

Researchers at Indiana University (Harste, Burke, & Woodward, 1979) have devised a transactional model of reading that in essence has a fluid view of interpretation at its core. That is, each reader reads a text uniquely and, therefore, interpretation is an open system. This view of the reading process is useful in that text is seen as an open system in which interpretation will necessarily vary among respondents. This component extends the interactive model beyond processing and suggests a reason for the disparity found among readers during the construction of meaning.

A reader and text come together to create a poem (Rosenblatt, 1978); however, that newly created poem must be congruent with the text from which it derives its potential if it is to be understood in light of the text from which it co-evolves, and if it is to be a transaction that has shared understanding. Rosenblatt (1938/1976) suggests that the reader must possess competence in the phonemic and syntactic systems of the language and be able to understand what the words stand for. She also writes about the reader's ability to complete a decoding of the text. Therefore, Rosenblatt does not ignore the crucial role of the reading of the text. The reader must be able to read the text at the word and meaning level in order to create the "poem." Rosenblatt cites recent research that children's errors in reading are often at the level of expectation or frames formed for texts rather than misreadings of individual words.

A transaction between reader, author, and text views the text as having meaning potential (Goodman, Shannon, Freeman, & Murphy, 1988). "The reader brings to the reading a life view, a set of values, and a set of schemas built through experience in a large number of language events" (p. 93). Therefore the act of reading is dependent on the individual's transaction between text and author intentions. This suggests that single-answer approaches to reading are not feasible because meaning is an open system. A "holistic view of teaching depends on a holistic view of the learner and of reading" (p. 130).

The problem with accepting the range of all interpretations for a text is that not all readers attend to what is written in the same manner. Some readers are unable to process certain information contained in a text. Consequently, the resulting interpretation will be limited by that surfeit of text-based data. Therefore, not all interpretations are equally error free. Remember the three second-grade children who thought erroneously that the princess in *The Swineherd* lived happily ever after? Nonetheless, the children listening to that story were busy constructing meaning based on what they already knew about the conventions of stories and about life in general. "Teachers should see that they don't rob children of the opportunity to learn for themselves by saying, 'That's right' or 'That's wrong' but rather, 'Well, does that seem right?' and 'How can you be sure?'" (New Zealand Department of Education, 1985).

To refer once more to the example of *The Three Bears*, it can be seen that a multitude of interpretations are possible based on a reading of one story; however, that story has certain elements that are fixed. There were three bears. They did leave their porridge to cool, and so on. If a child ignores or is unaware of certain elements of the text, it is helpful for the teacher to make observations to that effect, not necessarily for the sake of correcting those specific errors but for future reference with regard to that child's individual needs for instruction. Observation of how a child interacts with and constructs meaning from text will yield useful information in determining what strategies a child uses during comprehension. The great American "gotcha" game in traditional reading programs is no longer a sufficient rationale for determining what a child is capable of during reading time, nor is it an adequate method for measuring what children know when they read.

Whose Interpretation?

What transactional theory allows for is great diversity in interpretation of text and an understanding and acceptance of interpretations that differ from text. Remember Katie's summary of *The Carrot Seed*? "A boy planted a plant and his mother and dad said, 'It won't grow. It won't grow.' But he thought it would and he was right. So . . . so he ate it all. The end." If one rereads the actual text, one finds no reference to the boy eating the carrot at the end of the story. Katie did a bit of embellishing here to give her retelling of the story an appropriate finale. She hasn't really missed the key elements of plot or the main events of the story. What she has done is create a new poem and incorporate her expectations for the text, as Rosenblatt (1978) suggests. Katie's ending is very satisfying and follows a set pattern for narrative, not unlike the little red hen's eating all of the bread that she planted, harvested, and baked herself. Katie has a particular schema that she called upon, or instantiated, to extend the ending of this story. In some ways, hers was a more complete and traditional ending.

It is worth noting that background knowledge will cause the reader to focus on different aspects of the story, directly influencing interpretations. The question remains and is basic to each model just described: Is it necessary that the interpretation of the story coincide with the text itself? Each of the four reading models essentially focuses on this question, the role of the text and the relation of the reader to the text. A holistic view of teaching borrows freely from top-down, interactional, and transactional theories of reading but has less in common with bottom-up theories because of their rigidity regarding the reading process and interpretation of text.

The implications for the teacher's attitude toward the child's construction of meaning during the reading process, from the transactional view are several.

1. Meaning should be the goal of reading, which in itself should be purposeful.
2. Meaning will vary for each reader, depending on the reader's

own schema and the context within which the reader and text reside (Halliday & Hasan, 1979).

3. Meaning resides in the text and in the reader's head, and is shaped by a context, and when meshed together a transaction occurs; that is, a new "poem" is created. However, if the reader's ability to reconstruct meaning is the focus, the resulting poem will necessarily be text-congruent. Conversely, if the reader's ability to construct meaning is the focus, the resulting poem will not necessarily be text-congruent, for the re-creation of the text is not the goal of a transactional model.

THE BUILDING BLOCKS OF MEANING

Current theories of cognition view schemata as the "building blocks" upon which all information processing depends (Rumelhart, 1980). Any research which hopes to explore how children build meaning during the reading process must consider what schemata are and how they are utilized. Also, one can better understand how mature readers constantly make inferences based on the concepts that are stored in the brain. Schemata are essentially individual concepts that people hold in memory. Rumelhart (1980) writes

> a schema theory is basically a theory about knowledge. It is a theory about how knowledge is represented and about how that representation facilitates the use of the knowledge in particular ways. According to schema theories, all knowledge is packaged into units. These units are the schemata. Embedded in these packets of knowledge is, in addition to the knowledge itself, information about how this knowledge is to be used. (p. 34)

He writes that basically schemata are used in comprehension, storage, organization of actions, determination of goals and subgoals, allotment of resources, and in processing.

Essentially schema theory accounts for the complex network of concepts that are stored in memory. These generic concepts contain variables and are assigned values by individuals. For example, the notion of "restaurant" can be thought of as a generic concept that many people hold. Some restaurants have waiters or waitresses, table cloths, formica tops, silverware, plastic forks and spoons, can be considered fast or slow experiences. Individuals assign values to that concept. Do I eat out every night? Do I like expensive restaurants? Places serving seafood? Do I have a preference for real plates? Do I like being waited on? Do I prefer to go through a line where I pick out my own food? Are fast food places real restaurants? My concept of a restaurant might differ from your concept of a restaurant given all the possible variables and personal values that we attach to the basic concept of a place where you go to eat out. The child that I was liked fast food restaurants; the adult that I have become doesn't tend to think of fast food places as real restaurants. We constantly revise our own individual schemata over time.

The schema is a conceptualization of knowledge that includes objects, situations, events, sequences of events, actions, and sequences of actions, and contains the network of interrelations held among the constituents of the concept under consideration (Rumelhart, 1980). Any schema is necessarily limited or extended by the input available. If my restaurant experiences are limited to fast food places I might not be aware of how to use three spoons. Schemata are embedded within each other, make use of part to whole and whole to part processing. Thus as a reader encounters text that reader instantiates, or pulls out schema to fit with the textual context. The example below will help to clarify how readers pull out schema to make sense of what they read.

Context

My understanding of *The Three Bears* is vastly different on some levels from that of the 4-year-old child hearing the story before bed. I have had more than 40 years of experience that has shaped my reading and comprehending of that particular story. Context also shapes a reader's schema. If I live in the city where break-ins are prevalent I may view the story from a different perspective than will a child living in the country. As a city child I may also fear the woods as being a dark and strange place. Context shapes perceptions; even the examples that I provide in writing this text are shaped by my own personal schemata.

Writers depend on what readers already know. For example, a clock in a bedroom will be tucked into memory with specific values of "clockness" attached to it — sits on bed stand, has alarm, glows in dark, makes noise in morning, etc. (Anderson, Spiro, & Anderson, 1977). One fills in the gaps as one reads and literally recreates the text (Iser, 1980). R. E. Warren referred to this as text-connecting and slot-filling. Instantiation is the process of automatically pulling out that information which is needed to make sense or lend clarity to a situation encountered, in this instance during the act of reading. If information is stored generically in a network of concepts stored in memory then the process of accessing that information is necessarily an extremely fast process. Furthermore, refinements and revisions are ongoing and constant as new data or input is perceived by individuals. Therefore readers can pull out concepts with values already attached. Authors cannot spell out all elements of a story. Some components must be understood to keep the flow of the narrative moving in a forward direction. The reader will instantiate the entire notion of bedroom clock if the clock is said to be located in the bedroom, without a specific description of a bedroom clock being necessary. A kitchen clock has different attributes than one located in the bedroom. The author, however, need not define the features of each, because the reader draws inferences based on the instantiation of the correct schema and fills in the gaps of the text. Individual values attached to the clock found in the bedroom may vary, but the essential function of the bedroom clock has cultural expectations already established. However, the farmer accustomed to awakening at dawn with the crow of the rooster may have different expectations for the bedroom clock. The concept is only operable if there are certain attached values which are socially defined and agreed upon.

Fish (1980) argues that interpretations are communally determined. "Since all sign systems are social constructs that individuals assimilate more or less automatically, an individual's perceptions and judgments are functions of the assumptions shared by the groups he belongs to" (p. xxi). Bleich (1980) expands this idea by suggesting that the individual negotiates within that given framework. Consequently, the young reader has not taken on the complete values of society but is said to be in a formative stage of growth. Therefore, the child's instantiations of meaning may differ greatly from those of the adult. As teachers it is crucial that we acknowledge and accept the differences, or at least be open to listening to what the child has to say from his or her perspective of meaning.

The reader's expectations also influence the act of reading. Subjects told to read a narrative from a house buyer's point of view remembered different aspects of the story than those who were told to read from a thief's (Pichert & Anderson, 1976). The former subjects tended to stress real estate advantages such as room size and access to schools or playgrounds, etc., whereas the latter were preoccupied with hedges to hide behind and windows to crawl through. One remembers what one expects to remember. Memory is selective. One actively constructs text as one reads (Blachowics, 1977). What is known is integrated with what is presented.

In the search for meaning, readers will generally make every attempt to create a cohesive text. Readers will add information to a text to create congruity (Spiro, 1977; Blachowics, 1977), and if later given plausible information which conflicts with an unclear text the reader will reconstruct the text to fit the new information (Spiro, 1977). This search for meaning employs the use of inference. In Spiro's experiment with adults a brief narrative was presented that stated that an engaged couple disagreed on the desirability of having children, quarreled, and were eventually happily married. The conflict was left intact for the reader to process. Inferences had to be made as to the resolution of the two schema states—one of disharmony and one of harmony. The subjects were asked to recall the story as exactly as possible without adding any information. The results showed that subjects reconstructed the story and added information to make the story cohesive. Subjects "remembered" that the couple had sought counseling, decided to adopt, or hadn't really had a serious argument. When the story was reversed and the couple did not marry, the same reconstructive process occurred. However, when the story was presented without discongruent elements subjects made no errors in recall.

This bolsters the notion that the reader actively constructs meaning during the reading process. If a text is poorly written, the reader will still seek meaning, and apparently find meaning, but the content of that meaning does not necessarily reside in the text. This illustrates the active role of the reader in her search for meaning. Reading is not a passive activity, wherein the text is whole and the reader merely decodes. This type of research directly challenges the notion that all meaning is inherent in the text and not constructed in the mind of the reader. Halliday (1975) has concluded that children learn language while using language to learn. Goodman, Shannon, Freeman, & Murphy (1988) suggest that it is the need to use language to communicate that motivates language development; therefore, it is most easily learned when it is functional. Reading for enjoyment is certainly one of the functions of teaching children to read, and this cannot occur unless well-written texts are available for children.

Let me return for a moment to the 5-year-old children in my study who were preoccupied with the pigs' being eaten. None of the adults surveyed in the study mentioned the notion of being eaten up. It never even arose as a consideration. Yet 13 of the children talked about this concept. What this suggests to me is that it is not haphazard information. It is not a preoccupation with one minor point in the story, nor does it reveal the child's inability to think logically about thematic information. What this information tells me clearly is that children process information in a manner differently from adults. Knowing that helps me listen and perhaps understand the child's construction of meaning, because I am no longer looking for my adult answer, my adult point of view. Rather, I am giving credence to the child's verbalization. The 5-year-olds had no expectations for leaving home and making their way independently in the world and, as a result, this was not the schema that was instantiated.

HOW CHILDREN USE THE STRUCTURE OF STORIES TO BUILD MEANING

How do children construct story schemata? By listening to many stories and building knowledge about how story events are sequenced, children construct a set of expectations about how stories function. As a child encodes, the story schema acts as a general framework in which comprehension processing occurs (Mandler & Johnson, 1977). Furthermore, the framework acts as a guide that signals that certain facts are to be kept in mind. The story structure also increases the predictability of what is read, which simplifies processing.

Mandler and Johnson (1977), who formulated a general story structure for simple stories based on Rumelhart's (1975) story grammar, define a simple story as one that has a single protagonist in each episode. They proposed a tree structure "which makes explicit the constituent structure and relations between constituents" (p. 115). Events are related by their tree position and by the causal or temporal node connections. Other fixed or basic nodes include settings, beginnings, reactions, attempts, outcomes, and endings. The grammar is lengthy and complicated and will not be elaborated in this text (see Mandler & Johnson, 1977, for a complete diagram of their story structure); however, the application of the story grammar and its implications for recall will be explored.

Mandler and Johnson (1977) asked first-grade, fourth-grade, and university students to listen to two tape-recorded stories and then retell the stories using spontaneous recall. The stories were structured to conform to the story grammar developed by the researchers. Two were versions of tales used by Piaget in 1926, which had been altered for clarity. Each of the stories had propositions from one of the six major nodes from the story structure: settings, beginnings, reactions, attempts, outcomes, and endings.

Not surprisingly, the adults recalled more than the fourth graders and they, in turn, recalled more than the first graders, suggesting a developmental perspective on recall. First graders tended to recall settings, beginnings, and outcomes. They omitted the internal reactions of characters as well as story endings. Fourth graders performed similarly; in addition, their recall of attempts and outcomes was greater, but not significantly. Adults lagged in their recall of endings and reactions but were able to recall the other nodes.

The results show that children are sensitive to story structure and use retrieval strategies similar to those of adults. The major differences between children and adults seem to be that children stress outcomes rather than attempts and almost ignore reactions. Mandler and Johnson's research challenges Piagetian (1926/1960) research, which maintains that children confuse temporal order as well as cause-and-effect relations during recall. This study did not use probed recall, but other studies have found that children can answer questions about reactions and attempts (Berndt & Berndt, 1975; Lehr, 1988a; Stein & Glenn, 1978).

Children apparently focus on how stories begin and how outcomes proceed from actions, but this does not mean that they are unaware of internal reactions or attempts. Additions during recall produced interesting results. First graders made the fewest additions, but when they did, the additions were frequently irrelevant or fanciful. This usually occurred when the child lost the threads of the story early in the recall attempt. What this suggests is that the child was trying to fill empty nodes but had inadequate information to do so correctly. It is interesting to note that because the expectation existed for the child to tell about the story, some children made up information. Were they actually remembering the disinformation, having a bit of fun, or merely fulfilling their part of an obligation?

Using Mandler and Johnson's (1977) story grammar, Whaley (1981) found that third-, sixth-, and eleventh-grade children had expectations for story structure corresponding to the story grammar of Mandler and Johnson. In their responses to manipulated stories, children expected and included categories from the story grammar such as settings, beginnings, reactions of characters, outcomes, and endings. There were also age-related differences that corresponded to the findings of Mandler and Johnson. Similarly, Stein and Glenn (1978) systematically deleted categories and found that children tended to fill in the deleted category. Trabasso and Nicholas (1977) had similar results. Children are meaning makers and actively construct relevant information during reading! Children also had strong expectations for stories that had been manipulated (i.e., categories deleted, altered, or moved), and comprehension suffered when these expectations were not met, indicating that in reading, oral, and listening situations children have strong expectations for categories in stories.

To generate a developmental perspective, low-graded materials were used for all students tested regardless of age. For example, Whaley (1981) used stories at the second- and third-grade level. It is not surprising that upper level students would be more successful with the recall tasks than the first- and second-grade students. Would the previous researchers have found that college students had difficulty recalling internal motivation or stressed beginnings if appropriately graded materials had been used? Would probed recall have caused children to consider internal motivation of character in a way that free recall did not? In essence, did free recall indicate that young children do not consider internal motivation or beginnings, or did the method used preclude finding out what the children knew? Would the differences between first- and fourth-graders have been the same? Whaley points out the difficulties of presenting high school students with simple stories. Did this have a tendency to affect the results negatively? Would the use of real books with illustrations have made a difference?

To make a valid comparison it seems necessary to include narratives appropriate to each age level. Taylor (1980), in her study of recall of expository text, used two identical passages that were altered for difficulty for two grade levels. Removing the inequities, she reasoned, would more accurately reveal the structural expectations of readers or listeners.

Interestingly, Taylor's results for immediate recall indicate that developmental differences do exist across age levels, despite the comparisons between skilled fourth-grade readers and less skilled sixth-grade readers. Results of delayed recall, however, revealed no differences between the two groups. Furthermore, and contrary to other findings (Meyer, 1977; Waters, 1978), Taylor found that sensitivity to superordinate over subordinate concepts was not differentially recalled by subjects in the brief expository passage read. She suggests that this may have been due to the brevity of the selection; however, passages used by Waters (1978) were equally brief, yet his results were contrary to those of Taylor. Perhaps the disparity in the findings of the above two research projects lay simply in the content and interest level of the passages chosen.

Thematic Manipulation in Narrative Discourse

In experiments, Thorndyke (1977) manipulated story organization and found that comprehension and recall were dependent upon the inherent plot structure in the story, regardless of story content. He defined theme as "the general focus to which the subsequent plot adheres" (p. 80). He found that subjects tended to recall high-level organizational story elements over low-level details, and that they recalled a general structure rather than specific content as the story became schematized in memory. For example, remember the child's response to *The White Mountains*, which was a general statement about the plot: "Oh, that book was about a boy who escaped from his village so that he could be free from these giants that were controlling the minds of his people." The child generalized elements of the story to form high-level categories about escape and freedom.

Thorndyke manipulated story elements that altered plot structure by removing or changing the position of theme in narratives. The results demonstrated the importance of having an organizational structure for comprehension and memory with a standard hierarchy of goal-directed episodes, because subjects replaced theme statements in the traditional beginning position during recall. Readers are logical in their search for meaning. Placing the theme statement of a text in an initial position suggests structure and order during retelling. The reader literally pulls his or her thoughts together by focusing on the theme. All else follows logically and sequentially.

When thematic statements were deleted altogether, Thorndyke found that recall suffered and comprehension was lower. Apparently understanding the overall theme of a narrative guides the encoding of meaning, and without such an overarching concept, comprehensibility of narratives is difficult to ascertain. This again underscores the importance of well-written texts for all readers, and specifically for emergent readers. These data also suggest that texts that have no apparent theme will be difficult for fluent readers to comprehend. Consider primers for young children that wander aimlessly: Jack is up, Jill is down, the sun is up, the tree is down. As educators we had best choose our books carefully if we want to facilitate comprehension.

Interpretation of Main Idea

A series of studies with elementary school children suggests that the child is able to recognize the story's main idea but lacks the ability to generate main ideas of prose passages without specific instruction (Baumann, 1981; Dunn, Matthews, & Bieger, 1979; Otto & Barrett, 1968; Taylor, 1980; Tierney, Bridge, & Cera, 1978–79). Otto et al.'s early research with children in grades 1 through 6 tested whether children could conceptualize and generate a main idea in reading four constructed sentences (at first-grade vocabulary level and also at each grade level) with one clearly unstated main idea. The children's grade level and the readability of the paragraph were critical factors in determining quality of the responses; however, he found that children's responses were of low quality based on his scale of rating. For example, 29% of the second graders were able to compose an appropriate main idea statement as were 64% of the fifth graders. Responses having more abstract information in the body of the answer received lower scores. A correct answer was measured as one that contained both general and specific information relating to the text.

Answers that contain more abstract information, however, are developmentally at a higher cognitive level than those that include literal aspects of the story. Applebee's (1978) work analyzing the responses of children aged 2 to 17 suggests that the answer that is most developed is that which steps back from the piece and speaks in more general terms. The Purves-Rippere system refers to this stage as "interpretation," which is beyond the stage of perception and is based on characteristics of the work. Interpretation involves generalization beyond characteristics of the story. Applebee's four developmental stages in the formulation of response include:

1. *Narration.* This stage occurs in the preoperational stage, and the narratives of children generally lack integration.
2. *Summarization.* This stage occurs in the concrete operational stage, the point where children begin to categorize.
3. *Analysis* of the structure of the work or the motives of the characters. This includes understanding through analogy and typically occurs in the formal operational stage I.
4. *Generalization* about the work; consideration of theme or point of view. This occurs in the formal operational stage II and typically involves the adolescent's understanding of the work and its effect on the reader's own views.

Dunn et al.'s (1979) work involved the use of a lengthy prose passage that fourth- and sixth-grade subjects had to read and recall through writing. Their findings indicate that children with superior reading ability can recall subordinate- and superordinate-level information equally. The results do not necessarily indicate that students are unable to generate main idea statements. They do show that better readers recall more information at lower levels of importance when asked to write all that they can remember about a passage. Furthermore, the average readers remembered fewer details and recalled more superordinate ideas, perhaps indicating that although they cannot remember as much as the more fluent readers, they are able to generate the most important ideas of a passage.

Tierney et al. (1978–79) probed their subjects more directly when testing the recall of a prose structure by using interview techniques based only on information already given by subjects and an oral retelling of everything remembered. Tierney et al. made a distinction between explicit information contained in the basal selection and in the reader's response and implicit information not in the text but inferred by the reader. Results showed that poor readers are less complete in their recollection of propositions and in their ability to generate interpropositional structure than better readers. Comprehension of the children was perceived to be constructive and abstractive "for the purpose of acquiring a meaningful interpretation based upon their own schemata" (Tierney et al., 1978–79, p. 539).

Readers recall more explicit than inferred information during free recall and in probed recall are able to generate more inferential information, thus indicating that different processing strategies are operating. These differences vary across reading levels. Inference makes use of generation, whereas recall of explicit information involves retrieval. These findings are supported by Brown, Smiley, Day, Townsend, and Lawton (1977), who state "that young readers rarely render inferences without probing" (Tierney et al., 1978–79, p. 548).

Baumann's (1981) research is perhaps most complete in terms of the generation of main idea with subjects. Using unaltered text, third- and sixth-grade students were asked to read expository passages that were randomly selected from social studies texts. They read the passages twice, had a filler task to control for short-term memory, and then were asked to write a sentence on what the whole story was about. Afterwards they were asked to write all that they could remember about the story.

A second task required students to read a second passage and respond by identifying a main idea statement from a list of seven statements, completing multiple-choice questions that probed for main ideas or details, and examining a list of 12 statements to determine whether they were main ideas, details, or false statements. Findings indicated that students are able to produce main idea statements about one third of the time. Ability to identify the main idea in lengthy prose passages exceeds children's ability to put it into words themselves. That is, a child may tacitly comprehend the main idea of a passage but be unable to state it (Baumann, 1981). Studies showing that children do produce main idea statements have used extremely brief passages (Danner, 1976) that are not indicative of text children must typically read and understand in the classroom. Baumann's work supports the findings of Dunn et al. (1979), Tierney et al. (1978–79), and Taylor (1980), which showed that elementary students were unable to show "superior comprehension" in differentiating between superordinate and subordinate information.

When narrative prose is used, subjects show greater skill in comprehension of main ideas (Brown & Smiley, 1977; Christie & Schumacher, 1975; Lehr, 1988b). Children may have greater facility with narrative forms because of a well-developed sense of story (Lehr, 1988a; Mandler & Johnson, 1977; Stein & Glenn, 1978; Thorndyke, 1977; Whaley, 1981). Furthermore, a study by Boljonis and Kaye (cf., in Baumann, 1981) suggests that children have little exposure to expository prose before they are introduced to content-area books, which occurs around the fourth grade, and consequently have less knowledge about the structuring of nonfiction passages and are less adept at processing main ideas (Baumann, 1981). Boljonis and Kaye found that fourth graders showed superior recall of information presented in a narrative passage compared with a nonnarrative passage containing the same information (Baumann, 1981).

Also Baumann asserts that those studies using a listening approach (Brown & Smiley, 1977; Christie & Schumacher, 1975; Danner, 1976; Lehr, 1988b; Meyer, 1977; Waters, 1978) have achieved better results with main idea comprehension than those requiring students to read selections. He hypothesizes that listening promotes main idea comprehension and reading does not. Hildyard and Olson (cf., in Baumann, 1981) found that students showed different patterns of comprehension after reading and listening. Main ideas were produced after listening and details were supplied after reading.

Generation of Theme

Research has explored the child's ability to recall thematically relevant information after listening to narrative passages. Children as young as age 5 will delete irrelevant information and retell logically sequenced stories that are thematically centered. In the Soviet Union, Korman (1945, cf., in Yendovitskayz, 1964/1971) studied the narrative recall of 4- to 6-year-old children and found that the material was related in a logically sequenced manner and that certain episodes containing lower level information were deleted in the retellings, particularly those that were not pertinent to the main idea of the passage.

Christie and Schumacher (1975) extended this work by testing kindergarten, second-, and fifth-grade children. They purposely included children of 7 to 8 years old, the critical age "at which children are expected to begin abstracting relevant thematic information and recalling this information in a logical order (Piaget, 1926)" (Christie & Schumacher, 1975, p. 599). Students listened to the story and then taped their responses. Idea units were judged to be correct if they did not alter the meaning of the story.

The results demonstrated that children recall more relevant idea units than irrelevant and in logical order, thus challenging the idea that children cannot abstract relevant thematic information before the age of 7 or 8 and supporting Korman's basic claims. Christie and Schumacher (1975) conclude that the kindergarten child is more capable of "abstracting and producing relevant thematic information than has previously been assumed" (p. 601). The stories were manipulated and included intrusive detail, which was extraneous and distracting. Using real stories might have revealed different results. Also, Christie and Schumacher apparently did not analyze the retellings for thematic statements or categorizations that children may have made, so the results indicate that children remember stories in a general manner. Whether the recall was at a level of retelling or summarizing is not known. This information would be useful in analyzing the child's sense of theme.

Brown et al. (1977) had similar results when testing children's recall of the most important units in narratives. Recall of other levels of importance increased with age. Central to this study is the fact that Brown et al. used warm-up sessions to acquaint the children with the process of recalling the gist of the story. They also shared background knowledge about the narrative to be presented with the experimental group. The control group received a false orientation. The results support what is already known about the importance of background information: Relevant orientation increased the amount of units recalled.

Intrusions made during recall were divided into those that were considered theme relevant and those that were not. Results indicate that relevant thematic intrusions are a function of age. Younger children's intrusions are less related to theme, regardless of orientation. During probed recall children had a tendency to make more critical inferences than they did in their free recall. Brown et al. point out that the older children made more intrusions, and that technically the intrusions are errors. The authors refer to them as creative errors because they added cohesive threads to the story and ultimately made it more comprehensible. Young children also made these "errors," thereby suggesting the constructive nature of the reading act based on what is known about the world.

Similarly, Brown et al. (1977) found that good readers in the seventh grade, reading and listening to two passages, recalled more of the idea units in the story, particularly those units that were structurally most important, than did their counterparts who were less skilled readers. This reveals that poor readers experience a "general comprehension deficit."

Fluent readers seem to have the ability to identify themes of passages read if the structure of the passage is familiar. This familiar framework allows the reader to instantiate schemata that facilitate the comprehension process. If the reader encounters structures that are not familiar, the process of understanding the author's intentions and pulling out a hierarchy of meaning is weakened. This suggests that children need a wide range of reading and listening experiences to alleviate the stark differences between the expository and the narrative research!

Generation of thematic content is thought to be a developmental trend that entails minimally an implicit understanding of structure. Children show facility with narrative forms as a result of their familiarity with such a format. As has been shown in their recall response patterns, children are capable of remembering the main ideas in prose passages. They encounter difficulties, however, when reading lengthier nonfiction, such as textbooks.

Mal'tseva (1958, cf., in Smirnov, Mal'tseva, & Alova, 1971–72) asked 60 second, fourth, and sixth graders to compose an outline of a narrative text. Smirnov et al. does not explain how this was accomplished, nor do they provide examples of passages used or writing samples (of which the outlines of the youngest group tested would be particularly interesting). At any rate, Mal'tseva found that second graders expressed "chief thoughts" of the text 46.3% of the time, fourth graders 57.5%, and sixth graders 65%. These percentages are quite good considering the difficulty of the task involved; however, more information such as examples of passages used and outlines that children composed would be needed to ascertain how the researchers gathered these outlines.

An interesting finding of the experiment was that children were unable to express how to go about identifying the theme of a passage or how to check themselves as to whether their headings were correct. A major finding was that the children needed further instruction in the extraction of main ideas. This concurs with Baker and Stein's (1981) notion that children's ability to express how they function may be below their ability to actually do so.

As part of the continued treatment for subjects, Smirnov et al. (1971–72) trained students to generate and identify main ideas in passages. They were encouraged to state main ideas out loud in their own words and later to use these vocalizations as headings in their outlines.

Furthermore, Smirnov et al. trained subjects to explain how each operation was performed. In other words, the concepts were dissected in the hope that a type of meta-awareness would occur. Specific instruction of this type in extracting main ideas from passages had a tendency to increase the independent generalizations of students trained. Making a child aware of what a main idea is and how it can be identified seems to aid the process of generating theme in selections read.

Divergent Responses to Literature

Recent research has begun to take a look at how children construct meaning while reading and responding to literature. It has also begun to explore whether and how the child is able to interpret theme, understand character motivation, and make generalizations about the book. When I first began working with the child's developing sense of theme, there was virtually no research in this area with elementary age children. Young children were essentially out of the loop, because their notions of theme were often at odds with adult answers. Current studies are examining the quality of texts used in the classroom, which is critical in considering the child's attempts to construct meaning. The types of questions are certainly being examined. Convergent questioning does not encourage interpretation of text in interactive contexts. The child's perspective is also vital to any understanding of how children construct meaning.

Liebling (1989) found that the instructional method and the quality of the text influenced third-grade children's interpretation of "inside view" and "character plans" in fiction. Liebling compared different instructional settings using original high-quality texts and basal adaptations and essentially asked students to "weave an interpretation of the inside view and character plans with a recall of the plot's main events" (p. i). She evaluated their responses both qualitatively and quantitatively and found that using original texts and implementing sociocognitive instructional methods significantly affected students' interpretations of text. Liebling's particular method combines a view of the reading process that is sociocognitively based and examines literary form and content. Central to her method is the selection of original materials and an examination of the text to define important literary content prior to sharing with students, which then becomes the focus of response. The context for sharing is to be lively and open as students reconstruct the main events of the story. Her results support a social view of reading and interpretation in which children discuss text and build meaning in interactive contexts. Quality of text and type of questions asked were found to be critical indicators of success with interpretation. She used the original version of *Freckle Juice* by Judy Blume and a basal adaptation that deleted about a third of the text, which distorted the social sequencing of the story.

In individual interviews Liebling invited students to retell the story and found that recall was greatly influenced by the quality of text and the type of instruction that occurred during discussion of the book, which included divergent questioning techniques. Children were aware of character motivations and were able to offer extensive retellings of the original version of *Freckle Juice* by Judy Blume, including rich interpretations woven into their retellings.

In contrast, Cullinan, Harwood, and Galda (1983) found that fourth-graders did not interpret themes in novels with a great deal of success when compared with older children reading the same novels. The responses of the younger children were simpler and seemed to miss the subtleties of the plots. This supports a developmental view of the child's ability to discuss theme and also has implications for difficulty of text.

Two basic differences are inherent in both pieces of research. Liebling chose a specific book that was age appropriate for third-grade children, *Freckle Juice* by Judy Blume. Cullinan et al. used two novels that are perhaps more difficult for a fourth-grade child. In particular, *A Wizard of Earthsea* is a complex fantasy by Ursula LeGuin that is better suited for a middle school child. *Bridge to Terabithia*, the second novel, drew rather simple and at times shallow responses from children, which underlines the importance of building meaning in interactive and supportive contexts. The fourth-grade children in my study had a great deal of success in talking about themes, but the texts were simpler and included pictures.

Holland's work (Holland & Lehr, in press) with fourth-grade children reading *Bridge to Terabithia* shows that students had rich and complex reactions to characters and the tragic main event of this book by Katherine Paterson. Holland, like Liebling, worked extensively with the children in response discussions that were open-ended in nature and that encouraged a wide range of reactions to the book. Children wrote poetry and explored the thematic meaning of the book through artwork that was linked with personal text. Children built a literal bridge between the two main characters and described the characters in detail on large cutouts. One child interpreted each chapter in a color collage mural that evoked the mood and tone of the book through color alone. This supports earlier work by Cohen (1968) and Cullinan, Jaggar, and Strickland (1974) that stresses the importance of extending book experiences with oral language discussion and activities that include artwork.

Many (1989) explored the responses of fourth-, sixth-, and eighth-grade students to three realistic short stories. Their stance to the story was measured using a scale based on Rosenblatt's (1978) efferent and aesthetic categories. After reading the stories, students were asked to write a response. Additionally, the reader's level of personal understanding was rated on a scale beginning with literal and rising to generalized response. Many, like Lehr and Liebling, found that understanding of realistic stories at interpretive levels increases with age. Fourth graders in Many's study were able to respond beyond the confines of the text 15.5% of the time. They considered what characters might have done, or constructed a "global understanding" based on the text. This ability to apply the story events to the world increased with age. Over 40% of the fourth graders also "included some interpretation of story events or were able to go beyond the text and apply story events or generalizations from the story to life" (p. 29). Many suggests that the success of all three age levels, when contrasted to Applebee's (1978) findings, might be the result of the instrument used (Many, 1989), which is based on reader-response theory and gets at abstract generalizations.

Interestingly, the response to the rating question generated thematic information from some of the readers that was interspersed with opinion about the relative merit of the stories read. Many found that children who stressed the "lived-through experience" of the story seemed to understand the story better than their counterparts who took no apparent stance to the story. Those taking an aesthetic stance tended to interpret story events, make story-to-life connections, and were often able to make generalizations about the story. This suggests that an aesthetic response to literature can evoke imaginative and creative responses when the students find the literacy experience meaningful and relevant (Many, 1989). Efferent responses more closely resemble fact-finding missions, where students plug in the correct answers about literary elements and frequently respond with antagonism, as some of Many's examples indicate. "I didn't like the story at all. The story was too confusing. The story didn't tell anything much about the characters. The story didn't share the feelings of the characters. The story was quite boring and I didn't like it" (p. 9). Many found no link between stance and the grade level of the student. Identifying with characters or a story seems to evoke a rich personal response regardless of age. Many points out that a limitation of the study is the fact that the texts were the same for all three age levels. With this I concur; however, her results are exciting and again underscore the importance of eliciting a rich and varied response from students in experiences with literature.

2

Theme:
The Child's Perspective

Paley (1981) has described the growth of her kindergarten class through an entire school year with observations about the cognitive growth and development of her students. Her observations include records of storybook interaction as it relates to the encoding of meaning. Her goals for the children included the development of logical thinking accompanied by the language skills necessary to articulate those thoughts. Consequently, she provided a classroom atmosphere that valued the statements of the children and encouraged oral language as a means of responding to books shared in class.

After Paley's kindergarten class heard the story of *Tico and the Golden Wings* by Leo Lionni, Lisa's retelling of the story went like this: "There was a bird named Tico and he didn't have any friends because all his friends had black wings and they didn't like him anymore because he asked the wishingbird for golden wings" (Paley, 1981, p. 25).

Paley (1981) relates in *Wally's Stories* that she and the children did not agree about Tico. Whereas she viewed him as a nonconformist, the children unanimously saw him as a "threat to the community." Their observations are congruent with the story and reveal their own perceptions about being different. Tico is viewed as being nicer with black wings. The children do not respond to the fact that Tico originally had no wings. Wally asserts that Tico thinks he's better with golden wings, reflecting the jostling position common to the young child. Jill states that Tico has no right to be better and that the wishingbird was "wrong" to give Tico golden wings. This worldview wants all children to be on an equal footing. Deana puts the full blame back on Tico by arguing that he should not have asked for the golden wings. In conclusion, Deana's position, consistent with her kindergarten world, is that

32

Tico should share his golden wings and keep only one for himself (Paley, 1981, pp. 25–26).

In this conversation the teacher respects the consensus and does not insist that the children take on her view. Their views are not inconsistent with the story, and although they may not reflect the author's intentions or that of the adult, they are thematically possible based on the story itself. The children's sense of theme for this story is: "Do not make your friends jealous." It is this perspective that research must be open to explore, for it affords the teacher a serious look into the child's world and his or her attempts to construct meaning.

Given my experience with classrooms like Paley's and my understanding of research in relation to the child's ability to talk about themes in books, I set out to do a series of studies that would explore the child's developing sense of theme. In the first study (Lehr, 1985; 1988a; 1988b; 1988c) I worked with kindergarten, second-, and fourth-grade children, reading stories with the children in small groups and exploring their basic concepts about the books shared in individual interviews. I also measured their basic knowledge or exposure to children's literature in a variety of genres using the Huck Literature Inventory (Lehr, 1987) to determine what links there might be between a high exposure to children's literature and the ability to talk about themes in books. In a second study (Lehr, 1990) I worked with 4-year-old children in a similar fashion, reading and discussing books. In a third study (Holland, Thompson, & Lehr, in preparation) I worked with three colleagues in three distinct settings with three classrooms of third-grade children: an inner city, a small industrialized town, and a suburb. In this last study my colleagues and I were taking a close look at the interactive construction of meaning between the teacher and children using both fiction and nonfiction during read-aloud time, which I discuss in Chapter 5 in terms of classroom application.

The following pages describe the research settings in the classrooms used for these studies. In addition, several of the tools used for the studies were invaluable in terms of exploring what children know about literature and how they develop a sense of theme. These are described in some detail as are the studies' results. Research of this nature illuminates what we now know about the child's ability to talk about books at abstract levels. Furthermore, response studies of elementary age children challenge static views of child development that suggest children are unable to structure valid meaning during story telling. Gordon Wells's view of the child as meaning maker and books like Donaldson's *Children's Minds* have broken new ground for research into children's abilities to construct meaning. The following section explores the child's exposure to literature as measured by a literature inventory and how the knowledge gained from such exposure might impact on children's interaction during story-telling events.

A CHILD'S EXPOSURE TO LITERATURE

The Huck Literature Inventory (Huck, 1960), which was found to be a strong tool in predicting linguistic sophistication in Carol Chomsky's (1972) work with children, has also been shown to be useful in measuring a child's exposure to children's literature. Because the inventory was originally published in 1960, it was necessary to include more current titles and to delete those that are now less well known or not widely available. Therefore, I revised the inventory, with Huck's permission and guidance, to include a blend of old and new titles (Lehr, 1987).

The revision covers 63 items in five genres, taken from books determined to be readily available in libraries, classrooms, and bookstores, and thus generally identifies the child who reads and listens to literature both in the home and at school. The inventory is divided into four sections. Section one contains Mother Goose rhymes, section two poetry, section three fairy tales, folktales, and fables, and section four picture books of realistic fiction and fantasy. Although it certainly does not embrace all the good literature available, it aims at the widest selection possible.

Because home and school reading practices vary widely, this inventory does not identify children who may have had experiences with other types of printed material, such as books available in grocery stores, comic books, or children's Bible stories. (Keep in mind that Irwin found in 1960 that exposing children to read-aloud settings with "grocery store" books increased vocalizations of infants, suggesting that book interactions with young children stimulate cognitive processes. The interaction itself is extremely valuable for children, for it provides a focus on ideas and words, as well as illustrations.) What the Revised Huck Literature Inventory (RHLI) provides is a checklist of quality children's literature, with special attention given to both text and illustrations, not unlike the difference between reading romance novels and well-crafted pieces of literature. Certainly there is value in simply reading anything, but there are nonetheless distinctions in the quality of what is read.

Despite this basic kind of limitation, it is useful to establish a measure of students' exposure to well-crafted literature to explore the relationship between such exposure and the child's ability to construct meaning in book-sharing events. With the reappearance of so many classics in children's literature (like *Petunia*, written in 1950 by Roger Duvoisin) both in bookstores, as Reading Rainbow selections, and in book clubs, most of the titles in the revised inventory are still widely available to children.

I administered the RHLI to all of the children participating in the first study exploring a child's sense of theme, including the kindergartners, second, and fourth graders. A pilot test revealed that the mean was 39.54 for the 63-item test with a high score of 51 and a low score of 19. This indicates that the average child tested got about 39 of the 63 questions about the books correct; therefore, missing one third of the items would not be considered a low score. Given the wide range of books available, with approximately 2,000 to 3,000 published annually for children alone, a score of 39 is average.

The scores indicated that all of the children tested had some knowledge of the literature included in the inventory. A score of 51 indicated an extremely high exposure to children's literature. When I worked with individual classrooms of children, I found age-related differences in terms of exposure. Fourth-grade children, for example, had a higher average, presumably because they had had more exposure to the wide range of books available for a longer period of time.

Interestingly, certain questions were answered correctly by almost all of the children. For example, all in the pilot study were familiar with the rhyme "Little Miss Muffet," indicating a basic exposure to at least one Mother Goose rhyme. All but one of the children knew "Hey, Diddle, Diddle!" Compare this with scores for "The Old Woman Who Lived in a Shoe." All but one of the 12 children in the high-scoring group answered this item correctly, whereas only 3 of the 10 low scorers knew this rhyme. What these scores seem to indicate is the importance of parents' reading with children.

The poetry section revealed similar discriminating questions. Shel Silverstein's poem "Jimmy Jet and His TV Set" was chosen from a popular book by the author. Half of the children with high scores answered this item correctly, but none of the children with low scores were able to identify this poem found in *Where the Sidewalk Ends*.

Similarly, *all* of the children with high scores identified "The Owl and the Pussy-Cat" correctly, compared with only 4 children with lower scores. This is a traditional poem often included in early poetry collections for children. The fact that all of the high scorers were familiar with this poem indicated at least a basic exposure to children's poetry. That 16 children knew this poem also indicates its popularity in poetry collections and is a tribute to those parents, teachers, and librarians who obviously are sharing poetry with children.

In part three of the inventory, fairy tales, folktales, and fables were explored. Most children identified the common fairy tales about the three little pigs, Little Red Riding Hood, and the three bears. Surprisingly, a small number of children had had no exposure to these common tales. Children not familiar with common fairy tales may have had very little exposure to read-aloud settings in the home. Having such knowledge informs a teacher and adds to her pool of knowledge about learners in her classroom and also helps indicate a plan of action for read-aloud time with children. If basic fairy tales like these are not in a child's cultural cauldron of narratives, the child will miss much over the years in terms of references to these stories that many of us take for granted. They are a part of our rich cultural heritage and link us to storytellers of the past. They also include so many of the basic values that form the fabric of society that we sometimes forget that our children pick up these values at tacit levels: It's wrong to hurt other people, take someone else's property, let jealousy rule your life, trust wolves. You also know that the ultimate goal of childhood is to go off into the world, to build your own house, but the warning is that you had better be strong, that you had better make careful choices, that you need to be a risk taker, and trust your instincts.

The question on the inventory that was the highest discriminator between the high and low groups was the fable "The Tortoise and the Hare." All of the high scorers contrasted to only one of the low scorers identified this fable. Children with a high exposure to literature seem to know a variety of genres, compared to the paucity of genre variety recognized by the low scorers. It would be of interest to follow up and determine the home and classroom reading patterns of both groups of children. The scores seem to indicate that the high group continues to read or listen to books in volume, in a variety of genres. The low scores indicate the opposite trend, but this cannot be established from the inventory alone. It is an indicator that would necessitate observation in the classroom and perhaps interviews with parents, teachers, and children. Analysis of the inventory was helpful in showing what children already know about children's literature.

DESIGN OF THE FIRST STUDY

Children in kindergarten, second, and fourth grade were chosen from 20 classrooms in the same school on the basis of test scores obtained from the Revised Huck Literature Inventory. Twenty children were chosen from each of the three grades with ten in the high-scoring and ten in the low-scoring group. The children lived in a comfortable middle-class suburb of a large midwestern metropolitan city. The school itself was located in a noncommercial section of the city surrounded by well-kept moderately sized homes. There were libraries in the area with good selections of books, as well as several bookstores that catered to children's literature. The school also had many books available in classrooms as well as in the school library.

Setting

The school chosen for the study had two separate programs of instruction available for children. The first was a more traditionally based classroom, termed contemporary, which used basal readers, workbooks, and textbooks. Children in several of these classrooms were also observed listening to books being read aloud by teachers. The second program used a literature-based reading program and an integrated approach to teaching through thematic studies. It is important to note that parents of children in the literature-based classrooms opted for this special program and that their children were not automatically placed in an informal setting.

The school prided itself on its use of children's literature, and one could safely say that literature formed a large part of a child's school encounter. Therefore, it was not feasible, nor even desirable, to make a comparison between the two parts of the school. I was more interested in learning how children constructed meaning during picture book sharing than in making a case for literature-based versus traditional approaches.

Age of Children

I chose to work with kindergarten, second-, and fourth-grade children for a variety of reasons. My choice of the youngest group ultimately proved to be a solid decision, as evidenced by the second study I undertook with 4-year-old children. I outline the results of that study in Chapter 3. First, long-held notions of researchers regarding the theme-generating abilities of the preschool and kindergarten child have suggested that a child of this age is developmentally incapable of generating theme. Piaget (1926/1960) designated 7 to 8 years of age as the critical point at which the child begins to abstract relevant thematic information. Applebee (1978) in his analysis of children's stories points out that children below the age of 6 generally lack clear thematic centers in their production of stories. Paley's (1981) observations of kindergarten children indicate that this age group is aware of thematic content and that young children do encode meaning from stories on the basis of their own perceptions of the world. Consequently, this age group was included in the study to test this concept of thematic awareness and production.

I chose the second-grade children to show the range of responses possible for a child in the concrete stage of operations. A child this age has just learned to read independently and is expanding his or her repertoire of knowledge without total reliance on listening to stories read aloud.

Fourth-graders comprised the upper level of the population sample and provided a view of the child who is beginning to expand his or her awareness of expository structure. Because expository writing is structured differently from narrative forms, the child must become familiar with a new style of writing. This is not a style of writing with which younger children are typically familiar. Baumann's (1981) research indicates that children tested were not proficient at generating or identifying theme in content-area reading; therefore, this age group illustrates the narrative perspective of the child who is beginning to take on expository structures.

Materials

Books for this study were chosen from the wide variety of children's books available with no effort made to control vocabulary. As part of the study design, I used picture books familiar to the child, in natural book-sharing situations, rather than constructed materials in a clinical setting. The picture books reflected a concern for quality of text and illustrations as outlined by Huck et al. (1987). The child's age was also of concern, and every effort was made to choose books that would be considered appropriate to the child's cognitive development. A committee of experts in reading and children's literature assisted with the final selection of books.

For example, a picture book such as *The Seeing Stick* by Jane Yolen would not be a good choice for the kindergarten child because of the abstract theme of seeing the world without eyes; however, the same book would be an excellent choice for a fourth grader because of the maturity of the theme. The older child would be stretched with the thematic content, whereas the young one would be merely confused. Content must necessarily be of concern to teachers in choosing appropriate books for appropriate ages, and, as has been pointed out earlier, content has not been a major concern of recent research. Passages have

been maintained at low levels of vocabulary and have been essentially as
unlike real books as possible.

Three books in each of two genres were chosen for each grade level
(see Table 2.1). The two genres chosen were realistic fiction and folktales. *Realistic fiction* is a genre offering stories within the realm of
children's everyday life experiences, such as fighting with a friend or
sibling, being jealous, or doing something with a brother and sister. For
example, *Titch*, by Pat Hutchins, is about a young child who is always
left behind but who finally does something important, much to the

TABLE 2.1.   Books Read Aloud, Grade Levels, and Genres Used for Task One

REALISTIC FICTION

Kindergarten books
> *Titch* by Pat Hutchins
> *The Carrot Seed* by Ruth Krauss
> *New Blue Shoes* by Eve Rice

Second-grade books
> *The Hating Book* by Charlotte Zolotow
> *Let's Be Enemies* by Janice Udry
> *Say it* by Charlotte Zolotow

Fourth-grade books
> *Stevie* by John Steptoe
> *Thy Friend, Obadiah* by Brinton Turkle
> *When I was Young in the Mountains* by Cynthia Rylant

FOLKTALES

Kindergarten books
> *The Gingerbread Boy* by Paul Galdone
> *The Three Little Pigs* by Paul Galdone
> *The Three Billy Goats Gruff* by Marcia Brown

Second-grade books
> *Tattercoats* by Flora Steel
> *Snow White* by Trina Hyman
> *The Swineherd* by Lisbeth Zwerger

Fourth-grade books
> *Dawn* by Molly Bang
> *A Japanese Fairy Tale* by Jane Ike
> *The Stonecutter* by Gerald McDermott

surprise of his older siblings. The themes of books selected for the second- and fourth-grade children were more complex, such as the theme of acceptance in *Stevie*, by John Steptoe, yet still reflected children's likely experiences.

The second genre, *folktales*, was chosen because children are frequently exposed to folktales at early ages both at home and in school. In addition, according to Favat (1977), folktales are predictable and reaffirm a stable world view. Tucker (1976) notes that they contain concrete rewards and punishments, which children find particularly satisfying. Therefore, I predicted that folktales would be a familiar genre with readily identifiable themes.

This study emphasized content with quality illustrations and appropriately graded books because of the nature of the thematic exploration involved in the tasks. If the child's perceptions were to be explored in depth, then it was necessary that the picture books chosen reflect themes about which young children could verbalize, and themes that challenged rather than inhibited the older student. Table 2.1 shows the books used for the study by grade and genre.

Within each genre, I chose two books that I thought shared a common theme, and one book that did not. In order to verify that two books in each category could be identified as thematically similar, I read all of the books to a class of 20 undergraduate students enrolled in a children's literature course that I taught at Ohio State University. These students were asked to identify the two books in each genre that shared a common theme and to write that theme. From these results, I judged that two books in each series were easily identifiable by adults as sharing common themes. Consensus was higher for the realistic books. The folktales showed more diversity in the answers, which was consistent with the answers of the children tested. Table 2.2 shows the choices of the university students for thematically matched books.

Procedures

I worked with the children from November to January. Mornings were designated as the best times to gather data. Groups of two to five children attended two reading sessions, on different days, and in each session I read three books aloud to them in a comfortable room separate from their classroom. Realistic fiction was read aloud during the first session. Folktales were read in the second session. Children were then asked to draw a picture about the two stories that they thought had the same theme or told about the same idea; they were given 10 to 15 minutes to draw. Some children indicated that they were ready to be

TABLE 2.2.   Adult Choices for Thematically Matched Books

REALISTIC FICTION

Kindergarten books

Titch/The Carrot Seed	17
The Carrot Seed/New Blue Shoes	2
Titch/New Blue Shoes	1

Second-grade books

Let's Be Enemies/The Hating Book	17
The Hating Book/Say it	1
No response	2

Fourth-grade books

Stevie/Thy Friend, Obadiah	20

FOLKTALES

Kindergarten books

Three Little Pigs/Three Billy Goats Gruff	17
No response	3

Second-grade books

Tattercoats/Snow White	14
No response	6

Fourth-grade books

Dawn/A Japanese Fairy Tale	14
The Stonecutter/Dawn	4
No response	2

interviewed after drawing for several minutes, whereas others wanted more time. While one child was being interviewed, the others were allowed to continue drawing. They were within my sight but could not overhear the interviews with other children. They were also separated from each other so that they could not view each other's pictures.

First I asked each child to "tell me or show me which two books have the same theme or tell about the same idea." Next I asked the child a series of interview questions designed to aid in story retelling, adapted from guide questions developed by Goodman and Burke (1972). These questions encouraged the child to consider the stories from the authors' perspectives, to compare the stories to former book experiences, and to make personal evaluations about the stories. I used the following questions:

1. Match two titles. Why did you choose these two books? What are they both about?
2. Can you tell me what the whole story was about, in a few words or in short form?
3. Are these stories similar to any other stories you have read? How?
4. What were the authors trying to teach you when they wrote these stories?
5. What are the most important ideas in these stories?
6. Pick a story. Why did it end like it did?
7. Is there anything you would have changed?
8. Did you like the story? Why or why not?
9. Would you have changed the ending?

During the interview, the books were in visual range and within easy reach of the child. Children could handle the books as they talked, if they chose to do so. During the interview, each child sat close to me on a couch or rug.

Any child who was unwilling or not ready to be interviewed was allowed to continue drawing and be interviewed later, giving him or her time to think about the books. This contributed to the natural setting of the study and was helpful in adding to the comfort level of the kindergarten children. Interview transcripts were analyzed for whether children were able to generate a thematic statement for books heard. Thematic statements were rated for congruency with text and for level of abstraction. (For a fuller discussion of the rating scale, see Lehr, 1988b.)

All transcripts of the interview were examined for thematic content. I found some of the thematic statements embedded within retellings or summaries of the stories. I also combined some of the statements with statements made in other portions of the interview, because children's ideas tended to build as the interview progressed. For example, one fourth grader, when asked what the authors of *Dawn* and *The Stonecutter* were trying to teach, answered, "The two . . . are similar, I think. The more you're greedy, the more you can lose in trying to get what you want." The child was next asked why the story ended the way it did. His answer extended his previous statement: "He (points to book *The Stonecutter*) wanted to be greater and greater than anything else, and he wanted to be a mountain, and he started to get chipped away like he was less and less of himself." The perspectives of the questions were so diverse that only by combining several of the answers could one represent the child's complete thematic statement. Even a question eliciting the child's opinion about a story could lead the child to reflect that a character "was greedy and wanted everything for himself, and so I didn't like the story."

IDENTIFYING AND GENERATING THEMES
IN A LITERATURE SETTING

First, I was interested in finding out quite simply if children could link two books with similar themes, an identification task as opposed to a generative task. The setting was the school itself in rooms adjacent to classrooms. The children and I sat on a couch or rug together, which created a relaxed setting. They were generally eager to listen to the books I had to share and enjoyed listening and looking at the illustrations as I read. None of the children in the study were unwilling to listen to me read or to talk to me about the books. Because of my presence in their school and in their classrooms, I was not viewed as a stranger invading their setting. In fact, going out of the classroom with me was typically viewed as a positive event.

All the children interviewed attempted to match two books that they perceived as sharing the same theme. Table 2.3 shows the children's choices for thematically matched books. Children at all grade levels were more likely to identify realistic books with shared themes than folktales. Second- and fourth-grade children made the same selections as adults more often than kindergarten children.

You'll notice that most of the children's answers match adult choices for the same books with the exception of the folktale selections for the kindergarten children. This suggests that identifying themes of books is a fairly early strategy that children are capable of. When the adults chose different books with possible variations, the children generally followed the same pattern. There was more variance with folktales in all three grades, but you'll notice in Table 2.2 that adults also were more unified in their perceptions for realistic fiction than they were for folktales. As the theme statements of the children are analyzed, some possible reasons for this disparity will emerge.

Concrete Thematic Statements

Some children were unsuccessful in their attempts to link two books with a thematic statement. Many of the statements were too concrete. For example, one kindergarten child tried to link *Titch* and *New Blue*

TABLE 2.3.   Children's Choices for Thematically Matched Books

REALISTIC FICTION

Kindergarten books
Titch/The Carrot Seed	16
The Carrot Seed/New Blue Shoes	2
Titch/New Blue Shoes	2

Second-grade books
Let's Be Enemies/The Hating Book	20

Fourth-grade books
Stevie/Thy Friend, Obadiah	20

FOLKTALES

Kindergarten books
Three Little Pigs/Three Billy Goats Gruff	7
Three Little Pigs/Gingerbread Boy	12
Three Billy Goats Gruff/Gingerbread Boy	1

Second-grade books
Tattercoats/Snow White	12
Tattercoats/The Swineherd	8

Fourth-grade books
Dawn/A Japanese Fairy Tale	12
The Stonecutter/Dawn	4
A Japanese Fairy Tale/The Stonecutter	4

Shoes "cause both of them have blue." Such responses were based entirely on specific details. "It's snowing," was offered by one low-exposure second-grade child for *Tattercoats* and *Snow White.*

Some children were able to identify concrete similarities between two stories that were related to the shared theme but were unable to abstract and verbalize the theme. For example, one child linked *Titch* and *The Carrot Seed* by stating that "they both had things that were growing." In *Titch*, an underlying theme is the idea that a child eventually gets bigger and does bigger things. It could be argued that this child correctly identified a concrete aspect of both stories that leads to the shared theme. However, as it stands, the statement is too concrete. Similarly, the response offered by one second grader that *The Hating Book* and *Let's Be Enemies* share the theme of "to be your friend" is too vague. Although the concept of friendship is identified, the answer does not reflect what either story has to say about friendship.

Many children offered statements that were concretely tied to the plot. When asked why *Titch* ended as it did, one kindergarten child responded, "He needed to have something that was bigger. He wanted it to grow." A common response for *The Three Little Pigs* or *The Ginger-bread Boy* was "they both got eaten up." Another kindergarten child, Mary, added that *The Three Little Pigs* ended like it did because "you can't blow down brick houses."

Many second-grade students also gave statements that were literally tied to the plots, such as the second grader who said that in both *Tatter-coats* and *Snow White* "it's like there's both two people being mean on each one to another person." Other second-grade children pointed out that the main characters in *Tattercoats* and *Snow White* both had some-one who hated them, both were the prettiest, and both got married to a prince. These were basically plot summaries, which contained no ab-stracted levels of theme.

Also, in terms of plot, the outcome of the book was salient, espe-cially if harm came to any of the characters. For example, in response to *The Three Billy Goats Gruff*, one child stated that "they almost don't get where they want to be." Some second-grade children identified Snow White's plight as being more severe than that of Tattercoats, because Snow White dies. Consequently, some children said the two books were linked because "they *don't* get almost killed," or because "no one gets hurt in these two."

In response to *The Three Little Pigs*, one kindergarten child stated, "Build your house strong." This response includes information specifi-cally related to the plot of the story, but it is possible that the child used the words metaphorically, as an abstract statement of theme. Because the story is about the avoidance of real danger, and about tasks well done, which the first two pigs did not accomplish with straw and sticks, the idea of building a strong house is a suitable metaphor for the theme of the story. However, it is impossible to tell whether this is what the child intended.

Abstract Statements of Theme

An example of a thematic statement at a high level of abstraction is a fourth-grade response linking *Stevie* and *Thy Friend, Obadiah*: "Be nice to your friends while you still have them." This response steps back from the literal plots of both stories and links them successfully with an overarching idea. One kindergarten child linked *The Three Little Pigs* and *The Gingerbread Boy* effectively with this statement of theme: "Not to trust strangers that you don't know." Adults did not match those two books; however, 12 kindergarten children did. One second-grade response stated that in *The Swineherd* "you don't get everything and that's how life goes." "You can sacrifice things to make people happy," was offered by a fourth grader in response to *A Japanese Fairy Tale* and *Dawn*. His statement reflects a clear understanding of the concepts explored in the books and an ability to state an abstract theme shared by both.

CHARACTERISTICS OF A CHILD'S DEVELOPING SENSE OF THEME

Remember my earlier statements regarding Rosenblatt's (1976) idea of text and reader making a new "poem"? The majority of the theme statements given by children matched the text but were different from adult perspectives, suggesting that the idea of a new poem is right on the mark. However, statements that were not congruent with the text primarily originated in the low-exposure groups for all three grades and occurred most frequently with folktales. These children simply didn't have the same depth of experience with literature and had trouble talking about the books from a variety of perspectives that meshed with the text itself. Some characteristics of them that emerged after careful analysis of the transcripts included congruency with text, the ability to summarize, awareness of character motivations, and ability to make generalizations. Children had certain story expectations and at times used moralistic language in response to books.

Congruency With Text

The folktales were more complex and longer, had more events to remember, and included more character interactions than the realistic fiction. Thus, children who gave responses that were not text-congruent may have been having difficulty with comprehension or recall. "They're basically, they're both in foreign countries" was offered by one fourth-grade girl for *Dawn* and *The Stonecutter*, and when probed further she added that "they both had boats." Neither statement was congruent with the text in terms of thematic content. Children making statements that were not text-congruent also had more difficulty verbalizing answers for other questions about endings, important ideas, or exploring what the author was trying to teach. Children at the fourth-grade level were less likely to include information incongruent with the text than were kindergarten and second-grade children.

Some of the children indicated a basic understanding of a character's internal dilemma and struggle but responded with statements of absolute values that were not appropriate in relation to the larger context of the story. "Don't go across bridges" was offered by one kindergarten child as the author's message in *The Three Billy Goats Gruff*, which is not representative of the dilemma posed in the story. The child's perspective is that of avoiding conflict, without thought of the danger of starvation. This is consistent with the child's safely structured world, where basic needs are met in the home, but it is not consistent with the perceived need of the characters in the story. In this instance, the child did not take on the perspective of the characters and therefore did not grapple with the characters' dilemma. Thus, the theme identified by the child was not text-congruent.

Similarly, one second grader responded to *The Hating Book*, "Even if you don't think you like the person, it always ends up that you like the person." The answer indicates an understanding of the plot of the book but lacks a certain depth in relation to choices made by the characters. Answers that included such absolute statements occurred most frequently with folktales.

Comparison With Adult Responses

The majority of the children's thematic statements differed from any of those offered by adults. The kindergarten children's statements were distinctly different from the adult responses, whereas the fourth-grade statements differed more subtly from those of adults. One kindergartner said the theme of *Titch* was "share whatever you're doing," and justified her position with direct reference to the illustrations and the text, which initially show two characters ignoring Titch, and in the end show the three characters working as a team. Her thematic statement suggests a unique transaction between the child and the book perhaps outside the realm of author intentions. None of the adult answers mentioned the concept of sharing or talked about unfair situations in *Titch*. This occurred most frequently at the kindergarten level and suggested that the child can take on the perspective of another (Donaldson, 1978; Paley, 1981), although it may differ from an adult's view. Kindergarten children responded with answers that differed from those of adults more frequently than did second- and fourth-grade children.

Many of the answers of the kindergarten children showed less concern with becoming independent or overcoming evil than they did with being safe. "So he would learn that he should not have run away," was offered as an explanation for why *The Gingerbread Boy* ended as it did.

The fates of the two foolish little pigs and the foolish gingerbread boy were mentioned by 11 children. The kindergarten children's concerns were more literally tied to the stories than the adults' concerns and were stated with absolute values, indicating that they had formed their own perspectives of the stories based on their existing knowledge about how the world functions. For example, in response to *The Three Billy Goats Gruff* one child stated, "Bigger is better." Reflecting a slightly older perspective, but again one not shared by the adults, a fourth-grade child likened Tasaku's changing in *The Stonecutter* from man to wind to sun to mountain to deciding what one wanted to be in life. His answer missed the subtleties of greed and the misuse of power and instead honed in on a personal concern, finding an occupation.

Although many of the children's responses were not congruent with the adult choices, most of them *were* congruent with the text, which suggests once again that young children process meaning in literature from perspectives that differ from those of adults.

Ability to Summarize

Most children in all three age groups were able to summarize stories. In fact, a number of children, especially at kindergarten age, gave plot summaries rather than theme statements. This ability to summarize the story enabled the child to talk about concrete similarities between stories. Some of the summaries were given when the children were asked, "Can you tell me what the whole story was about, in a few words or in short form?" In addition, asking children to respond to specific questions related to the story gave them a focus for constructing meaning.

In linking the two selections for realistic fiction, Mary (kindergarten) successfully summarized the plot of *Titch*: "They both (referring to the two books in front of her) have a plant that grows. . . . They (pointing to older brother and sister in *Titch*) get all the biggest things. He (pointing to Titch) ends up with the biggest." When asked why the story ended as it did, she responded, "He needed to have something that was bigger. He wanted it to grow." She summarized the story, and could identify the concrete similarities between *Titch* and *The Carrot Seed*, even though she could not generate an abstract statement of theme. Note Mary's dependence on the physical text to help order her statements and identify her use of referents. Without the text physically present, Mary might have had more difficulty summarizing.

Elizabeth (kindergarten) also summarized *Titch* in response to my question about the ending of the story: "Like older brothers and sisters had bigger things. All their stuff is bigger. She only got the littlest things." But in the end, "She got one of the biggest things. . . . Cause they all got the big stuff and she wanted something big." Eight of the ten kindergarten children in the high-exposure group were able to summarize at least one of the stories heard among the realistic fiction selections. Most second- and fourth-grade children were able to summarize stories in one or two sentences.

Most, but not all, children in kindergarten were able to summarize when they were asked to tell what the story was about in a few words, or when probed about the story. This ability to summarize enabled children to talk about concrete similarities between stories. In contrast, Applebee (1978) found that children of this age were unable to summarize and instead had a tendency to retell entire stories. The structure and content of the interview questions used here might account for this difference. During the interviews, I specifically asked children to retell the story in a few words or in short form, and I specifically asked what the most important ideas were.

Awareness of Character Motivations

Children in all three grades talked at length about characters and their internal motivations. Responding to how characters behaved or exploring what they needed was often included in summary statements, which frequently involved following a character's actions through the plot of a story. Focusing on the character's dilemma provided a format for talking about the theme of the book.

One kindergarten child enlarged upon the theme of sharing in *Titch*:

> They're going real fast up the hill. And here they won't let him try to fly the kites. Here they couldn't let him try their instruments. Here Titch he had to hold the nails and they had to the hard jobs. That's not fair. . . . Right here they won't let him put any dirt in or hold it. They only let him handed the seed. . . . It grew bigger until it was bigger than them . . . at the ending the plant grew out and it got those two.

This answer indicates an awareness of internal reactions of characters and a sensitivity for Titch's plight as the youngest child. This child's view of being the smallest included a level of frustration with an added form of retribution. His world view included a system of concrete rewards and punishments and provided a satisfying ending. This sensitivity to the character in the story indicates a clear understanding of what the story is about; however, in terms of moral development, as described by Kohlberg, young children tend to view behavior as being right or wrong without considering the subtle nuances of situation or intent (Huck et al., 1987). Luke identifies strongly with Titch but has little sympathy for older siblings who seem to ignore Titch. The entire response to the character of Titch shows how this child is reconstructing the plot in a way that is meaningful for him.

Carey (age 8:0) stated in response to *The Swineherd*: "The princess learns a lesson. . . . She was someone that wanted just about everything and that's how she learned her lesson. . . . You don't get everything and that's how life goes." These sentences illustrate a concise understanding of the story, through analysis of the character's internal motivation. This response is also a summary statement of the story. Children who were able to talk about a character while summarizing a story were typically able to generate themes. The questions provided a focus; however, not all children were able to summarize a story or talk about a character's motivations.

In talking about characters and their actions, children were also able to link the book experience to their own lives. Titch was viewed sympathetically by many kindergarten children because he was little and "big kids have big things and little kids have little things," but "it doesn't matter if you're little or not . . . cause if you're little you might get better things."

Benny stated that "you can't always have things your own way . . . cause you have to let your friends have things their way sometimes." His analysis referred directly to *Let's Be Enemies*; however, his words also came out of his own experiences with friends. In responding to *The Hating Book* and *Let's Be Enemies*, another second-grade boy gave a lengthy discussion of his neighborhood peer structure and how he and his little sister related to other children and handled disagreements.

Fourteen kindergarten children mentioned internal reaction or motivation of character at some point during the interview. Knowing how or why the characters responded as they did in particular episodes was often included in thematic responses. This result contrasts with Mandler and Johnson's (1977) finding that young children omit internal reactions of characters during spontaneous recall. The variety of perspectives probed by the interview questions included may have acted as a catalyst in this respect. This supports the idea that young children can take on the perspectives of others (Donaldson, 1978; Paley, 1981).

However, as discussed earlier, not all children were able to understand or talk about a character's motivations. For example, the child who said the theme of *The Three Billy Goats Gruff* was "don't go across bridges" was unable to perceive the billy goats' motivation for crossing the bridge (hunger). Such children often gave responses that were not text-congruent.

Second- and fourth-grade children identified with characters and expected characters to change, whereas kindergarten children typically did not want to change characters' actions, nor did they wish to restructure events. The exception was with folktales, where kindergartners wanted the two little pigs "not to be eaten up"; however, children responding at this level gave no indication that they understood the internal motivation of the two pigs as characters—that is, that they were lazy, lacking motivation, or simply did not have the foresight to prepare against the threat of danger.

Interestingly, 12 kindergarten children matched *The Three Little Pigs* and *The Gingerbread Boy* as being thematically similar, whereas adults chose *The Three Little Pigs* and *The Three Billy Goats Gruff*. The reason most often cited by the children was that "they both got eaten up." This coincides with some of the more basic needs described by Maslow (Huck et al., 1987) in his hierarchy of needs, ranging from basic physiological to aesthetic needs. "Safety" needs are to be met early in life if the child is to develop fully. Young children I interviewed were preoccupied with safety and "belongingness" needs, which underscores the point that children understand stories quite differently from adults and have different perspectives based on their own social, emotional, and cognitive growth.

At the second-grade level children suggested a more active role for characters in changing what they didn't like in the stories. Kindergarten children offered answers that were more passive; Titch was a victim of sorts, whereas themes for *The Hating Book* and *Let's Be Enemies* ranged from "she wanted to find out why her friend was mad at her. . . . She was misunderstood," to "make friends and don't let an argument separate you." Fourth-grade children talked about changing characters and their actions; they also wanted to alter endings with both genres. For example, in *Thy Friend, Obadiah*, children wanted to delete Obadiah's act of cruelty toward the seagull. Other children wanted to alter the ending to *Stevie* by John Steptoe, so that Robert could be with Stevie again to show that he now liked him. In *A Japanese Fairy Tale* children wanted the hero to regain his good looks, because he had sacrificed them willingly.

Ability to Analyze and Make Generalizations

Children, particularly those in the high exposure to literature groups, were able to analyze and make generalizations about the stories. This ability to talk about the story from an abstract perspective oc-

curred differently among the students. Some offered theme statements
right away when asked what both of the stories were about, whereas
others discussed plot and character first. About half of the second- and
fourth-grade theme statements from the children in the high-exposure
groups (8 of the 20 total responses for second grade and 10 of the 20
responses for fourth grade) met the analysis and generalization levels set
in Applebee's (1978) Developmental Formulation of Response Categories. This finding was interesting, because Applebee asserts that children
in the concrete operational states of development are typically unable to
analyze and generalize about stories. However, in this study children
were given access to the books as points of reference during the interview, after hearing them read aloud, and they were also given time to
draw a picture of what the books were about. This procedure presumably focused the children on the thematic content of the stories and gave
them an opportunity to consider themes for the books (Siegel, 1983).

Carey's (age 8:0) statements about *The Swineherd* reflect an ability
to analyze and make a generalization about the story. Remember her
eloquent statement about the self-centered princess? "The princess
learns a lesson. . . . She was someone that wanted just about everything
and that's how she learned her lesson. . . . You don't get everything and
that's how life goes."

Statements like Carey's indicated an awareness of not only the plot
but also the internal workings of a character and the ability to take this
information and apply it to life in general. In terms of critical-thinking
skills, this statement reflects a depth of understanding of this character
and others like her and the ability to take that information and generate
the overarching concept for the story. Children who were able to talk
about a character while summarizing a story were typically able to
generate themes. The question provided a focus.

Fourth-grade responses for *Dawn* and *A Japanese Fairy Tale* further illustrate the language that the 9- or 10-year-old child brings to an
understanding of literature. "You can sacrifice something for something
else" (Chris, age 9:2). "You can sacrifice things to make people happy"
(David, age 10:1). The language used and the concepts revealed in these
statements were at generalized levels for stating theme.

Moralistic Language

At times children responded in absolute terms. Their answers offered no alternatives or choices for characters and were often stated in
the negative.

Children offered statements that reflected personal value systems, such as "don't run away from home" (kindergarten response to *The Gingerbread Boy*) or "share whatever you're doing" (kindergarten response to *Titch*). What was noteworthy was the child's attitude toward life, the definite black/white value system that emerged in a discussion of stories and how characters behaved. At this level of thematic response, children viewed events somewhat unidimensionally. Rather than seeing life choices as a complex weave, they tended to react moralistically, almost parallel to morals given for fables. For example, Tana's (age 9:7) response in reference to *The Stonecutter* was: "Be what you are and don't change it." This type of decisive statement was meant to be an endorsement of how things should be. It became an overstatement of the stonecutter's dilemma, recommending a static state in order to avoid problems.

By contrast, other answers showed a delicate sensitivity to the themes of the books. "Well, don't underestimate your friends; they can be nice people" (David, age 10:1, in reference to *Thy Friend, Obadiah* and *Stevie*). Statements like these tended to include qualifiers that revealed students' awareness that other options or choices were available.

Children also offered warnings, which can be characterized as similar to adult admonitions that are typically given to children of this age. This was most apparent with folktales. Pete (age 5:0) stated that you should "be careful walking on bridges" and that you should "stay away from wolfs." The statement has several layers of meaning and at a very literal level is a caution to the billy goats, pigs, gingerbread boys, and others in a similar position. However, like the statement discussed earlier, it may also have been intended by the child metaphorically. That this may be so is suggested by the same child's statement that these books taught you "not to trust strangers that you don't know." Kindergarten children were concerned with the literal safety of characters: "Never go across dangerous bridges." Their answers reflected their status as young children who are still dependent upon others for their safety and well-being.

Physical Use of Texts

Children used the books as references during the interview and opened them, pointed at illustrations, browsed while thinking about an answer, and, at times, even hugged the book while explaining an answer. This literal use of the book decreased with age. Seventeen kindergarten children opened the book as they talked. The three children not opening or touching the books seemed ill at ease during the interview sessions and, when invited to open the books to help jog their memories, would not take the invitation, even though it was repeated several times.

The second-grade children used the books as references quite differently. They pointed to and held the books. In contrast, fourth-grade children rarely opened or touched the books but would occasionally nod in the direction of the book under discussion. This indicated a literal movement from the concrete toward the abstract across age levels in using the physical text as a reference.

Story Expectations

At times children had strong prior expectations for story parts. Consequently, children instantiated familiar story frames to fit with prior expectations (Anderson, Stevens, Shifrin, & Osborn, 1977; Spiro, 1977). As suggested in studies with background building, the children filled in confusing or missing information on the basis of predictable patterns they had evolved for stories (Pichert & Anderson, 1976).

Zwerger's retelling of *The Swineherd* does not end typically. Yet three children used the predictable "they lived happily ever after" response to the story when verbalizing themes. This suggests the child's strong sense of story and prior expectations for story parts to behave in a predictable manner.

As Spiro (1977) and Anderson, Stevens, Shifrin, & Osborn (1977) have suggested in studies with background building and the instantiation of meaning, the children had background knowledge that definitely did not mesh with the idea of a princess sitting alone out in the rain at the end of a "fairy tale." Instead, children instantiated a happy ending schema to complete the tale in a satisfying manner. The role of prior expectations in terms of predicting what will be read on the page is a strong factor in building reading and listening fluency.

CHILDREN'S RESPONSES TO
REALISTIC FICTION AND FOLKTALES

Children offered a richness and diversity of responses to the two genres used in this study. The majority seemed most relaxed talking about realistic fiction, presumably because it is closer to their life experiences than tales based on the struggle between good and evil, finding the right man or woman, or learning how to avoid unpleasant stepmothers or nasty kings. Interestingly, however, some of the richest themes and discussions arose from the folktale selections.

Responses to Realistic Fiction

Andy (5:0) was able to go beyond a simple concrete answer and add several general components about the theme of *Titch* and *The Carrot Seed*. The following interview typified the manner in which the children talked about realistic fiction.[1]

I: Why did you choose those two?

A: First of all it didn't grow and then he got the biggest carrot. And on this one Titch got a bigger got something that his brother and sister didn't get.

I: Can you tell me what one of the stories is about in a few words or a short form?

A: I'll have to read it then.

I: Oh yeah? To remember it you mean.

A: (pause as he looks through *Titch*) His brother Pete had a kite that flew high over the trees and his sister had one that flew over the house and Titch just had a little pinwheel.

I: (later) What do you think that the authors were trying to teach you when they wrote those books?

A: That it doesn't matter if you're little or not.

I: How come?

A: Cause if you're little you might get better things. (pause)

I: Did one of those little guys get better things?

A: He got a better thing (points to boy in *The Carrot Seed*) and he got a better thing (points to *Titch*).

I: Why do you think someone little would get a better thing?

A: Cause big kids have big things and little kids have little things.

I: Why did this book end like it did? (*The Carrot Seed*)

A: Because his parents and his brother said it wouldn't grow and it did.

The chain of logic can be connected in the following way: "It doesn't matter if you're little or not . . . cause if you're little you might get better things . . . cause big kids have big things and little kids have little things." He began with the concrete and through a series of questions was able to generalize the theme of the story. This movement toward building meaning was typical at all age levels but most apparent with

---

[1]Throughout the dialogues, I = interviewer, and the other letters indicate the names of the children just mentioned.

the kindergarten and second-grade groups of children, especially those with a high exposure to literature. Fourth-grade children often responded immediately with thematic statements rather than embedding them in discussions of the stories.

Andy generalized his thematic information about the book from elements in the story and his own instantiation of meaning based on background knowledge about how the world operates. His own life experience at home and at school formed the basis of his meaning structures and was apparent in his answer (Duckworth, 1972). This concrete connection of story to real-life experience buttresses White's (1984) notion of how knowledge gained from books reinforces life experiences as well as how life reinforces the book experience. Most of the children interviewed made connections between their concrete experiences and the books heard across age levels. This supports Hardy's (1977) view of narrative as a primary act of mind. To talk about meaning in stories is to "story" itself.

General responses.   An example of a more general response that did not focus on theme but did begin to grapple with main ideas of the stories was Kurt's (6:3). It illustrated the developmental processes at work in a child's early attempts to generate a thematic statement.

> **K:**   (turns pages of book) They're about (pause) This one's about a plant, I mean this one's about a little girl that has little toys and this one is about a growing carrot. . . .
> **I:**   OK, and how is that the same? How is that the same idea?
> **K:**   Cause they both have growing things.

Kurt was not able to state the theme of the story concretely, but he was able to identify components that would be included in a thematic statement. In kindergarten about half of the responses occurred at this level or lower, which included *all* of the low scores on the RHLI. Children with low exposure to literature accounted for all but one of these vague kinds of responses. Within this framework a developmental perspective began to emerge, in relation to a child's exposure to literature. Among second graders 20% of the responses were at this level, among fourth graders only 10% were at or below this level, none of which came from the high-exposure group.

The question that seemed most effective in serving as a catalyst to generate thematic statements when the initial question regarding children's choices was not successful asked the children what they thought the authors were trying to teach when they wrote the books. The perspective of the question was outside the book itself and suggested that the author had a point of view when writing the book. This in itself may have assisted children in distancing themselves from the literal elements of the book and may have opened up a new line of reasoning for some of the children questioned. Questions about what the author was trying to teach, or what the most important ideas in the story were, guided children to state theme, whereas "retell" or "recall" questions would not have led the children to explore theme. Children were willing to discuss the concepts of the books because the questions continued to probe for what they knew about theme. General questions that ask the child to tell all that he or she can remember about the story do not serve this purpose but rather act as a net that will grab anything the child wishes to include.

At times children offered vague statements that could not be linked to any solid idea. Important ideas for *The Hating Book* and *Let's Be Enemies* were identified by Amy (8:1) as "to be your friend." The thought goes nowhere and leaves more unstated than stated. No point of view is suggested, and the "your" does not link to a general *you* or a specific character from the book. Amy and certain other children were unable to bring thoughts to completion throughout the interviews in conjunction with other types of questions.

Pete's (5:0) answer typified the kind of response that was considered too vague and was offered by all ten of the children in the low-exposure kindergarten group, six of the children in the low second-grade group, and only three of the children in the low fourth-grade group, indicating that ability to talk about theme in realistic fiction increases with age. When asked what the most important ideas in *Titch* were, he replied that "instruments can break." This answer had nothing to do with the story of *Titch*, except for a superficial link to an illustration that showed the children with instruments. The child attempted to generate a thematic statement but was unable to. At another point in the interview he tried again to link ideas in *Titch* and *The Carrot Seed*.

P: They're something like it, like carrots and popcorn.
I: How is it alike?
P: Cause there's two foods in it.
I: What do you think both authors were trying to teach you when they wrote those books?
P: Teach you they're both the same.
I: What's both the same?
P: The books.

Children at the fourth-grade level seemed better able to character-
ize theme for realistic fiction across group levels and really did not
include theme statements that did not mesh with the text. Developmentally this indicated a greater facility for adhering to the text when
discussing realistic fiction.

Negotiating meaning.   A conversation with Michael (5:4) illustrated
the importance of negotiating meaning throughout the interview session as
terms became defined and the search for theme continued. It also illustrated the impact that other books can have on book-sharing experiences and
the encoding of theme. Michael had heard the sequel to *Titch* and linked
both books when talking about theme. The second Hutchins book deals
even more strongly with the concept of size and outgrowing clothing and
becoming bigger. This background knowledge about Titch's character was
intertwined in Michael's repertoire of knowledge and affected his answers,
which were congruent when taken as a whole. In fact, this prior knowledge
actually enriched Michael's answers and gave them a depth not found in
many of the other children's answers. Michael's statements show how context builds with subsequent book encounters to form a cohesive whole.

> I: All right Michael, which two books do you think tell about the
>   same kind of idea?
> M: Ehhhh . . .
> I: You can think about it . . . (pause)
> I: You've got to pick two books that tell . . . are alike, that tell
>   about the same idea. (He points to *Titch* and *The Carrot
>   Seed*.) Can you tell me why?
> M: Cause they both grew a plant.
> I: Is there anything else?
> M: The bike and the no bike. (He points to the picture in *Titch*
>   with a bike.)
> I: Anything else?
> M: Nope!
> I: Nope. What were they both about?
> M: Do you know what a clue is?
> I: A clue? What's a clue?
> M: No. You have to guess. I do.
> I: I don't know. What's a clue?
> M: You have to guess. If you guess and the clue is . . . you have to
>   say part of it.
> I: You want me to give you a clue?
> M: Yes.
> I: Hmmmm . . . You want me to give you a clue? OK. I want

> you to look at this book right here and tell me what that book was about. That's your clue. In a few w —

M: No you have to say the name of a part of it.

I: OK. You tell me about Titch.

M: She grew a plant and she had two big brothers and they had to need big things and the girl had to have little things. Big brothers and they had big things and her had little things. The big kids have the big things.

I: What else . . .

M: Nothing!

I: Nothing else?

M: Nope!

The context taken as a whole reveals what the child brings to the book-sharing experience and how he networks information to create cohesiveness in his response to literature. Isolating events might suggest incongruency; however, experiences with books can be seen as linked events that build on each other and give texture to a child's response. Michael was at first unwilling to talk about the books, or perhaps he didn't understand what it was that I was asking. I don't have a clue as to why, but after I asked him several questions, he decided that we would abandon my agenda. He then set his own and asked for a clue. Not realizing that the agenda was changing, I took a while to pick up his cues. He patiently explained to me what a clue was, and when I finally realized what it was he wanted, I gave it to him. I had to be corrected several times along the way, you'll notice.

The point is that Michael and I negotiated meaning. We set up a dialogue that could not have happened if I had insisted on following my own set format. He didn't give a particularly elaborate statement about *Titch*, but you'll notice that he did have things to say about the book and that he did understand some of the book's underlying concepts. He talked about characters' needing big things and little things but didn't take it the final step in terms of talking about "whys." Nonetheless, Michael illustrates how teachers can nurture talk about books that encourages children to crawl into characters' skins and think about what is going on behind the scenes. Michael gave me no more than what he decided I'd get, and that's important to remark on as well. Children have their own agendas and their own limits. When Michael was done, I allowed him to be done.

Active protagonists. At the second-grade level the idea of theme was viewed more pragmatically, and the burden of responsibility to rectify a bad situation was often placed on the protagonist in the story. In reference to *The Hating Book*, Sara (7:5) stated "that it has to be some kind of reason that your friend splits up . . . and just try to still get back together and don't just give up." She viewed not giving up as the key idea in the story. Adult answers characterized *Let's Be Enemies* and *The Hating Book* as the highs and lows of true friendship. There was no real mention of not giving up or looking for the reason when conflict arose. Laura (7:7) added the component of not being understood. "She wanted to find out why her friend was mad at her. . . . She was misunderstood." Brad (7:9) suggested that being friends and not being bossy was what the authors were trying to teach. At the highest level of abstraction was Dan's (8:5) response: "Make friends" and don't "let an argument separate you." He realized that arguments can and do separate people and was able to generalize the story from that perspective. The answers of the second graders were pragmatic and indicated that they were better able to deal with an ordering of the world than were the younger children. The characters were more in control of their actions, and second-grade children suggested that they not be mere victims but take an active role in changing what they didn't like in their worlds. This corresponded to the tone of the fourth-grade children as well, although the fourth graders were more willing to alter themes of stories to fit their notions of how the world should ideally be structured.

The idea of a balanced slate or eradication of improper internal motivation seemed important to the older children. Internal motivation of character was most clearly defined with the fourth-grade children in that they wanted characters to behave or act as they would in real-life situations. This suggested an ability to tinker with themes at an abstract level and showed that an older child not only understands or can generate theme but has a desire to alter theme at a cognitive level by way of responding to stories. The question that acted as a catalyst for this type of response asked the child how he or she would change the story, allowing the child to take on the perspective of the author.

At the same time, the fourth-grade children more than the others seemed to need reassurance that their answers were acceptable and that they would not be counted wrong. Several boys checked up on themselves the following day and asked which of them had been right. They were relieved to hear that there was a broad range of acceptance. This preoccupation with right and wrong responses was not apparent with the younger children.

Responses to Folktales

Although many children were able to link books with similar themes, they were not necessarily able to justify or explain their choices, which may give credence to Baker and Stein's (1981) position that ability to identify theme may be after the level of ability to verbalize meaning. In the low-scoring group for the RHLI, few children were able to generate thematic statements for folktales. Of the 30 children in this group, across grade levels, only 6 were able to generate theme statements. Of the 30 children in the high group, across grade levels, 24 were able to generate themes for folktales. In contrast, for realistic fiction, 11 children in the low group and 28 children in the high group were able to do so. Children with the higher exposure to literature seemed more comfortable with both genres, perhaps indicative of their familiarity with a variety of genres.

Children expressed a strong interest in folktales across grade levels during interviews, challenging Favat's (1977) notion that interest in folktales peaks by age 6 to 8 and declines sharply thereafter. Fourth-grade children repeatedly expressed their enjoyment in hearing the tales, and some stated that they read folktales/fairy tales independently for enjoyment. Part of this may have been due to the introduction of fairy tales from other lands, or tales that were new to the children. This was not, however, the case with *Dawn*. Many of the children were familiar with *Dawn*, by Molly Bang, and expressed apparent enjoyment as well as anticipation during the oral reading of the story.

Rehashing the plot.   Children exhibited a wide range of abilities in the generation of theme with folktales. Becky (7:9) typified the concrete answer for *Tattercoats*, illustrated by Diane Goode, and *Snow White*, illustrated by Susan Jeffers. "Because they both have somebody that hated them because and they were both prettiest in the land and they both got married to a prince." She identified the female character in *The Swineherd* by Lizbeth Zwerger as being different from Snow White and Tattercoats, in that "she wasn't as pretty . . . she's real mean." As an inference the fact that the princess wasn't as pretty could refer to her mannerisms and her personality. There is no other indication in the story or illustrations that would suggest she is less pretty than the other two princesses. Can it be that this child identified beauty in terms of actions?

One of the second-grade children stated that *Snow White* teaches you "to don't open doors to strangers" (Don 8:2). This paralleled statements made by kindergarten children regarding folktales where characters were eaten up and showed a literal response to the book based on survival rules for everyday life.

The second-grade children had less to say about the folktales than the other two groups. Three of the boys did not like fairy tales, viewing them as foolish or silly and expressing a preference for realistic novels. For this study it would be difficult to determine if other children shared this view but did not express it. The second graders' attitude, however, reveals something of the nature of what children want to read and respond to and has strong implications for how teachers might structure reading time in the classroom and make a variety of choices available to readers.

Relevant episodes.   Five children in grade 2 chose the books that did not match *Snow White*. When asked to explain this choice, the children offered the following type of explanation:

> Nothing happens to the princess in this one. They don't get almost killed. (Stephanie 8:1)

> Because book two had a part that had hate in it and these two don't. (Mary 7:11)

The reason for not choosing *Snow White* was the severity of the cruelty she suffered.

Being married was a preoccupation of the second-grade boys and girls interviewed, as was being the prettiest and being in love. Six of the girls mentioned beauty and love in their statements. Boys were more concerned with the lesson the princess learned, or the evil in *Snow White* that was overcome. Both sexes mentioned the hate that prevailed in *Tattercoats,* and there was a general condemnation or censure of the old grandfather who refused to forget about his daughter's death and build a new life with his granddaughter. The most common type of thematic response was that the books were about loving others and not being mean.

Children's concerns with these selections differed from adult subjects' answers on several points. Four of the fourth-grade children chose *The Stonecutter* and *Dawn* as matched selections (as did four adults) and were able to substantiate their choices with information from the text. For example, Marie (9:5) made her choice of *The Stonecutter* and *Dawn* based on the fact that metamorphosis occurs. "Cause well this one, Tasaka can change into all these things. And in this one Dawn's mother changes into a bird. Well she was a bird first then changed into a mother. Then she changed into a bird again."

Her thoughts were too generally stated, but they were text-congruent. Dick extended this attitude toward change by stating the following:

> The Stonecutter he tried, he didn't want to be a stonecutter anymore so he went to god. He went to the mountain god and wanted to

> change and wanted to change and so he changed into a whole bunch
> of different stuff and in this (*A Japanese Fairy Tale*) he went to god to
> the god and he wanted to be, they both went to the god to see what
> they wanted to be. (Dick 10:2)

His continued repetition and rephrasing suggests a verbal thought process, a working out of his ideas aloud as he attempted to state theme.

The notion of greed appeared in four of the fourth-grade children's
responses as a linking idea between *The Stonecutter* and *Dawn*. Four of
the adult subjects also linked those two books based on the idea of greed.
Some of the children linked the other two books but chose to talk about
The Stonecutter in terms of theme. As Jeremy (9:5) said: "He gets a taste
of his own medicine."

At another level of theme a preoccupation with being right appeared with the older children, as it did concerning realistic fiction.
Andrew (10:2) concluded his statement of theme for *The Stonecutter*
with, "But I picked these two. Was I right or wrong?" He had chosen to
explore his feelings regarding the book that appealed to him, but he was
concerned that there might be a hidden agenda, and although the interviewer had not steered him away from his topic of choice, Andrew was
worried that he might be responding incorrectly. Informal talks with
the fourth-grade children as they walked to and from classrooms revealed a deep concern for being right or correct. Children would say,
"See, I was right. I told you I was." Children wanted to be reassured
that their answers were right, but they also enjoyed the informal sessions
and wanted to hear more stories, longer stories, as one boy suggested.
The children clearly enjoyed being given further opportunities to talk
about themes in books as an extension of the read-aloud sessions. Reading aloud to children has often been relegated to early grades. In this
school, however, children were read aloud to at all ages, and their
enjoyment of these sessions was apparent. In several classrooms, research times conflicted with daily read-aloud times and children stayed
in the classrooms until read-alouds were finished. This happened with
all three grade levels, and was most apparent in the literature-based
classrooms.

With folktales the children injected much more misinformation
about the text into their comments than they did with realistic fiction.
The stories were more complex, longer, had more events to remember
and more character interactions, but were also more familiar to the
children. Most of the children had at least heard versions of the folktales
used or had heard one book at home or in the classroom. Statements not
congruent with the text came from eight of the kindergarten children in
the low group, seven of the second-grade children in the low group, and

eight of the low fourth-grade group. In the high-exposure groups, one kindergartner, three second graders, and two fourth graders included vague or incorrect information in their responses.

Realistic fiction seemed more accessible to these children, in part because of the shorter length and in part because of the concrete nature of the stories. The folktales were too remote or complex to command attention, and the children were unable to piece them together individually as cohesive stories with meanings that linked to other books.

Consider this discussion with Patricia (10:2) with regard to *Dawn* and *The Stonecutter*:

I: Tell me or show me which two books have the same theme or tell about the same idea.

P: I picked these (points to *Dawn* and *The Stonecutter*).

I: OK. Why did you pick these?

P: Well they . . . well they're basically . . . they're both in foreign countries.

I: What else is alike about them? What are the ideas that they share, the themes that they share?

P: (pause) They both have boats.

I: OK. In a few words tell me what this one is about (points to *Dawn*).

P: Well this girl goes like on a little journey in a sailboat or whatever that is.

I: What about the girl in the story?

P: Well her mom had . . . she had a baby. Well it was born in a goose egg as a goose girl . . . (mumbles)

I: How did that story end?

P: The mother died.

I: Why did she die?

P: Cause (pause) I don't know. (pause) Person killed her or whatever the man was.

I: You think that man killed her. How did he do that?

P: With his beak.

I: What about the other story? What is that about?

P: Well this Chinese girl goes to a ugly looking (laughs) Chinese man.

I: uhhum.

P: Well she gives him the piece of paper (mumble) cause I guess she's gonna go somewhere.

I: Are these stories similar to any other stories you have read?

P: No.

I: What were the authors trying to teach you when he or she wrote these stories?

P: About what happens in foreign countries.

I: How is this one different from that one?

P: Well that one's sort of like a . . . you could say a cartoon one (points to *The Stonecutter*) and those are just like regular old stories.

I: Is there anything you would have changed?

P: No.

I: Did you like the story?

P: Yeah.

I: What did you like about them?

P: Well it sort of taught me that what sort of happens in foreign countries.

I: Can you retell one of the stories that I told you last time?

P: This little boy's mom told him that a little boy was coming to stay for the week and he didn't like it really and then they . . . he finally came and he had to play with him and the little boy would always have to have things his own way and then at the end the . . . he went to . . . he was walking and talking to the little boy and his friends saw him and they were calling him names and everything and after a while the boy started liking the kid.

Patricia was probably the least involved student in the fourth grade. She didn't really seem to like the folktales, and she was reluctant to tell much about them. Attention span and comprehension were perhaps factors affecting her answers. You can see, however, that she remembered quite a lot from *Stevie*, one of the realistic fiction selections. Patricia's continual reference to "foreign countries" when talking about *Dawn* and *The Stonecutter* and her confusion about the events of the stories suggested an unwillingness or inability to understand stories that did not link directly to her own frame of reference or worldview. Patricia's conversation suggested a limited range of response for this type of story genre and a limited interest in stories about other cultures. This indicated the lack of rich background that Pearson (1981) refers to, which builds up over time with exposure and familiarity. This lack of background knowledge also had a limiting effect on Patricia's ability to generate theme and again points out the importance of allowing choice in book-sharing sessions.

Compare Patricia's response to the folktales to Melissa (10:2):

I: Why did you choose these two titles? What are they both
      about?

M: I thought the . . . this man gave something so that someone
      else could be happy. Well in this one she gave something so
      someone else could be happy too.

I: Are these stories similar to any other stories you have read?

M: Yeah. *The Fisherman and His Wife*, because it was like *The
      Stonecutter* because he kept asking for more . . . his wife did
      rather . . . and he wanted to be the same thing again and
      . . . (mumbles) but in this case he was the mountain instead
      of the wood stonecutter.

I: What were the authors trying to teach you when he or she
      wrote these stories?

M: Maybe I'm not really sure . . . but to give more than we re-
      ceive.

I: That's a good thought . . . (pause) I'm writing that down.
      How are those two stories different from that one?

M: Well in these two as I said, they were giving happiness, but in
      this one the spirit was giving happiness but he was just taking
      it and taking it and not giving anything back so he ended up
      like the mountain.

I: Uh huh, go ahead.

M: And, well, he wanted to be the same thing again but the spirit
      couldn't do anything and so ended up being the mountain and
      well he kind of felt badly taking all of it instead of being
      happy the way he was.

I: Pick a story. Why did it end like it did?

M: Well, gee, well, I think *The Japanese Fairy Tale* ended like it
      did because they were happy, and well I think if you did
      anything else it might've turned out overdone. I think he did it
      just a perfect way.

Melissa had a lot to say about the folktales she heard. She linked *The
Fisherman and His Wife* to *The Stonecutter* thematically, indicating the
connections children make and the importance of having a cauldron of
stories available to aid literary comprehension. She was able to talk
about *Dawn* and *A Japanese Fairy Tale* succinctly in terms of giving
more than we receive, a generalization that links both books. She also
considered author intentions with the last question and decided that the
story ended appropriately. Her use of the term "overdone" suggests the
ability to consider literary elements. Her interpretation of the stonecut-

ter's final intent is different from an adult's in that she attributes re-
morse to the character. She says that the stonecutter in the end felt bad
about taking everything the way he did instead of remaining content
with what he had originally. As an adult reader I don't give the stonecutter that much credit. I perceive him as greedy, wanting more, and
only stopping because the spirit had had enough. I don't know what the
motivation of the spirit was. I certainly would not have been as patient.
As for the stonecutter, I think he didn't have much regard for human life
and would have continued destroying whatever got in his way. Melissa is
more of an optimist and suggests a hopeful ending, in that she states at a
tacit level that his heart at least changed. Kids are hopeful and that's
why children's literature usually contains hopeful elements.

COMMENTS

Kindergarten children were able to identify thematically matched
books 80% of the time for realistic fiction and 35% for folktales, thus
indicating that thematic identification is a fairly early developmental
strategy.

In terms of their ability to generate a thematic statement, children
with low exposure to children's books, as tested by the Revised Huck
Literature Inventory (Lehr, 1987), most frequently responded at levels
too concrete or too vague to be considered thematic responses. In contrast, children familiar with a broad range of children's literature typically responded to interview questions with thematic statements that
were essentially correct with regard to concrete elements.

Some developmental trends were observed across age levels. As children got older they were better able to talk about the themes in stories.
Children with a lower exposure to children's literature also improved in
their ability to talk about meaning in books; however, their statements,
even as a function of age, were more concretely tied to the plot of the
book, and they were less able to step back from the text and talk about it
in general terms.

Most, but not all, children in kindergarten were able to summarize
when asked to tell what the story was about in a few words or when
probed about the story. This ability to summarize enabled children to
talk about concrete similarities between stories. In contrast, Applebee
(1978) found that children of this age were unable to summarize but
rather had a tendency to retell entire stories. The structure and content
of the interview questions used here probably account for this differ-

ence. During interviews, I specifically asked children to retell the story in a few words or in short form and specifically asked what the most important ideas were.

Most, but not all, children at this age level were also aware of the internal motivations or reactions of characters. For realistic fiction, 70% of the kindergarten children mentioned the internal thought processes that motivated character actions in the stories. Explanations of how or why the characters responded as they did in particular episodes were often included in their statements of theme. This result contrasts with Mandler and Johnson's (1977) finding that children omit internal reactions of characters during spontaneous recall. The variety of perspectives probed by the interview questions may have acted as a catalyst in this respect. The current results support the idea that most young children can take on the perspectives of others (Donaldson, 1978; Lehr, 1990; Paley, 1981).

At times children had strong prior expectations for story parts, regardless of their exposure to literature. Consequently, children instantiated familiar story frames to fit with these prior expectations (Anderson, Stevens, Shifrin, & Osborn, 1977; Spiro, 1977). As suggested in studies concerned with background knowledge, the children filled in confusing or missing information on the basis of predictable patterns they had evolved for stories (Pichert & Anderson, 1976).

About half of the second- and fourth-grade thematic statements from the children in the high-exposure groups (8 of the 20 total responses for second grade, and 10 of the 20 responses for fourth grade) were at analysis and generalization levels in Applebee's (1978) Developmental Formulation of Response Categories. Children were given access to the books as points of reference during the interview, and they were also given time to draw a picture of what the books were about. This procedure presumably focused the children on the thematic content of the stories and gave them an opportunity to consider themes for the books (Siegel, 1983).

Younger children, and children with a lower exposure to books in all three grades, tended to speak in absolutes, whereas older children and children in high-exposure groups tended to offer more qualifiers in their responses to books, indicating more background knowledge about the world.

Children were more successful with the identification and generation of themes for realistic fiction than for folktales. This may be due to differences in relevant background knowledge. Realistic fiction is closer to the child's experience. Common folktale themes, such as greed, sacrifice, gaining independence, and overcoming evil or danger, are abstract concepts, especially when related in settings removed from everyday experience. Regardless of their exposure to literature, children were able to successfully *identify* books that shared themes for the realistic fiction selections but were less successful with folktales, in terms of matching adult perspectives. This finding underscores the importance of background knowledge in a child's ability to recognize themes. It also underscores the importance of considering why the child offers the answers that he or she does rather than automatically discounting those answers.

IMPLICATIONS

The study has several implications for future research. Children in kindergarten, second-, and fourth-grade all responded enthusiastically to having copies of the books available to them throughout the study. This made a difference for many children, and contributed to the high quality of their responses. The books were referred to, opened, and touched constantly throughout the interviews.

The interview format, which encouraged children to consider the story from several different perspectives, was also helpful in eliciting a wide range of responses from children in all three grades. Children need encouraging contexts in which to query and offer their insights. Several fourth-grade children made this clear to me when they answered and then asked timidly, "Is that the right answer?" Giving children the opportunity to talk about their ideas regarding the book without worrying about the "right" answer can help them discuss themes and explore character motivation and elements of plot.

Because exposure to children's literature correlated highly with the child's level of thematic awareness, future studies might include classroom interventions to provide students with a rich literature background in a variety of genres. We know that giving children opportunities to listen to books and to read books in the classroom can increase the child's background knowledge about the world and thus improve the child's ability to comprehend (Pearson, 1981). We also know that rich oral contexts are important in developing a child's ability to talk about the meaning that he or she is constructing. We do not yet know how such opportunities affect the child's developing sense of theme.

3

A Preschool Child's Developing Sense of Theme

Children's books are an integral part of preschool classrooms, where they are often used to allow children to explore stories individually with a teacher as well as in organized group story times during the day. It has been suggested that reading with young children, as well as addressing immediate affective goals, may also be important to their acquiring the comprehension skills necessary for later developmental reading programs (Joels, 1987). This exposure to stories has a tendency to increase prior knowledge of narrative forms (Flood, 1977; Lehr, 1988a; 1989; Mandler & Johnson, 1977; Stein & Glenn, 1978; Whaley, 1981), thus fostering the child's ability to generate organizational structures for recalling main ideas. But what is it that young children understand when we are reading them a story? How does the child perceive the meaning of the story, and how does he or she tell you what is understood?

Cochran-Smith (1984) discusses the role of story reading and suggests that "children's efforts to make sense of stories are constructive rather than a function of memory alone." Comprehension is rather "the result of an integration of memory and the internal mental operations performed by the hearer of a story" (p. 9). Additionally, story events are like "dialogues" and function as "conversationally interactive experiences" (p. 18). Researchers have found that when the mother scaffolds the child's labeling during story events the interaction provides a context of give and take, which consists of a structured sequence of dialoguing where children learn the rules of turn-taking (Ninio & Bruner, 1978). Snow and Goldfield (1982) additionally found that components of the book-sharing situation included predictable contexts where the child took in new information and later applied it to similar contexts. "Book-reading can be a conversationally interactive experience wherein a routinized exchange between reader and listener occurs" (p. 19). Cochran-Smith's (1984) work in a preschool setting has described how books are used and perceived by children, teachers, and parents. Experiences with books for preschoolers were "embedded" within the wider context of the belief system of the community, the organization of the nursery itself and events that occurred at times other than story sharing. Rugtime in this classroom provided the occasion for listening, sharing, and constructing meaning within joint contexts. Children told stories that were jointly constructed using books as catalysts, with the result that they created a thematically and narratively connected story.

Similarly, Taylor (1983) writes, based on her studies of family literacy, that "story sharing was intricately woven into the social processes of family life, with a broad panoply of purposes, facilitating communication between parents and children and forming one medium for the development of a shared social heritage" (p. 67). Children are immersed in stories from their earliest years. A young child in Taylor's study illustrates this point. Nan, at the age of 1 year 11 months, sat with her pile of books and "read the story, rhythmically making the sounds of reading, and then stopping every few seconds to turn the book for [Taylor] to see the pictures." This child, at such an early age, was already mimicking reading behavior. The fact that she "read" the story and paused to show the pictures to the listener suggests a child who hears a lot of stories read aloud. Over time, one might ask what her sense of the story is. What kind of meaning is this child busily constructing?

DESIGN OF THE SECOND STUDY

Because kindergarten children are able to construct themes from their own perspectives, my study of this age group (the second of three studies on how children construct theme) focused on the ability of 4-year-old children to identify and generate themes for children's stories. Specifically, I wanted to explore the attitudes children hold toward books and the act of reading, particularly as these relate to their ability to discuss the theme of a story. I also wanted to describe the 4-year-old's ability to generate, as well as to identify, theme using children's literature. Below I briefly describe how I went about this, because some of the interviews and tools developed were useful in exploring young children's attitudes toward literacy, and some of the methods differed from those used in the earlier study with older children.

Subjects

I worked with ten 4-year-old children in a morning preschool program that met from 9:00 to 11:30 on Monday, Wednesday, and Friday. I became a visible part of the classroom, sitting with my pile of books in a corner, talking to children as they passed by, and they frequently stopped to hear or read a story. I brought in a variety of books and read some of them aloud during read-aloud time. I allowed the children to talk, to interrupt with their ideas and thoughts. When the children came down the hall a short distance to my office, I continued with the same relaxed routine. I was perceived as a "book" person.

Instrumentation

I used a brief interview, which was a simplified version I adapted from the Burke interview for use with older children and consisted of the following six questions:

Interview for Exploring Preschool Attitudes Toward Books
1. Do you like to listen to stories?
2. Who tells you stories? When?
3. What are some stories you like? Why?
4. Do you like to read stories yourself?
5. Who do you know that reads a lot of books?
6. What do you have to do to learn how to read?

Additionally, I used a standard interview to assess the child's understanding of, and ability to retell, a story, also adapted from the earlier interview used with older children (Goodman & Burke, 1972). If a child did not understand a concept, it was explained in one or two additional sentences that used different words to get at the concept. And if a child gave a statement, the interviewer would probe with words like *why?* *how?* or use the child's own words as a question. The book used with the children for this task was *Titch* by Pat Hutchins.

Interview Exploring Theme with the Preschool Child
1. Tell me the story again.
2. Is this story like any other story you know?

3. What do you think this story is trying to teach you or tell you?
4. Did you like this story? Why?
5. What do you think is the most important thing that happened in this story?
6. What is the most important idea in this story?
7. What do you think this story is about?
8. What happened at the end of the story?
9. Would you change the ending of this story? How would you change it?

Because I videotaped the sessions, I constructed a checklist of behaviors, both verbal and nonverbal in nature, to observe during the retelling sessions. As I mentioned, my earlier study with kindergarten, second-, and fourth-grade children indicated the importance of book availability during the retelling sessions; therefore, the checklist provided a more formal means of observing the behaviors of the children. The retelling observation checklist consisted of:

1. Child touched book.
2. Child opened book.
3. Child pointed to something in book.
4. Child used book as reference while talking. [opened or closed]
5. Child retold story while flipping through book page by page.
6. Child made specific reference to character or action and pointed to same in book.
7. Child did not touch book.
8. Child did retell story.
9. Child attempted to retell story but did not complete retelling.
10. Child attempted to retell story but did not successfully complete retelling until opening book.
11. Child did not retell story.

Materials

Books for this study were chosen from the wide variety of children's books available, reflecting the same concern for quality of text and illustrations as outlined in Huck, Hepler, and Hickman (1987). Some of the titles used with the children in the classroom were *Where's Spot?* by Eric Hill, *The Amazing Hide and Seek Alphabet Book* by Robert Crowley, *The Very Hungry Caterpillar* by Eric Carle, *A Dark Dark Tale* by Ruth Brown, *Happy Birthday Moon* by Frank Asch, *Haunted House* by Jan Pienkowski, *Whose Mouse are You?* by Robert Kraus, and *Titch* by Pat Hutchins.

Procedures

I read and talked with the children both individually and in groups over a 6-month period beginning in the first part of the school year (September–March). Early mornings were designated as primary data collection time (9:15–10:30). Children attended three individual sessions on different days.

In individual sessions with the children, I invited them to read Jan Pienkowski's *Haunted House*. Because Halloween was approaching, the book generated a great deal of enthusiastic participation from the children, and they wanted to return to my office for subsequent sessions. This information is provided to indicate the willingness of the children, which is a vital factor when one works with this age group. Ironically, even after the final session in March, many of the children still wanted to visit my office and still wanted access to the *Haunted House* book.

In a second individual session the child was given the Interview for Exploring Preschool Attitudes Toward Books and was again invited to read *Haunted House*. Children also listened to *The Very Hungry Caterpillar* in the small-book format. I had read this book aloud to the entire class previously in the large-book format and perceived it as a favorite among the children. They were enchanted with the small-book format, which was not much larger than their own hands.

In session three the children listened to *Titch* by Pat Hutchins. None of the children were familiar with the book. I then interviewed them using the Interview Exploring Theme With the Preschool Child. Children had access to the book at all times but were not told to refer to it. Following the interview children were asked to respond positively or negatively to a list of possible themes for the book *Titch*. Then they were invited to read *The Very Hungry Caterpillar* to me and again had access to the *Haunted House*.

I've divided the discussion of the findings into three sections. Section one discusses attitudes of the 4-year-old child toward books and reading, with particular emphasis given to conversations with several children who had less to say during the book discussions. Section two explores the 4-year-old child's ability to generate themes during individual book discussions. In this section I provide three detailed case studies of conversations with children. Section three considers the 4-year-old's ability to identify themes, with specific examples from transcripts.

PRESCHOOL ATTITUDES TOWARD BOOKS AND READING

Almost all of the children whom I talked to stated clearly that they liked listening to stories. Children mentioned parents, siblings, baby-sitters, and grandparents as people they perceived as active readers. Most of the children indicated that they were read to all the time or every night. Stories were an intrinsic part of their lives, as well as the lives of primary caretakers.

Compare their experience to Laurie's, who stated that she only heard stories from "daddy on his day off." Laurie had less to say about books in general than did the other children. She basically did not speak during the interview after *Titch*. Her typical response was a shake of the head or a shrug of her shoulders when asked questions about the books. Laurie identified herself as a nonreader, but she had this to say about learning to read: "Read. Read the same what you write." Laurie saw reading and writing as being interchangeable. She identified a favorite title as being *Three Little Bears*. As I observed Laurie reading some of the books offered to her, I noticed that she turned the pages and studied the pictures silently, yet intently. Her responses to my questions consisted of nods and shrugs, yet she was attentive as I read. Laurie didn't talk a lot, so it was difficult to assess what she knew about the books she heard; however, she did listen and look through books during every opportunity I gave her. Reading with Laurie was not interactive. She functioned as a passive listener. This is not to say that she did not attend to the story or enjoy listening. In fact, later during probed recall, Laurie was able to successfully identify all of the themes for *Titch*, again done nonverbally.

Reagen's response when asked how often she heard stories was "not a lot of times." Reagen differed from Laurie in that she verbally told me she didn't know how to do what I asked of her. Reagen identified *The Very Hungry Caterpillar* as a book she really enjoyed because the caterpillar turned into a beautiful butterfly. Other than that, Reagen essentially shrugged or offered "I don't know" as an answer. She did, however, laugh a lot during the reading. Her nonverbals were expressive and indicated full participation, including laughing, pointing at pictures, and turning pages. After a lengthy session where I did most of the talking and reading, Reagen asked me to read *Titch* again. She later identified several of the themes in *Titch* by answering simply "I think yes." Both Reagen and Laurie seemed hungry for book experiences, Reagen more openly identifying her enjoyment and Laurie more timidly.

Although Brian was highly verbal during this interview, offering numerous titles and people who read to him and acted as models for him, and described at length how and where he read at home, he had virtually nothing to say later during the book discussions. Essentially he listened attentively to the stories and nodded his head or shrugged his shoulders in response to questions. Probing did not elicit any response.

Alex was similar in that he talked about going to school to learn to read. He related a story about cats when I asked him who told him stories. He couldn't wait to get the *Haunted House* open and returned to the book a number of times on different days. He had a lot to say as he looked through this book. In a later session, during the reading of *Titch*, however, he listened carefully and had little to say except "no" at the end of the story. Whereas some children said "I don't know" in answer to a question, Alex frequently said "I don't want to tell you," or he pointed at things in the books. All four of these children had little to say after this first session together, although their nonverbals indicated interest in the books shared and an ability to identify themes. More about that in a moment.

Book Preferences

Many of the children were immersed in print at home. Most of them mentioned specific titles of books that they liked. Most of these would be considered "popular" or "grocery store" books. A sampling of the titles given by the children includes *In the Dark*, *The Crazy Little Bubble Gum*, *The Crazy Little Bonkerhead*, *The Snake in the Key Lock*, *Sesame Street*, *A Snore's Book*, *The Bumpy Bus Ride*, *Rowing Home*, *Mousie*. Several of the children mentioned titles of books that I had read in class. Others mentioned fairy tales by name, like *Goldilocks and the Three Bears*, or as a genre, fairy tales. One child (Matthew) mentioned *Curious George*. "That's a funny one, huh?" Interestingly, most of the titles mentioned would not be books considered "quality" literature for children. Only a few were in the Revised Huck Literature Inventory. Children did, however, seem familiar with folktales and were read to a great deal in their preschool during rugtime. The favorites mentioned from home seemed to be grocery store books and pop series taken from cartoons, for example. The majority of the children, however, were savvy about books and read-aloud sessions.

Learning to Read

Children had mixed attitudes toward the reading process. Consider these responses: "I can't read, but I can read this one because I already know the words" (Reagen). "I can't read because I don't know the letters" (Alex). "I can't read and I can't tie either. You have to wait until you go to school" (Alicia). Durkin (1966) found that children who read early perceive themselves as readers and pester their parents until they get the answers they want about reading. Durkin also found that parents of children who do *not* read early believed that children should wait until school to learn to read or said that they were fearful of teaching them incorrectly at home or afraid that their children would be bored in school if they learned how to read too early.

Five children stated that they could read and mentioned specific titles to illustrate their point. Whether they were reading conventionally was really not of interest to me in this interview. I was more interested in their perceptions about themselves as readers, because so much of the reading research talks about children building on positive attitudes toward reading and taking on the behaviors of the reader in the process of becoming a successful reader.

When asked who they knew who reads a lot of books, the children mentioned family and friends and two included themselves. "My buddy Jenny, I do, everybody does," was offered enthusiastically by Brian. Anthony pointed at the researcher and said "You!" This suggests the importance of modeling positive reading attitudes for children. Durkin found that early readers had parents who valued reading and books and education in general.

When asked what one had to do to learn how to read, three children said that they must wait until school. One child suggested that you must spell. Another said he read already, and four stated that you must practice, read some, write, listen, and tell. Here is a sampling of what the children who acted like readers had to say about reading:

BRIAN: "I read a lot. Sometimes I do my homework and stuff. Lay in bed and do it. At my desk."

MEG: "I listen to mom. She tells me stories and I tell her stories."

LINDA: "Practice. It takes times, so you know how to read."

BRYANT: "Just talk. Read stories."

Many children already perceived themselves as readers. They were aware that one must be an active reader in order to be a successful reader. There is a strong sense that the print bears the message and that reading is as natural as talking. Notice that Meg listens to her mom read and that the events are highly interactive. This suggests a parent who not only models but also values what her child has to say and takes the time to listen. All of the children are well on their way to successful literacy.

EARLY DEVELOPMENT OF THEME:
A STUDY OF ONE CHILD'S RESPONSE

Most of the children provided comments about *Titch* that identified important information from the story and indicated an early development of theme. Many of the children also talked as the book was read, sharing thoughts about their families and friends; however, the children did not verbalize themes. They were able to focus on important components of the story in a general manner, and the stories helped them make links to events that were occurring in their personal lives. Consider this conversation with Meg during and after the sharing of *Titch*. Meg was a lively youngster who had plenty to say about the books shared.

> I: (reads text, turns pages) "Titch was little. His sister, Mary, was a bit bigger and his brother, Pete, was a lot bigger. Pete had a great big bike. Mary had a big bike. And Titch had a little tricycle."
>
> M: My sister had little, little bicycle.
>
> I: Does she?
>
> M: Guess what happened?
>
> I: What?
>
> M: With a car.
>
> I: With a car?
>
> M: Yes. My sister's bike got run over by the car and smooshed.
>
> I: It got run over by the car and smooshed? Oh my goodness! She left it behind the car?
>
> M: No. Like it was halfway out and she hit the back wheel.
>
> I: Uh-huh?
>
> M: And it crashed up like. The two things on the outside the red thing.
>
> I: Mmmmm?
>
> M: It rolled and it fell in part of the garage.

Notice how the mention of a bicycle made Meg think of her sister's small bike that was smashed by a car. It was important for Meg to share that story about her sister's bike being smashed by her mom's car. Reading is interactive. Young children must be given the opportunity to share what they know during book events, which will frequently trigger information that the child links to life experiences (White, 1984). In this instance, it was the objects mentioned in the story upon which Meg focused.

I: Ooh, people were upset about that, weren't they? Well let's find out what happened to Pete and Mary and Titch. "Pete had a kite that flew high above the trees. Mary had a kite that flew high above the houses. And Titch had a pinwheel that he held in his hand."

M: I have a pinwheel too.

I: Do you really?

M: I have my favorite color, pink, oh, I mean red.

I: Red, oh, I'll bet it's neat. And his is blue. Did you notice that? "Pete had a big drum. Mary had a trumpet. And Titch had a little wooden whistle."

M: I have a whistle too.

I: You do? You have lots of things that Titch has. "Pete had a big saw. Mary had a big hammer. And Titch held the nails."

M: Well, I have a little play saw.

I: You do? You saw things? "Pete had big spade. Mary had a fat flower pot."

M: I had that.

I: Yeah? "But Titch had the tiny seed. And Titch's seed grew and grew and grew." Now, I want to ask you if you can tell me the story about Titch again.

M: Um, let me look at the book, too. OK?

I: Sure, of course.

M: (turns page) My sister has that.

I: Um-humm.

M: I don't have that.

I: No.

M: I have that.

M: (turns page) I have that. (turns page) I have that. (pats book) I have that. (pats book) I have that.

I: Mmmm . . .

M: I have that. I have that. I have . . . not that.

I: Nothing on that page?

M: I have a seed. It grew to about this tall. (points to space over her head)

I: Really. What was it?

M: It's a plant.

I: A plant?

M: It's taller than yours. (points at one on my shelf)

I: You have a bigger one.

M: Yeah.

Meg listened to the story and identified with various objects that Titch and his siblings owned, systematically comparing her possessions to those shown in the book, reminiscent of Marie Clay's (1979) notion of how children generate lists of everything they know when first learning to write. Children personalize the story experience. They become a unique part of the events and they identify with the objects in the story. Meg identified with Titch and related how she too had a seed; however, hers was larger than the one in the book. You'll also note that it was important for Meg to take the book herself and go back page by page to see what objects the children had.

I then asked Meg questions about the story. Meg became distracted at this point. She didn't have the answers for my questions, and she got up and wandered around the room. At that point she saw the television monitor and saw herself on TV. It did not, however, distract her for long, because the children were used to seeing the monitor turned at an angle. The interview was becoming too long and Meg let me know immediately! Surprisingly, she continued and went back into the book for answers. Not finding what she was looking for, she turned the tables and asked me to tell what happened in the story.

> **I:** What do you think is the most important thing that happened in this story?
>
> **M:** Let me see. (opens book; turns pages) Whoa. What do you think is what happened in this story?
>
> **I:** Well, you tell me first what you think is most important in this story.
>
> **M:** The tricycle.
>
> **I:** OK. What about it? Why is that important?
>
> **M:** Fall down the hill. . . .
>
> **I:** OK.
>
> **M:** What do you think?
>
> **I:** Ummm, I don't know. Let me think about that. What do you think is the most important idea in this story?
>
> **M:** Well, matter of fact, bike, a spinning wheel.
>
> **I:** A spinning wheel? What do you think the story is about?
>
> **M:** (points)
>
> **I:** What? What are you pointing at?
>
> **M:** A flower.
>
> **I:** A flower. OK. Why is it about that? How is it about that?
>
> **M:** (taps book)
>
> **I:** What, who's that? Oh, that's Titch. What happened at the end of the story?

M: Let me see. (turns page) It grew bigger.
I: Yeah? Why did it grow bigger?
M: Cause there's a seed in there.
I: Would you change the ending of that story?
M: What do you want me to change it to?

Meg began to point out the elements that she perceived as being important. She knew that the flower (plant) growing bigger was central to the story and pointed to that. She was unable to articulate why it was so important to the story, and in response to my question about why it grew bigger, her answer was extremely concrete. It grew bigger because of the seed inside. I drew the same kind of concrete response about changing the end of the story, which was typical for this age. She threw the book on the floor. Other children thought I meant to change the endpapers or to physically change the last page of the story. By the time children reach kindergarten, they will begin to understand the nuances of that question. Most kindergarten children didn't want to change the endings of stories except not to have characters eaten up in fairy tales.

On a general level Meg responded to the question: "What do you think this story is about?" "A flower." She then pointed at Titch and tapped the book. Meg was unable to articulate a theme statement and was unable to expand on this basic information.

Compare this to LeMarr's response when asked, "What do you think is the most important thing that happened in this story?" LeMarr responded: "The plant got bigger." He later identified the relation between the three children in the book. "He's bigger and he's bigger and he's little." LeMarr pointed to the characters in the book as he spoke. Both children, generally speaking, were able to locate the central components of the story—the plant and Titch, the youngest child.

Compare Meg's concrete response to *Titch* to her answers regarding the identification of theme.

I: What I'm going to do . . . I'm going to read to you some things about the story. They may be about the story and they may not be about the story and you just say yes or no if they are or they aren't. OK?
  Is this story about not sharing your toys?
M: Um, no.
I: Is this book about being left alone?
M: (shakes head no)
I: Is this book about doing something important?
M: I think it is, yes.

I: Why do you think it's about that?

M: Mmmmm, I just don't really know. I'm not a very good
      knower.

I: You're not a very good knower? Is this book about being mean
      to others?

M: No.

I: Is this book about doing something with a brother and a
      sister?

M: (emphatic) Yes!

I: How is it about doing something with a brother and sister?

M: (shrugs shoulders)

I: Is this about being the smallest?

M: Yup.

Meg was able to successfully identify the themes for *Titch*; however, she was unable to elaborate her answers, indicating that identification of theme is an early strategy learned by children. Finding the words
to tell why begins to gel in kindergarten for children familiar with
books.

Retelling a Story

Meg was able to retell the story of *The Very Hungry Caterpillar*
successfully. She used the book as a referent and told the story to me
page by page, which suggests that children can retell stories in a logically sequenced manner with a thematic center. This coincides with Cochran-Smith's (1984) findings based on retelling social events but contrasts
with Whalen-Levitt's (1977) child script for *The Good Bird*, which was
essentially a cataloging of animals in the storybook (age 3:9). It is likely
that Meg's familiarity with this story and her slightly older age (4:5) had
a good deal to do with the differences, as well as my scaffolding as she
retold the events of the story. Linda's retelling, however, was independently achieved and recaps the events of Carle's story.

I: Are you going to tell me this story now? (*The Very Hungry
      Caterpillar*, which was read to Meg several days before)

M: OK. OK. Can you read this part? (points to first page of story)

I: In the light of the moon, a little egg lay on a leaf.

M: He was starting to pop out. Out popped a caterpillar. I'm
      hungry. (turns page) The next day he had one apple. The next
      day he had two pears. The next day he had three plums. The

next day he had four, four? four? strawberries. The next day he had four strawberries. Is this five?

I: Mmm, mmm.

M: Next day he had five oranges? or peaches?

I: Oranges.

M: Oranges. Next day he had a piece of cake. Slamamia. Is this slamamia?

I: Uh, pickle.

M: Pickle. And a salamia.

I: Swiss cheese.

M: Salamia? Salamia and a cupcake and a pizza and a lollipop and a sausage and a watermelon. The next day he ate all the leaves. That was much more better. So the next day he built him a little house. He crawled into it. When he came out, he was a butterfly. Is there anymore?

I: That is so good! I liked that very much!

This 4-year-old was able to successfully tell the story of *The Very Hungry Caterpillar*. She followed the illustrations with her own version of the story and was quite successful in her retelling. Notice the sophisticated language that Meg knew, as well as the sequence of the story. Illustrations are a powerful cuing system. It was important to Meg that I help her get started, however. She was familiar with the conventions of stories and could not remember how this particular story started. Eric Carle's story is predictable and follows a logical sequence with numbers, making retelling an easy task for this 4-year-old. The illustrations match the text as well, making this an exceptional book for emergent readers. Notice how her attempts were scaffolded by me. She wasn't sure how many pieces of fruit there were, what type of fruit was pictured, whether salami was pronounced correctly. Given that information, she continued with her retelling and told the story in a logically sequenced fashion.

Linda also told the story of *The Very Hungry Caterpillar* using the book to show the pictures.

L: One day, an egg lay on the leaf. Pop-out came an eensy teensy eensy weensy caterpillar. One day he was hungry and he ate one pear, one apple, two pears, four strawberries, five oranges. But he was still hungry. One piece of chocolate cake, watermelon . . . ate ice cream, ate pickle, sausage, lollipop, cherry pie and the . . . He ate a watermelon and he was still hungry. Wednesday . . . And when it was Wednesday again he ate another leaf and the next day he was a great big fat caterpillar. He made himself a great big fat cocoon and then he turned out to be a lovely, lovely (turns book around to show picture) butterfly.

Notice her use of book language, like "eensy weensy" and "but he was still hungry." In addition, she heightened the drama at the end of the story by turning the book around as the cocoon opens and the butterfly emerges. Linda was a natural storyteller, and all of the elements of the story were included.

Matthew's retelling of *The Very Hungry Caterpillar* was interactive in nature. He discussed the story as he went along, starting off by making observations of the dedication page.

M: Why do you have this in here?
I: That tells who the book is for and who wrote the book and drew the pictures.
M: (turns to first page of story) It's night time here, isn't it?
I: Yes.
M: I don't like night time.
I: Why?
M: Because I just hate it.
I: What do you like better?
M: The light. There's a little caterpillar there. He ate how many apples? How many apples did he eat?
I: One.
M: He ate two pears, one plum, no three, two pears, three plums, four strawberries, five, five oranges. How many of these?
I: One of each, a little hole through each one.
M: He ate five bites of all of this leaf. Then he was sick.
I: Mmmm.
M: Then he went into his caterpillar place and he turned out to be a beautiful butterfly.
I: He did! A lovely butterfly! Thank you for reading that for me.
M: Know what? Yellow is my favorite color and purple and pink!

Matthew's version of the story was highly personal and related to his own likes and dislikes. Matthew had trouble with cause and effect. For example, he mentioned that the caterpillar was sick out of sequence, not realizing that it was the leaf that made him feel better. The brilliant colors of the last page of the story generated a list of Matthew's favorite colors.

LeMarr was the only child who retold the story of *Titch*. He too told the story interactively and used the book as a guide. He frequently waited for me to respond before continuing with a segment of the story.

L: Titch was little. (pause)

I: Yes.

L: And he had two brothers.

I: Mmmm.

L: He had a big bike and she had a big bike and he had a smaller one. And he had a big kite that flies high and she had a kite that flies way up to the house. And he's not here. (pause)

I: Well, where is he? Turn the page.

L: And so he had a . . . (pause)

I: Pinwheel.

L: pinwheel . . . and he had a big drum and she had . . . (pause)

I: A trumpet.

L: He had a little whistle.

I: Mmmmm.

L: And he had a big saw and she had a big hammer and he had the nails and he had the . . . (pause)

I: Spade. It's like a shovel.

L: Spade. She had the bucket and he had the little seed and it growed and growed and growed.

Certain words brought LeMarr's retelling to a complete stop, words like *trumpet, spade, pinwheel*. LeMarr also waited at the end of each phrase for some reaction from me. Shared reading. He was able to retell the story successfully while I scaffolded the event (Ninio & Bruner, 1978; Bruner, 1983). He later identified the most important thing in the story as the plant's getting bigger. He also explained the relative size of each character. "He's bigger and he's bigger and he's little." He was unable to state why the information was important but knew that size was central to the story.

With regard to *The Very Hungry Caterpillar*, LeMarr related this. My comments are in parentheses.

L: Red and juicy. The sun came up. The moon came down. And now . . . what was on the leaf? (an egg) An egg was on the leaf. That's an egg? (Yes. A little egg.) A egg was on there and the sun came up. What's his name? (I don't know.) Then . . . and the sun came up. What's behind this one? (You tell me. What is that?) A pear. (What's he doing to it?) Eating it. What's he doing in this one? (He ate through the apple and now he's eating through the two pears. But he's still hungry.) Ate through the two pears. He ate the three . . . (plums) Plums. (He ate through four strawberries.) Four strawberries. He didn't eat . . . What ate these? (That's salami.) No, he didn't eat these. How's he gonna eat these? He ate and ate and ate and he was full. He ate that and that and that and that and that and that and that and that and that and that. And even that. He walked on the leaf (pause) inside of here. A butterfly.

Bruner (1983) has written about the role of parents in scaffolding events for their young children. Notice how my role was to help the story move forward, supply missing bits where needed, but essentially let LeMarr take the lead. The same process was used with Matthew.

Linking Life Experience to the Book Experience

Another type of response to *Titch* related real-life experiences to the book experience, much as Meg did in telling about her sister's bike. Linda set the agenda immediately by telling me that she wanted to read *Haunted House* and *The Very Hungry Caterpillar* after hearing *Titch*. *Titch* reminded Linda of "the furry little bunny story," which had a "little round cotton baby with lift-up pages." She went off on an explanation of how she was going to a birthday party and that she had to bring a favorite teddy bear. Linda then related Titch's experience in the story to an important event in her life and in doing so indicated a good deal of knowledge about the story.

I: Do you like this story?
L: Mmmm. I like it.
I: Why?
L: Cause it reminds me that I might be having another baby.
I: Really?
L: Cause my mom is really fat.
I: Is she? So it reminds you of something like that. What do you think is the most important thing that happened in this story?
L: That plant.
I: Why is that important?

L: Cause it grew and grew and grew and grew all over.

I: What's the most important idea in this story?

L: (pauses) The bike?

I: Why?

L: Mmmm. The bike is smaller and has that. (points to tricycle)

I: What do you think this story is about?

L: Titch being little.

I: What happened at the end of the story?

L: The plant grew.

I: Would you change the ending of the story?

L: What?

I: Would you change the end of the story?

L: This is how you could change it (she turned the pages backward starting at the back of the book).

I: How could you change it?

L: Going backwards.

Linda wanted to tell about her new baby in the family. This suggested strongly to me that children need to be encouraged to talk during or after book-sharing events. As did the other children, Linda identified important information that leads to themes about the book. Like Meg she was unable to express a concrete thematic statement. Like her peers, she knew that Titch was little, she knew that the plant grew and that this was an important event in the book. When asked about the most important idea in the story, she was able to point to the illustration of the tricycle that Titch labored to get up the hill while being left behind by his older brother and sister, an illustration mentioned by most of the children. Of all the illustrations this double-page spread concretely shows the gap in size and ability between Titch and his siblings. Linda also reacted concretely to the question about changing the end of the story when she began flipping the pages backwards.

Identifying With Characters

Alicia was intrigued with the part of *Titch* where the three children are going up the hill. She was concerned that Titch couldn't go up the hill, identified her as being sad, and suggested that she get a bigger bike. We discussed the size of the bike, and she showed me with her hands how big it would have to be. When she saw the children flying kites on the next page, Alicia stated that Titch was now happy. Notice that she labeled Titch as a girl and that she was trying to problem solve for Titch. If a bigger bike could be acquired, Titch would not have trouble with the hill and consequently would not be left behind, which the picture implies. When she saw the children flying kites and Titch with a pinwheel, she seemed relieved that Titch was happy. Children at this age are concerned with how characters feel. Even though they identify strongly with the plight of the character Titch, they want Titch to be happy and they want a balanced state of affairs.

Matthew identified Pete as the biggest, and on the last page of the story when Titch's seed grew, he asked:

> **M:** Why do they look that way? (points to the older brother and sister)
> **I:** Why do you think they look that way?
> **M:** Because they don't want it to grow that high.

At this point Matthew was considering the internal reactions of characters. He assumed that the two older children did not want Titch to do something bigger than they had done. Later he identified Titch as being "very small" and responded to the question about the most important idea in the story.

> **M:** Know what? I think when I grow up, the important thing is going to grow up.

Later, when probed about the theme of *Titch*, Matthew suggested that Pete and Mary should be nice to Titch and that Titch felt bad. Matthew stated that he didn't like Titch to feel bad and showed me in the picture just where it occurred and said that it was because they had the bigger things.

Matthew, like Linda, was able to take the book experience and relate it to his own life. In many ways his statement can stand as a theme statement, because the story of Titch is about growing up. In the context of the interview Matthew was unaware of his theme statement. He simply offered some information about himself in response to the specific question about the most important idea in the story. He generalized the story that he had heard and meshed it with his own perceptions of reality after exploring the internal reactions of the older children. Of all the children identifying general components of the story that relate to unformed thematic elements, Matthew's statements were the most focused, the most specific.

None of the children in this study were able to specifically generate a theme statement for *Titch* during the interview exploring theme, nor during the retelling of *The Very Hungry Caterpillar*. They were, however, able to verbally identify key thematic elements of the story that can be perceived as precursors to theme statements and retell stories using the book as a referent. This suggests that 4-year-old children are already beginning to sift through elements of plot and character and are developing a sense of theme, which is evidenced by their ability to identify thematic story elements and retell a story. The crucial linking, the explanations, develop at a later age. By the age of 5 some children are already able to make concrete thematic statements and summarize stories (Lehr, 1988a).

CAN FOUR-YEAR-OLD CHILDREN IDENTIFY THEMES?

After *Titch* was read and our discussions were completed, I asked the children to identify possible themes for *Titch* by saying yes or no as I read a list of statements. I read the following statements aloud.

Thematic Choices
1. Is this book about not sharing your toys?
2. Is this book about being left alone?
3. Is this book about doing something important?
4. Is this book about being mean to others?
5. Is this book about doing something with a brother and sister?
6. Is this book about being the smallest?

The theme statements could have been worded in a more complex manner; however, I chose to word the statements simply and directly so that children could easily identify them with the story. All of the children responded to the statements verbally or by shaking their heads yes or no, and all of the children correctly identified a theme statement for *Titch*. Only two children had a lot to say during this probing of the story.

Bryant chose theme 1, talked about sharing toys and other objects, and went through a lengthy search of the illustrations pointing out things to share. He supported his answer by stating that "kids don't share." He took information from the story and created a moral. He talked about sharing a TV, which was not in the story and was perhaps more directly related to his own life. He went through the book looking for a television and even though he didn't find one ("There's no TV in here"), he stated that sometimes they (Titch, Pete, and Mary) do share a TV. It was more likely that Bryant shared a TV at home with his siblings. On the basis of his perceptions of the text and illustrations,

Bryant viewed Pete and Mary as older children who would not share their "bigger" toys with Titch, even though Titch has toys in every picture. Therefore, his construction of meaning was logical and firmly rooted in his view of the world. It differed from the text at points but was uniquely his own and difficult to separate from his own experiences at home with siblings. Bryant did not detach himself from the story. He also correctly identified two other theme statements for *Titch* but had nothing to add after his discussion on sharing.

Matthew was most detailed in his answers when he identified themes 5 and 6. Consider the following conversation where Matthew explored the internal motivation of the characters.

> **I:** Is this book about doing something with a brother and sister? [theme 5]
>
> **M:** Yes
>
> **I:** How is it about that? Why do you think it's about that?
>
> **M:** Because they should be nice to him.
>
> **I:** Are they?
>
> **M:** No.
>
> **I:** How are they not nice?
>
> **M:** Because I don't think they're nice. Because I don't like him feeling bad.
>
> **I:** Who feels bad?
>
> **M:** (touches book and points to Titch): See?
>
> **I:** How do you think he feels?
>
> **M:** Bad.
>
> **I:** Why do you think he feels bad?
>
> **M:** Because they have the bigger things.
>
> **I:** Why do they have the bigger things?
>
> **M:** Because they're bigger. Whoever's bigger can carry bigger things.
>
> **I:** That's true.
>
> **M:** You know what?
>
> **I:** What?
>
> **M:** One day I was at a camp and I could push a very big ball in the water.
>
> **I:** Could you really!
>
> **M:** Uh huh. Long long time ago.
>
> **I:** That's really interesting! I'll bet you felt kind of neat about that. Is this book about being the smallest? [theme 6]
>
> **M:** Uh huh.
>
> **I:** Why do you think it's about that?

M: (points at Titch) Because he felt small.

I: Why is he so small?

M: Because he didn't grow up as high — as tall — as the other ones.

Matthew identified with Titch and talked a great deal about feelings. In fact, Matthew talked throughout the reading of *Titch*. He understood about being the smallest and growing into a bigger child and being able to do bigger things. He understood that the smallest can feel left out, and his answers indicated that bigger children are not always nice to smaller children. He cited a personal example of when he did something big. At the age of 4 Matthew showed an understanding in relation to the internal reactions of characters. My offering of a concrete statement of theme acted as a catalyst for Matthew. He began to frame the story, attaching motivation to actions of characters. The probing was general but allowed Matthew to give substance to his ideas.

COMMENTS

This study supports patterns that are consistent with previous research. Paley (1981) found in her work with kindergarten children that 5-year-olds are prolific meaning makers. She set up a classroom that was highly interactive, where her children were encouraged to voice their opinions, and disagree with hers. Children shared constantly and related experiences in books to real-life events. Paley scaffolded book discussions but did not dominate. Rather she encouraged her students to explore the meaning in books.

Taylor (1983) writes that "the children are also learning of reading as an interactive process, for the parents spent much of their story-reading time relating events in the stories to the everyday lives of their children. Donna King spoke of making associations with the story, while Jill Langdon spoke of the many experiences that they shared through books" (p. 70). Her picture of family literacy is one that nurtures and explores meaning in a variety of ways with children. Books are used as catalysts. They relate to real life, so that when one of the children in her study heard a story about a lost giraffe, the mother used the story as an opportunity to underscore the value of not wandering off. The child responded by recalling a time that he had gotten lost. Books inculcate children with society's values. Therefore, we had better choose our books wisely and allow interaction to occur during read-aloud sessions as children construct meaning.

Unlike kindergarten children in my previous study, none of the 4-

year-olds in this study were able to summarize the story, which may have had an effect on their ability to generate a theme statement; however, some children were able to retell a story using the book as a guide. Nor were these four-year-olds able to generate theme statements when probed after reading *Titch*. Most of the children were, however, able to talk about thematic elements, an early development of sense of theme. Children also considered internal motivation of characters, and most related the book experience to life experience. When given theme statements from which to choose children were able to identify a theme statement about the story. This suggests that 4-year-old children are busy constructing meaning from the information that surrounds them. They may not have the information clearly organized into hierarchical structures, but they are categorizing information and making connections between direct experiences and knowledge gained from literature. Pearson (1981) suggests that books are where children pick up much of their information about the world, which in turn facilitates comprehension — so sharing books can become an important building block for children in the storing of knowledge and may assist them in creating vital meaning structures.

Teachers can provide children with a network of information upon which future experiences with books build. Exposing students to high-quality literature in the classroom can increase children's background knowledge about the world and extend their perceptions of the world through discussion. Oral language before, during, and after the book-sharing experience (Flood, 1977) is to be valued because it allows a child to respond to the book, explore thematic meaning, and sort out new information, as the children in my study did.

4

Illustrations, Drawing, and Writing: The Link Between Art and Language

Reading researchers have had a tendency to separate text from pictures in research situations in order to focus on the child's ability to read text without picture clues. In fact, many researchers have stripped the reading context completely by removing meaning from research situations, asking subjects to read words in isolation. This approach to reading is contrary to what is known about how children learn language, how they learn to read, and how they build meaning while using language to read or listen to stories. Schemata cannot be instantiated where no context exists. Part of this context is the book itself, and this has been largely ignored in reading comprehension studies. Shuy (1981) states: "Research shows that good language learners begin with a function, a need to get something done with language, and move gradually toward acquiring the forms which reveal that function. They learn holistically, not by isolated skills" (p. 106).

The social situation in which children hear books read involves a very specific cultural routine. In the United States the book-reading experience in the home typically involves one or several children, usually siblings, a book with text and illustrations, a caretaker (often a parent, grandparent, or baby-sitter), close physical proximity (often the caretaker's lap or a child in bed with a parent perched nearby), and a familiar setting (often the child's home or that of a relative or babysitter). In the preschool setting many of the same home characteristics are present. The group may be larger, the setting may be an area rug, and the teacher may sit in a rocker and share the pictures at the end of each page, although this is not always the case. Again, all is familiar to the child.

Another component of the lap situation may be the interactive nature of the experience (Cazden, 1966). Again, the child often responds freely to the illustrations and story as they are read aloud. Heath (1983) suggests that this level of interaction may be culturally determined. Flood (1977) has found that interaction during, before, and after the lap experience can elicit a higher range of response from children. As children grow older, the school book-sharing experience changes. Often children will remain seated at their desks, and talk during the read-aloud session will be minimized. However, one component essentially remains: Pictures are shared during read-aloud experiences, and if they are not, the children will frequently demand to see the pictures.

Pictures are part and parcel of the early reading context. This is a cultural phenomenon. To strip the context of pictures changes the social situation dramatically and must necessarily affect the child's ability to construct meaning. Denburg (1976–77) suggests that reading is facilitated by pictures that enhance text. Readers integrate a variety of strategies in order to make sense of the text, which include strategies incorporating illustrations.

Current research views illustrations as beneficial for reading and listening comprehension when the pictures give redundant or additional information to the reader (Bransford & Johnson, 1972; Levin, 1981; Rohwer & Harris, 1975; Schallert, 1980). Subjects tested performed better on comprehension tasks that provided both textual and pictorial information. Levin (1981) concluded that content-relevant illustrations facilitate children's learning of that content.

A study by Cappa (1957) with 2,500 kindergarten children suggests that children find illustrations most appealing, even over story content (Huck et al., 1987). Fenwick (1975) took a look at books checked out of a library in a junior high school and found that those with numerous illustrations were frequently checked out. Children are accustomed to books with illustrations.

In my own research (Lehr, 1988b) with primary age children, I found that illustrations are an integral part of the read-aloud situation. The children listened and looked as I read. They followed the story carefully and referred to the pictures throughout the sessions. In addition, when talking about the themes of the books afterwards during individual interviews, the children pointed to illustrations to make points about the actions of characters or story sequence, used them as points of departure to talk about the book, as guides while telling what they felt about a chain of events, and hugged them close while talking. In short, having the book available as a referent made an impact on what the child had to say about the book. Kindergarten children pointed to the character Titch in the book *Titch* by Pat Hutchins, and then told how they felt about being the smallest. Obviously we can read and tell stories without pictures; however, in my own research I saw how children used the illustrations as referents, essentially as cuing systems to organize their thoughts about the stories. The kindergarten children were more reliant on the books, whereas the older children typically pointed to the book as they spoke rather than to individual pictures or characters.

IMPORTANCE OF THE READING CONTEXT
TO CHILDREN'S RESPONSES

Print Settings

Harste, Burke, and Woodward (1979) refer to the child who learns to read in a total environment. These "print settings" include size, shape, color, as well as the configuration of the print itself, a semiotic system based on signs from the environment. The child may not recognize a STOP sign without the benefit of context (on the corner), color (bright red), shape (octagonal), and social situation (being in a car, approaching a busy intersection, and coming to a complete stop). Children learn to recognize written symbols within the framework of meaning. Separating the text from the context can render the young reader helpless and unable to function at full capability.

In a similar manner, children hear stories in the context of lap situations with real books. To test the child's knowledge of meaning that context cannot be stripped to minimal components. Pictures are a part of that setting and therefore contribute to the child's building of knowledge structures. How that occurs is not yet known and is open for further study.

Children's Illustrations

Siegel (1983) worked with fourth-grade children in the area of interpretation by asking students to draw sketches of meaning for books read. By employing the use of art it was felt that meaning could be communicated that would not otherwise surface if language were the only vehicle available. Sketching was chosen because it required students "to take the experience of reading as an object of thought" (p. 9). Siegel discovered that the social situation affected the interpretation of what was read and how it was represented. The nature of sketching allowed a reader to reconsider the initial meaning-world and engage in signification rather than mere representation. That is, students related what was read to the specific context and moved from perception to interpretation.

Children's sketches included signs and symbols for elaboration and explanation, which were not solicited by the researcher. Children independently linked pictorial and written symbols in order to achieve clarity and organize ideas. Many of the written conventions used by the children were meaningful only in light of the cultural context. This suggests a natural tendency of children to use a wide range of signs in constructing meaning and attempting to communicate or share that meaning.

Color and size coding, for example, are only meaningful in a shared cultural context "when intertwined with other codes that they have the potential to signify" (Siegel, 1983, p. 31). For example, STOP in and of itself means "don't continue on your present course," but in conjunction with red and an octagon it has culturally encoded meaning that is situation-specific, distinct from any other use of the word *stop*. A distinction of semiotics (the study of sign functioning) is the notion of shared codes for successful communicative acts. This blends in well with Siegel's major finding, that interpretations by the children in her study cannot be explained in terms of reader and text alone but instead require a consideration of the total reading event. This has implications for the total reading context.

Response to Picture Books

Barbara Kiefer (1989) has done extensive work in the area of children's responses to picture books and has found that "picture books of many types and in many styles, created by sensitive artists (and authors) for audiences of many ages, can become the focal points for a variety of reactions and responses" (p. 81). She also suggests that giving children frequent opportunities to respond to picture books may in fact "develop deeper cognitive and affective understandings and a more critical aesthetic awareness" (p. 81).

Her work supports the notion that young children respond physically to picture book stories, in terms of holding books, bodily movements, artwork, or reenactments of stories. Children also respond to picture books through writings. Kiefer reports that one fifth-grade child's response to *Mossgown* by William Hooks perceived the colors in the illustrations as evoking seasonal moods. "In the front part of the book the colors were winter, in the middle part the colors were summer colors" (p. 82). The child experiences the book as a totality. Text and illustrations become the combined vehicle for creating the mood of the story.

Kiefer additionally discovered that children responded to picture books in their discussions and writings by conveying information about what happened and pointing out details. Children also made links between books, connecting and comparing the work of different authors and illustrators as well as different works by the same author and illustrator. Children are great observers of details, moving perhaps from section to section rather than taking in wholes (Coles, Sigman, & Chessel, 1977; Kiefer, 1989). This might explain way children notice as many details as they do about illustrations in picture books. Kiefer suggests that children also make inferences about characters, events, and themes, and that they make connections between the pictures in books that they read and their own lives. This supports White's (1954/1984) diary entries about her own preschool child's linking of the book experience to real life.

Illustrations are an integral part of the book experience. The fact that children in the upper grades not only choose books based on how many pictures are in them but also prefer a high ratio of pictures to text (Huck et al., 1987) attests to this. Stripping the research context of illustrations, or even suggesting that children will become more competent readers without illustrations, does not seem justified.

One must assume that the interaction between text and illustration, the balance that is achieved in picture books, is a total experience for children. Therefore, high-quality illustrations are as important to the learning process as well-written text. If readers can be impeded from accessing meaning because of poorly written text, they can also fail to learn from aimless illustrations, such as those found in many primers. Meaning getting will not occur in a vacuum.

CONSTRUCTING MEANING BY DRAWING AND WRITING

Children construct meaning using all of the sign systems available to them (Harste et al., 1979; Siegel, 1983). By asking the children to draw sketches about books shared, a teacher will find that their drawings contain information that might not surface with dialogue alone. Children are also sensitive to the art of the picture book and frequently want to respond to books with artwork of their own (Kiefer, 1989). In the words of one fourth-grade child in response to *Song of the Horse*: "The illustrations just catch your eye and then you don't want to let go. You just want to get hold of it and keep it till you've done all the illustrations" (Kiefer, 1989, p. 82). Children are aware of the many complex choices that artists make. They are able to talk about illustrations with descriptive language, and they notice detail that illustrators have carefully wrought. Kiefer writes:

> I found that many children like to take time with picture books and that picture books that are artistically demanding or puzzling like *The Grey Lady and the Strawberry Snatcher*, *Outside Over There*, or *Song of the Horse* are books that engender the most long-lasting and deepest responses on the part of children. It would seem that when artists are intensely involved in the creation of meaning through the medium of the picture book, they have the potential to destroy complacency, to uncover needs, to pique curiosity, to evoke enthusiasm, and to arouse passion. (pp. 86–87)

It is not surprising, therefore, that children wish to respond to picture books with their own artwork.

In a similar fashion I explored the child's interpretation of theme by asking students to draw a picture describing the books read to them, telling what they were both about. I viewed this activity as an opportunity to help the children focus on the meaning of the story; therefore, it occurred prior to the individual book discussions. The children's pictures were rich and varied and support Siegel's and Kiefer's premises. In the following section I discuss the illustrated responses to realistic fiction and folktales of kindergarten children, second graders, and fourth graders.

Kindergarten Children

Kindergarten children draw pictures about realistic fiction. Almost all of the kindergarten children drew pictures of both books chosen for theme identification. My invitation to them was to draw a picture about the books that they thought were similar and to write about their picture. Three children decided to draw a picture about one book, which I discuss below. Only one child drew a picture about the story he did not choose.

Alex chose *Titch* and *New Blue Shoes* as thematically similar, yet he chose to draw a picture about *The Carrot Seed*. When asked to read what he wrote next to his picture, Alex *said*: "Harold. This book was the wrong one." In actuality he *wrote* that "Harold's dad (said) it will not grow." Why did Alex respond as he did? Was he simply alerting me that his choice was to respond to the book that meant something to him? His verbal statement identifies *The Carrot Seed* as *not* being thematically matched to the other books. Notice the written connection he made from *The Carrot Seed* to the character of Harold in *Harold and the Purple Crayon*. Other children did this as well, which is not surprising, because the two characters are similarly drawn by the illustrators.

Alex later related *Titch* and *New Blue Shoes* to the theme of size. "Her shoes are getting small" (reference to *New Blue Shoes*). "The big brother has a big bike and he has a little small one" (reference to *Titch*). And later he said that they are "about size, bigger and smaller." He did not perceive the child in *The Carrot Seed* as having a problem with size, or being smaller. Instead Alex focused on the father's negative response to the boy's efforts to grow a carrot. His picture does not show a final resolution of the problem, as most children did in their pictures. There is no large growing carrot. Alex leaves the dilemma intact.

Ryan drew a picture of a monster and a bat with the accompanying letters: TEUNTUN. When asked to read his caption, Ryan said: "Count Dracula planted a carrot." Ryan was preoccupied with Dracula and bats, a month after Halloween, and made them fit into the theme of the story. Later in his oral discussion he matched *Titch* and *The Carrot Seed* and said they were about growing things and that both had a seed. His retelling was brief and to the point. "All the people said, 'It's not gonna grow, it's not gonna grow.' But it did grow." This illustrates to me that Ryan clearly understood the story and chose to combine his interests with the plot of the book during the drawing activity. His caption does not match his writing under the picture and shows a child in the prephonemic stages of spelling development. Children like Ryan need to be given the freedom to explore their own agendas, even when teacher's seem paramount. At the age of 5 Ryan was already savvy enough to attend to his own needs and placate those of the teacher as well.

Andy drew a picture of Titch and an older sibling and decided to concentrate on the writing aspect of the assignment. His caption overwhelms the page and reads: "First of all the carrot didn't grow. Titch got a good thing." Andy combined both books verbally and visually. Later, Andy had much to say about both books, as has already been discussed in Chapter 2. Interestingly, when asked to retell one of the stories, Andy went back to the book and said, "I'll have to read it then." After a retelling of *The Carrot Seed*, Andy ended by saying "it surprises 'em." This refers to the character's parents who said the carrot would not grow. This child had a lot to say about the books, and his ideas were well developed during the interview. His picture shows relative size only, yet his written words talk about beginnings and outcomes, perhaps setting the stage for the rich discussion that followed. This child was more adept with words, both written and spoken than he was with drawing. His desire to communicate with words took precedence over drawing.

Other children drew pictures about both books chosen as thematically similar, which provided a format for later discussion. Laura's oral discussion after the art activity was richly textured with descriptions of *Titch* and *The Carrot Seed*. She had this to say about *Titch*: "He sort of felt left out, cause all the big kids had bigger stuff and he didn't." She related *The Carrot Seed* to the character of Harold in *Harold and the Purple Crayon*. Both characters are similar and the illustrations are both spare with little background. She was able to retell the story of *The Carrot Seed*. "A little boy planted a seed. Everybody said it wouldn't grow and the little boy said it'd grow. And one day it did."

Compare that language to what Laura wrote on her drawing of both stories. (See Figure 4.1.) This refers to *Titch*.

A BoY haD a SaStar anD a BriTher Tha Thot That thaYar Smarter cas Tha Yor BiGoY The liite BoY Plant a seD The BeG BoY YoS So SiPriSt.

[A boy had a sister and a brother. They thought that they were smarter cause they were bigger. The little boy planted a seed. The big boy was so surprised.]

Laura created a conflict for the story based on character motivation. She attributed negative motives to the older siblings and resolved the conflict by relating that the little boy did something that surprised the older brother. Laura did not restate the ending of the book in this picture story in terms of the size of the plant; however, she did talk about growth later in her oral discussion of the book. The idea that it grew successfully was what she stressed. Her illustration of *Titch* shows no plant growing at all, but it does show three characters with distinct size differences. Notice the rich detail in the features of the characters. For *The Carrot Seed* Laura drew a boy in overalls with a baseball cap, pushing a large carrot in a wheelbarrow with a wheel. She used red, blue, green, orange, and brown markers. Laura not only drew two pictures that compared the books chosen as thematically similar, she also wrote captions that were parallel. "The boy planted a seed. The plant grew into a carrot." Her picture, combined with her writing, is a complex response to both books and indicates a depth of comprehen-

The BoyPlant
The Plant GreinaiseD
a caret

a Boy haDa sasta anD
a BritherTha Th e
That thayaesmart or
cosTha yor
Bigot
The liite Boy
PlantaiseD
The
Beg
Boy
Yos
So
SiPrist

FIGURE 4.1.   Laura's detailed drawing coupled with her message is a complex response to *Titch* and *The Carrot Seed*.

101

sion. On one level Laura has combined both stories and drawn two panels that show conflict and resolution, which are parallel for both stories.

In her oral discussion of the books Laura was able to retell the story of *The Carrot Seed*. "A little boy planted a seed. Everybody said it wouldn't grow and the little boy said it'd grow. And one day it did." In response to a question about changing anything in the story, Laura said: "He sort of felt left out, cause all the big kids had bigger stuff and he didn't." The captioned picture Laura drew provides a different sort of glimpse into her thought processes. What did she find central to the story? What is it that Laura comprehended? Through drawing, writing, and oral discussion one can see that Laura's response to the books was focused on the notion of growth and being excluded. One can see that this child, at the age of 5, is focused on the story, is able to consider the central tenets of the text, and has a depth of response both in art and writing that perhaps influenced her verbal discussion about the books. The fact that Laura emphasized the success factor involved in the stories and related that to size and feeling smarter indicates a child who understands and is able to verbalize some of the social structures that are operative in the real world. Does Laura have older siblings? Is Laura an oldest child? Has Laura experienced some of the same feelings of powerlessness or the smugness of those larger and older, much as Titch did?

Michael drew the most detailed picture showing both *Titch* and *The Carrot Seed*. (See Figure 4.2.) He also wrote extensively about both books and had much to say later during the interview. Michael's picture shows Titch alone wearing a huge smile with Mary and Peter standing nearby, mouths open with surprise. Between them is a pot with a large plant and the caption: "Titch wanted it to grow bigger." From the beginning Michael focused on Titch's success and the older sibling's surprise at his feat. Later, when asked what the authors were trying to teach, Michael elaborated: "If your brother has an older thing, you still have part of it — and sometimes it's the most important part." Later he identified that important part from the story. "Titch had the seed." When asked why he liked the story, Michael had this to say: "At the end Titch got something that he should have got. He got something that his big brother and sister didn't get." His discussion of *The Carrot Seed* also relates the character in this book to *Harold and the Purple Crayon*. His caption for that elaborate picture reads: "Harold and the Seed. Harold's dad said, 'It won't come up.' Harold did it." This picture shows two frames from the story, the family standing by while Harold watches his enormous carrot growing and another showing Harold bent to the ground with a carrot on his back, literally depicting the enormity of

FIGURE 4.2.   Michael's detailed picture links *The Carrot Seed* to another well-known book, *Harold and the Purple Crayon.*

what Harold has grown — what Harold has accomplished. Father stands in the middle smoking a pipe, while mother stands taller with a bit more hair and a big smile on her face. Michael chose to focus on the father's negative reaction to Harold's efforts in his writing. These pictures and captions provide a lot of information about how Michael has processed the information in the books. Both pictures and captions reveal that this child understands the plots of the stories, the basic dilemmas posed, and the satisfaction shared by Titch and Harold at the end of the stories. "Harold did it." Can anyone doubt that the 5-year-old child is capable of constructing thematic meaning with books?

Art as a response to picture books also provides another type of meaning building for children. Two kindergartners drew pictures but did not write anything about them. Richie's picture shows a large plant and a large carrot and a little person beside it, all done in red marker. (See Figure 4.3.) He later said that the two books were alike "because they both have seeds in them and they both grow." His retelling of *Titch* consisted of three words: "Being tall-brother." His retelling of *The Carrot Seed*: "Didn't grow and then it growed." Richie did not want to talk. He did want to draw. He did not want to write, nor would he talk about his picture. He got angry at each question and shrugged, glared, or grimaced. I suspect he cooperated as much as he did because he liked hearing the stories and didn't seem to be a child who knew stories or had much to say about them. Drawing allowed Richie to share his thoughts visually. For other students like Richie, art would provide a format for sharing information. Richie was not comfortable talking in the classroom, and I did not observe him speaking out during class time. Drawing is an effective vehicle for exploring meaning, because Richie's picture clearly compares both books and shows the importance of the two plants as well as their large size. He did not use as much detail, color, or words as other children did; however, drawing allowed him an avenue for expression and provided me with a view of Richie's perceptions of the books.

As his teacher in the classroom, allowing and encouraging Richie to express himself through art would give him the opportunity to focus on stories shared without forcing him into social situations with which he was uncomfortable. The art itself would provide me with a solid glimpse of his comprehension strategies, particularly when I gave focused assignments. "Draw a picture showing what you think is the most exciting part of the story." "Draw a picture showing the part you liked the best." "Draw a picture showing what happened first." "Draw a picture showing what Titch did that was important." All of these invitations to explore with markers, paints, colored pencils, and craypas,

FIGURE 4.3. Richie has had little experience with books and was uncomfortable and angry while drawing.

would also include the invitation to write at the bottom what the story was about, but would never include the threat that he must. Through Richie's art, I gained a window into his thought processes, and hoped that eventually he might be willing to tell about his pictures, at least in individual conferences where the social threat was minimized. Perhaps he would dictate a caption to me that we might attach to the bottom of his picture on a strip. I recommended that he spend time with these two books and let them become familiar friends. Perhaps he would ultimately create a mural showing the sequence of the story. Comprehension and understanding can be evidenced in a multitude of ways, and as teachers we need to be flexible for the Richies of the world because we don't want to build in failure, nor do we want to force children to give us that which they aren't ready to give.

Kindergarten children draw pictures about folktales.   In my second session with Richie, I read three fairy tales aloud (*The Three Little Pigs*, *The Billy Goats Gruff*, and *The Gingerbread Boy*), and I still found him reluctant to speak. His picture, done with purple crayon and purple marker, was more detailed this time and showed a large creature on four legs behind two smaller animals, all with rounded horns (the three billy goats). (See Figure 4.4.) They are going across a bridge, and a circle wearing a sad face is beneath them (the troll). Although he drew a picture about the three billy goats and the troll, Richie chose *The Three Little Pigs* and *The Gingerbread Boy* as thematically similar and explained why. "They both ate them." In the oral discussion Richie stated four times that characters got eaten, which the troll did not do to the three billy goats. This made quite an impression on him, yet he said that he did like the stories! He was more willing to talk in the second session. He clearly enjoyed hearing the stories and was preoccupied with being eaten up. Interestingly, his picture shows the characters who successfully met and conquered danger without being eaten.

During the oral discussion quite a few children, as mentioned earlier, focused on the characters' being eaten, yet several of the same children drew their picture about the three billy goats going over the bridge to safety, as Richie did. Although they verbally focused on not surviving, their drawings suggest that they wanted to depict characters successfully going across the bridge with a troll beneath. Jane's picture shows three small goats and a gigantic troll. Her caption reads: "We want to go to the hill to get fat." Later she stated that the authors were trying to teach you "don't go across dangerous bridge. Don't hurry out to get cookies out of the oven real fast (because) it would pop out and run away." In response to "Pick a story. Why did it end like it did?" Jane replied: "The goats got what they wanted. The ginger-

FIGURE 4.4 Richie's second drawing included more details. He also engaged in more friendly dialogue about the story.

breadman didn't get what he wanted and they wanted the ginger-breadman and the fox got it." In relation to the big billy goat gruff and the troll, Jane said that the "big goat came and he just crumbled him to pieces." Jane's second picture shows the gingerbreadman in a container like a cookie jar with the old man and the old woman looking on. She identified a successful venture and chose to put the cookie in a jar where he belongs.

Tony simply drew a bridge and a "B." He was preoccupied with the chant from *The Three Billy Goats Gruff* and *The Three Little Pigs* and verbally linked the books because of the threats to the characters. "This one says I'll poke your eyeballs out and crush your bits and bones and body and this one says I'll huff and I'll puff and I'll blow your house. See?" He repeated the chants over and over and used a dramatic voice. When I asked him if he would change anything in the stories, he responded with "make the pigs safe." He had trouble focusing on drawing, and his oral discussion rambled on with the chants being repeated at intervals.

Luke also drew a bridge with no other props. His caption said, "I will crush you to bits and bones." In the oral discussion he too linked the goats and the pigs as sharing a similar theme because the wolf caught the pigs and ate them and the troll threatened to do the same. He picked up on the violence in the story and the difficulty of survival, in contrast to the foolish-ness of the gingerbread boy. Luke decided that the authors were trying to teach that "bigger is better right here on billy goats gruff." "How is bigger better? What do you think that means?" "If somebody comes up to say something mean you can maybe do something to hurt them." I responded with, "And why do you hurt them then? Do you want to hurt them?" Lucas replied, "No, they might do something mean." "Well, then, why did this guy hurt the troll?" "Because he was gonna try to eat him up." He was directly referring to *The Three Billy Goats Gruff* and their dilemma: survival, not violence for the sake of violence, but in order to protect self.

Similarly, Liz's picture shows three happy pigs and two goats crossing a bridge. She wrote no caption but said later that "some bad thing was both after them in the stories." She also stated that they all have happy endings and that she would have changed it so "that the pigs weren't aten up," a typical response for many of the kindergarten children. Interestingly, her picture shows three happy pigs all making it to safety. She heard the story and processed the fact that two pigs were eaten; nonetheless, Liz changed the ending of the story and saved the two pigs. Keep in mind that the picture was her first response to the books and that the words telling about what she would change came later. This indicates a flexibility in relation to narrative. Ironically, Liz did not deal with the gingerbreadboy's demise. Perhaps the fate of cookies is more firmly fixed in her mind.

Three children choosing *The Gingerbread Boy* and *The Three Little*

Pigs as similar drew elaborate pictures of the gingerbread boy. Chris's picture shows a giant cookie with a raisin mouth and raisin buttons and the caption CBRG, dictated to me as reading "gingerbread." (See Figure 4.5.) He too verbally stressed the idea of being eaten. "They both ran away. He was gonna get eaten and they were gonna get eaten." He identified the most important ideas as being "building your houses with bricks. You might have a terrible storm or tornado. Your house might be blown over like the wolf did." He made a link between fantasy and reality, metaphor and real life. He knew that the idea was to have a secure shelter. Whether he applied this to life in general or houses specifically cannot be determined.

Laura drew the cookie as it is about to hop up on the fox's nose. Her caption reads: "The little gingerbread man ran away." (See Figure 4.6.) On the reverse side of the paper she drew three detailed pictures of pigs with hoofs and curly tails. The caption reads: "The three little pigs ran away." She later told me that the fox tricked him and ate him up. The authors were trying to teach you "not to run away and not to let a stranger come in," both of which apply directly to the dilemmas in both stories. Her art focused on the characters as they were in the middle of the story, not on the outcomes of the story, yet she understood the fate of the characters and applied this information to real life on two levels. Don't run away and don't let strangers in. Laura knew about wolves and foxes and the tricks they can pull on you. And can one assume that Laura was applying this book knowledge to her own life and the admonitions she received about not letting strangers in?

Children's responses to the three folktales differed from adult perspectives dramatically both verbally and in their artwork; however, they did not miss the themes of the books. Rather they drew pictures of characters actively involved in survival or making inappropriate choices for survival. Children typically drew pictures of characters before they were eaten. Their captions suggest characters in the act of trying to get away. "The three billy goats trying to get away from the troll and the troll is trying to eat them up," describes one picture. Lisa shows the troll attacking the largest goat and the third pig standing safely in his house. (See Figure 4.7.) Michael's picture is similar to Lisa's except that his third pig is standing safely outside his brick house. Only one picture, drawn by Mike, shows the wolf falling into the pig's stewpot. (See Figure 4.8.) Later Mike said this about the wolf: "He's dead and gone . . . because he build a fire by him." The smoke coming out of his chimney suggests that it was a big one!

Children understand about danger and dilemmas and how characters try to avoid getting eaten up. I think that folklore most dramatically illustrates this when one considers the real pitfalls that confront animal characters. These are harsh realities, and they must use their wits to escape the jaws of the wolf or the fox. Don't forget the childhood nightmares and fears

FIGURE 4.5. Chris's elaborate cookie is accompanied with invented spelling for the word "gingerbread."

The Little ginger Bred
man ran awa

FIGURE 4.6. Laura's message that "The little gingerbread man ran away" emphasizes a hopeful ending for the story.

FIGURE 4.7.   Lisa's artwork stresses the independence and safety of the main characters.

FIGURE 4.8.   Mike's picture of a wolf splashing into the stewpot included this explanation later: "He's dead and gone . . . because he build a fire by him."

that these children have, especially when the lights go off. I can still remember some of the nightmares that I had as a small child. Thank goodness my mother and father shared lots of tales with me. As Bettelheim (1976) says, folktales like these don't terrify our children; rather they help them sort through the chaos that is out there and perhaps ultimately help them make good choices and solid decisions about their own safety and well-being. One cannot underestimate the power of strong narratives for children as they go about this business of growing up. As my own children continually remind me, it's not an easy process.

Second-Grade Children

Second-grade children draw pictures about realistic fiction. I found more diversity with the second-grade children in terms of their artistic responses to literature. I again invited the children to draw a picture about the two books chosen as thematically similar. Their responses indicated much more variety in terms of using captions, using a series of panels to explore the theme, responding to one book or both books with two separate pictures, and giving characters in the study dialogue through the use of bubbles.

Ashley (age 7:11) chose to show both books. Interestingly, she drew two detailed pictures of two boys holding hands and two girls frowning and sticking out tongues at each other. (See Figure 4.9.) Her caption focused on being mad. Her oral retellings of the stories were thorough, and she recognized Maurice Sendak's artwork in *Let's Be Enemies* and remembered the picture of Max being mad at his mother, which she likened to a part of the book shared. She also made the comment that Sendak's colors were better in *Where the Wild Things Are!* As I emphasized earlier, children can create intricate details in their own artwork, and they are also acute observers of detail in the work of illustrators. Ashley personalized this story and compared it to vignettes about her sister. Could it be that this is the reason that she focused her art on two girls in conflict? One brings one's own schema to any reading with personal values attached.

Children like Rebecca were able to draw elaborate frames with dialogue written in bubbles above characters' heads. (See Figure 4.10.) Rebecca's caption showed parallel conflict and resolution. "They both hate their friend and at the end like them again." She considered two books, stepped back, and gave plot summaries one step removed from the literal plots. Rebecca said very little during the interview, yet her art and writing show the level of understanding at which she appreciated the books shared. Using her art and captions as a springboard, I would later ask Rebecca in the classroom to tell or explain or give examples of how they both hated their

FIGURE 4.9.   Ashley's pictures focus on both aspects of the books: making up and being angry.

TheYwere Both MaD at echa othe

friends, using her own words as catalysts. Additionally, I would encourage her to write and draw other episodes from the story that illustrated the conflict between the friends.

Barry's stick drawings were quite unsophisticated when compared with the detailed drawings of other children. His characters all had a unisex look about them, the only elaborate detail being huge hands with five digits. Characters had no feet and the hair was done in green. Yet Barry drew two pictures for each book showing sequencing of events with bubble captions where characters were exploring playing or walking together. His remarks later during the interview showed that he understood the basic theme about friendship and that characters changed because "it would be lonely and (they) wouldn't have anyone to play with." The most important idea was "how friends can be. How we can be enemies like for a week or so and then be friends." Barry's art was simple, yet it helped him focus on the major themes of the book and explore how the characters interacted with each other. Ken too used primitive artwork but had much to say about the books in individual discussion.

Amy had the same idea but developed it more fully. She sectioned her paper off and began a series of panels showing two elaborately dressed characters with striped tops and matching slacks. Her caption shows resolu-

FIGURE 4.10. Characters speak with bubble captions.

tion: "They were friends then they got mad at each other. Then you get to have pretzels with each other."

Anne illustrated her page with lively and colorful figures and dialogue bubbles and captured the essence of both books, yet she had little to say during the interview and seemed confused and unable to focus. (See Figure 4.11.) Having her picture and writing gives me a more precise view of her interaction with the book. It also tells me that just because a child is not verbally active during class discussion, the child may have comprehended the book and have many levels of response, which become evident through art and writing. Being unable or unwilling to tell verbally is not an indication of lack of understanding, yet how often do we as teachers assume that, because a child doesn't answer a question or contribute to a discussion, he or she probably doesn't know or have an opinion about characters or events in a story?

In a similar fashion Betsy illustrated both books but has all four characters in livid poses. (See Figure 4.12.) The anger really comes through in her pictures. Her first caption fully develops the theme and, instead of repeating it all again, she simply writes: "The same thing with this book." Children are practical and I assume that they don't like busy work any more than I do. Later in our conversation together Betsy explored the nuances of misunderstanding the words of a friend and stressed how important communication is in friendship. "Tell them what you think . . . because if you don't you might get mad at the other person for nothing, for something that they didn't really do." Her picture focused on the anger that erupted over a misunderstanding, and in the discussion she basically resolved that anger and explored resolution.

Sarah had by far the most sophisticated drawings because she took specific elements from the stories and showed them in action. (See Figure 4.13.) Her picture shows one of the boys in *Let's Be Enemies* riding in a wagon, crowned like a king, wearing a purple robe and acting, as we all know, extremely bossy. Many of the children used the word *bossy* in reference to this character and had had experiences with bossy friends, which they related. Sarah actually showed this character in the act of being obnoxious, raising his arm imperiously as the other boy pulls him along in the wagon. She focused specifically on the problem. From her picture it is clear that she understands this kind of character.

For the two girls in *The Hating Book*, her drawing shows two characters in dresses, which was the root of the misunderstanding. One is turned away, the other staring at the first helplessly. Her drawing again focuses on the problem, whereas her caption focuses on resolution. "The reason I liked this story is that it showed what to do if your friend split up with you. All you have to do is ask them why they were acting like they were." For Sarah

FIGURE 4.11.   Anne's picture and captions were more elaborate than her verbalizations about the book.

FIGURE 4.12. Betsy's illustrations erupt with the anger that the characters feel.

FIGURE 4.13. Sarah chose to focus on the imperious nature of this main character.

books are practical helps in dealing with problems. In this case, communication is the focal point in friendship. In our discussion later, Sarah talked about how there has to be "some kind of reason" you don't get along and that one shouldn't give up. These were pretty sophisticated responses to literature and showed an awareness of how the system works.

Other children used the drawings as summarizing devices for the stories. "This book is about two boys that are friends, then enemies, then friends. This book is about two girls that are not friends and then they are" (David). Succinctly put. Or they showed sequencing of the story through a series of pictures that told the story with captions.

Allowing the children to explore the theme of friendship with large sheets of blank paper produced a good deal of variety in their responses. By not being confined to one mode of response, they developed their own formats for merging pictures and print. The skills that are evidenced through this linking of art and writing include sequencing, writing dialogue, comparing two similar stories, summarizing a story, showing details from the story, and understanding conflict/resolution.

Second-grade children draw pictures about folktales.   This series of three folktales caused more confusion than any other set of books read to the children. Children seemed less sure of themes and had more difficulty articulating them, stepping back from literal elements of the stories shared. An analysis of the illustrations indicates that most of the children drew pictures of the princess and prince at the end of the story or the princess standing alone. Some of the characters are elaborately dressed in fancy ballgowns and crowns. Others are in castles in what appear to be throne rooms, getting married.

The generic princess was the most common figure to appear in pictures. All of the princesses illustrated are basically beautiful and well dressed. Children seem to visualize their princesses as finished products, not struggling to get there. None of the illustrations really reflect the other qualities of princesses or scenes described in the stories, like a tattercoat princess, a sulky princess, a child princess hiding in the hut of seven dwarves, or a princess dying when poisoned by the queen.

David wrote that Snow White and Tattercoats "were both just plain people. Then they were both princesses." He was the only one who mentioned the idea of change, the process of becoming something. His illustration shows the house of Snow White and the castle of Tattercoats, both with an unidentified figure in the window.

The idea of beauty and love was illustrated and mentioned by most of the children, with only a few children drawing or talking about the roles of the antagonists specifically. Lauren's caption shows parallel development in

both pictures. "The queen hates the princess. Grandpa hates the Granddaughter." Her picture shows the happy ending and does not match her
captions, which mention the conflict in the stories and specifically name the
antagonists.

Only one child drew a picture of the wicked stepmother in *Snow
White*—standing in front of her mirror. The figure is glamorous and wears a
beautiful purple gown. In a second panel she has drawn Tattercoats with
long, flowing blonde hair, red cheeks, a well-developed figure, and a lovely
gown. A Barbie doll figure to be sure! Her oral caution to readers is that
"you shouldn't lock yourself in your room just because someone died." One
might have thought that she would choose to draw the grandfather sitting in
his castle at his window crying a river of tears.

Barry is the only child who shows the princess in Zwerger's retelling of
The Swineherd getting what she deserves at the end of the story. The prince
is saying, "You have been bad," while the princess is saying, "I am sad."
Barry rightly concludes during our discussion that the "princess learns a
lesson." His art is detailed but primitive. His figures have stick arms and legs
with balloon bodies. The heads have no hair or other features save eyes, yet
his four panels for both stories have lots of activity, with one hidden figure
even yelling from the castle portcullis, "Get out!" One stick figure performs
a deep bow and says, "I have found her." Obviously, Barry's illustration is an
organizing device for his thoughts regarding the story. His captions show
what he considered important events in the story. Notice that he relates the
swineherd's admonition to the princess and that she acknowledge her grace-
less ways. For *Snow White* Barry relays the queen's rage ("Get out!") and
the woodcutter's completion of his duty ("I have found her"), two interesting episodes of the story to relate.

Some of the children used simple line drawings with detailed captions
that neatly summarized the plots of the stories. Rebecca's caption was the
most detailed. "They were dressed in rags and they both married a prince
and they both had great beauty and someone didn't like her." Concretely,
her writing links both stories and literally retells the stories of Snow White
and Tattercoats. Her picture was very simple and had little detail, showing
one blonde princess reaching out. Only one child verbally linked *Tattercoats*
to the traditional Cinderella version, *Tattercoats* being the English version
of the Cinderella story.

To conclude, the children were more easily able to relate to realistic
fiction that dealt with themes common to their lives. The folktales that
considered evil acts and love and marriage were more removed and caused
them to focus on concrete elements of the stories such as the marriage of the
prince and princess at the end. Their illustrations reflected this concrete

stance toward the stories and focused on the happy endings rather than the violent aspects.

Fourth-Grade Children

Fourth-grade children draw pictures about realistic fiction.   All of the fourth-grade children drew pictures for both stories, except for one child who wrote captions. The focus of the 19 children was typically on both the written and the artistic expression of their ideas. Some children had rather lengthy captions and included bubbles for characters to speak. One child separated two characters through the word *dislike* and bridged the same two characters through the word *friendship*, paralleling how the young boy felt linked to Stevie at the end of the story. This facility with words shows the ability of the older children to play with forms, figures, and language, in a sense distancing themselves from concrete representations and exploring new ways of linking ideas. Other children focused primarily on the writing; their pictures were rather simply drawn. Contrasted to this were pictures with elaborate detail, even down to the bows on shoelaces and the hook protruding from the seagull's mouth in *Thy Friend, Obadiah*. There was a good deal of variety in the illustrations as well, from tiny, accurate pencil sketches, to cartoon sequences, to parallel pictures showing relationships before and after, with an emphasis on the pesky nature of the characters in both books.

Jon's (9:9) picture shows two characters, both drawn with exacting detail, one in a negative stance, the other looking dejected and in a lower position. (See Figure 4.14.) The characters are linked by a descending arrow with the word *dislike* written on it. Ironically, both characters are the same size. Below them two characters are pictured with their hands clasped, linked by the words *friendship, friendship*. This linking was symbolic, however, because Stevie was gone by the story's end, suggesting that although the characters were no longer together, the child understood that the relationship was no longer negative in the mind of the main character, revealing personal growth. Later during the book discussion Jon said that the authors were trying to teach that the characters "didn't really bother to judge the other person by the thing. They didn't stop to talk with him. When they thought back it made them realize that they were nice." His illustration actually gives a clearer picture of his understanding of the themes of both books than does his verbal explanation.

Melissa, however, had a lot to say about both books and wrote a detailed caption with detailed illustrations, which were much simpler than Jon's. She wrote: "I think that the storys were like each other because there

FIGURE 4.14. Jon combines words and pictures to create symbols showing themes.

about friendships. They were about gaining and missing friends. it also had (in both) a lot of memories." Additionally Obadiah says: "Stop following me," to which the bird replies, "I love to follow you." Melissa's illustrations seem to be an organizing device for her thoughts. She later linked both books to *Jonathan Livingston Seagull* and *Serendipity* and said that all of the books basically teach a lesson, which she defined as "be kind to people . . . they could turn out to be your friend." Melissa, like six other children, made connections to pests in other books, ranging from *Dear, Mr. Henshaw; Superfudge; The Eighteenth Emergency* to *Tales of a Fourth Grade Nothing.*

Many children framed the sequence of the story in a cartoon format with bubble dialogue emphasizing the dilemma of the story, that of being followed or being bothered by someone else, and ending with a parallel structure in which both stories end with friendship. Some show the dejected character in *Stevie* at the end, whereas other illustrations reflect a basic contentment that the negative attitude toward Stevie no longer exists.

Christie is typical of the child who seemed unable to focus at the beginning of the book discussion but was able to state a theme for *Stevie* and *Thy Friend, Obadiah* after being asked what the stories teach. "You can get mad at people and you can still be friends." Simply put and basic to the story. Early on she identified that both books had pests and that they reminded her of *Dear, Mr. Henshaw*. Compare that to the captions in her illustrations that show the pests in both stories with this written below each picture: "Care, love and friendship." Her thoughts later on during our discussion were interesting and explored the idea of friends as pests and even suggested that getting mad is not a permanent state, yet she mumbled and left sentences hanging and seemed unable to complete certain claims that she began to make. Confining children to one mode of response can be a limiting experience for them. Oral discussion, art, and writing encourage children to sort out meaning and to make connections between different book experiences through different modes of expression. By combining the child's thoughts one begins to see how children interact with books and how they process that information in a variety of written and spoken forms.

Jill's illustration shows in a detailed fashion how Stevie and the narrator are now friends. (See Figure 4.15.) Both, in fact, are wearing sweatshirts with numbers on them. In an opposite panel Jill has Obadiah removing the large hook from the seagull's mouth. Her captions, "It was about a boy how did not like the boy but then when he was gone he was sad" and "It about a bout (boy) who hate a bird. But when the bird was gone he was sad," show resolution rather than conflict.

Jill's focus is on how the characters changed as they realized their

Book One

It was about a boy
how did not like the
boy but then when
he was got he was
sad.

Book Two

It 'about a bout
who hate a bird. But
when the bird was
gone he was sad.

FIGURE 4.15. Jill's drawings focus on the change that the characters underwent.

errors. This is borne out in her statements about the endings of the stories. In *Stevie* he "thought about the good things that happened, not the bad things." In *Thy Friend, Obadiah* "he felt kind of clumsy because he didn't have his bird around . . . and then when he went on another walk he saw the bird and he thought about leaving it but then he decided that he was trying to be my friend so I'll be a friend to him and so he took the hook off the bird and they were friends again." She summarizes by saying "they hated a person and then they got to like them." Everything that Jill said about the books during the oral discussion is shown in the scenes she drew about the books.

Patricia has already been mentioned as a child who was restless and seemingly disinterested during the book-sharing events. She chose to draw illustrations from each book, giving each drawing a full side. Her caption for *Thy Friend, Obadiah* includes a negative response to the seagull, defining its pesky role and the act of deliverance by Obadiah. Ironically, her seagull stands almost as tall as the boy and has a large hook caught in its mouth. In the picture for *Stevie*, Patricia shows two happy children together outside. Her caption, however, states that "he had to play with him." She told me later that the lesson was to "like people and to be nice to them." Patricia's language was confusing in that her use of referents was unclear. She continually talked about *he* and *him* without clarifying which child she was referring to. Her pictures are much clearer and show that she actually was able to sort out the characters.

David (10:1) compared both books to Garfield and Otie's escapades and said that they turn out to be friends after Otie got dragged to the pound and Garfield helped him. He wrote on his illustration that "the people that got buged didn't like the bugys at first, but when the bugys left the people who were being buged got worried or sad." His initial illustration is scratched out, and his second, smaller illustration shows the protagonists in a state of conflict with Stevie and the seagull. Later David told me that the authors were trying to teach you the following: "Don't underestimate your friends." David's illustration shows the motion of the stone flying through the air as it hits the bird, the part of the book that bothered him the most. It was the part he said later that he would like to change.

The responses of the fourth-grade children were diverse, their concepts well developed, and their illustrations revealing about the variety of their responses and thoughts in relation to hearing the same books read aloud. Many children focused on the conflict; others chose to detail resolution; some showed their dissatisfaction with characters' actions. None of the children seemed to miss the basic point of the story shared. In fact, many seemed to identify with having a pest around, like the characters in the story.

Fourth-grade children draw pictures about folktales.   Jon (9:9),
you'll recall, used word symbols to separate or join his characters in his
illustrations of realistic fiction. His response to the folktales was equally
distinctive. He chose *The Stonecutter* and *Dawn* as being thematically similar. (See Figure 4.16.) His caption reads: "They wanted something better for
themselves and ended up with less than they had before." His picture rather
than showing characters from the story, uses symbols generally meaningful
to a 9-year-old boy. Jon has drawn a new basketball and hoop across from
an old, used ball and hoop. Below is a very used vehicle. A character stands
in the middle, having thrown away the old ball, and faces the new ball and
hoop. Later Jon talked about the character in *The Stonecutter* wanting to
be the best, yet losing more than he gained and ending up with nothing. He
concluded, when asked, that the authors were trying to teach you that you
are "better off with what you have." His illustration shows the connections
children make from book to life experiences. Being a mountain is obviously
less of an enticement than acquiring a basketball court and car.

Geoff chose *Dawn* and *The Japanese Fairy Tale* and drew elaborate
illustrations of Munakata and the goose. (See Figure 4.17.) His caption
states that "in both stories the character that brought out meaning in the
story had to give up something very rare to them." Later he referred to the
concept of sacrifice and patience. Similarly, Jessica's drawing told the story
in both picture and caption form. (See Figure 4.18.) The face of the mountain shows the pain of the character as it dies. Interestingly, Jessica has
made her caption an integral part of the mountain. Greed obviously kills.
Nearby a stonecutter stands ready to strike the symbolic deathblow. Above,
Dawn's mother is making silk from her own feathers and is also going to die.
Jessica has made the bird half human, as she has the mountain. During our
conversation Jessica drew a parallel between the character in each story
who wanted to take everything and the one who wanted to give.

Steve typified many of the children who drew sequences of the story
with detailed thematic statements. He wrote: "One of the main Charictars
wanted More More and then ending up losing more than he got. this is true
in both stories." He later said that the authors were trying to teach that "the
more you're greedy the more you can use." This is an interesting contrast to
Jon's idea of ending up with less than what you started with. Steve also
talked about how the mountain started to get chipped away, becoming less
and less of himself. The concepts behind the images in his pictures include
Tasaku trapped inside the mountain in a human form, the internal argument of the man as he debates whether to open the door, and a step-by-step
transformation of the goose. The pictures are done simply in black marker
but convey a wealth of information about both books. Contrasted with
Jessica's picture where the mountain is the man, Steve's picture shows a man
trapped but separated from the mountain.

They wanted something better for themselves and ended up with less than they ~~had~~ before.

FIGURE 4.16. As with realistic fiction, Jon chose to create symbols representing the themes of the stories. Notice that the symbols hold personal meaning.

FIGURE 4.17. Geoff's exacting pictures of the main characters match his ability to write about the theme of both stories.

FIGURE 4.18. Jessica's drawing reveals the pain of the main character as he is literally trapped in the mountain.

Melissa's art is typical of the picture that has several faces and concentrates on the caption, which in her case reads: "*Caring*. Those books were all (e.i) were about caring about someone so much that you give your life for them. (or almost, somting you would not whant enyone to be like.)" During our discussion she compared the two books to *The Fisherman and His Wife*, saying basically that the authors were trying to teach you to give more than you receive. She linked the concept of giving to being happy.

Christie linked *Dawn* and *The Japanese Fairy Tale*, saying that "the bird sacrificed his feathers and the guy sacrificed his looks." She decided that "the stonecutter was greedy." Her art shows a scroll that symbolizes the teacher and has the caption "about a ugly teacher." The sailboat has the caption "a story about dawns mother." Her statements are much more sophisticated, but she chose to draw two symbols that represented the characters who sacrificed something, a rather abstract way of dealing with the actions of the characters.

David (10:1) drew a detailed picture of a ship with the caption "giving up something to make some one Happy." He also showed Dawn off to the side, ostensibly getting ready to sail off in search of her mother. His oral comments compared the idea of the goose who "gave her life to make Dawn's father happy" to the princess's teacher who "gave his good looks to a very ugly baby." He then compared both books to the television series "V," which he identified as dealing with sacrifice as well. Just as he had suggested character changes in our discussion of realistic fiction, David would have changed the looks of the ugly tutor in these folktales as well. During both of our interviews he made strong links to television or cartoon characters, suggesting that he relates ideas across a variety of media and that there is a definite impact from those particular audiovisual forms on how he structures and relates concepts.

As they did to realistic fiction, the children responded diversely to these stories in their art, their written captions, and their oral representations. One cannot say that drawing led to lively discussions about the themes of the books. One can conclude, however, that giving the children the opportunity to explore the meaning in the stories in diverse ways extended their responses to the books. A worksheet or a quiz or a tight, teacher-led discussion with a preset formula for answers would not have encouraged the children to build meaning for themselves. These instructional methods merely teach children to parrot, not to think for themselves. From the rich descriptions given above, one can see that children are capable of depth and breadth of understanding in relation to what they read. Comprehension is a complex processing system that is unique to each individual. In the next chapter I explore concrete ways of creating experiences for children in the classroom that extend and enrich the book experience through art, writing, and oral discussion.

5

Classroom Profiles: Exploring Themes in the Classroom

Can anyone doubt the importance of reading aloud with children? Reading aloud gives children access to the same material, allowing all the listeners to participate in a story. They can then discuss the story together and analyze what choices the characters had and made, what choices the author had and made, and what choices they themselves might have made in similar circumstances. Wells (1986) states:

> What is so important about listening to stories, then is that, through this experience, the child is beginning to discover the symbolic potential of language: its power to create possible or imaginary worlds through words — by representing experience in symbols that are independent of the objects, events, and relationships symbolized and that can be interpreted in contexts other than those in which the experience originally occurred, if indeed it ever occurred at all. . . . For ultimately . . . they will need to be able to answer (and also to ask) questions that go beyond naming and rote recall. They will need to follow and construct narrative and expository sequences, recognizing causes, anticipating consequences, and considering the motives and emotions that are inextricably bound up with all human actions and endeavors. In a word, they will need to be able to bring the full power of storying to bear on all the subject matter of the curriculum. (pp. 156–157)

ENCOURAGING ACTIVE THINKERS AND LIFELONG READERS

Wells's (1986) longitudinal study in Bristol, England, found that the frequency of listening to stories was an important indicator of reading comprehension at the age of 7 and a predictor of oral language ability upon entry into school. "Children who had been read to were better able to narrate an event, describe a scene, and follow instructions" (p. 157). Additionally, these children seemed better able to "understand the teachers' use of language" (p. 157). Reading stories to children seems to contribute to the child's ability to talk about his or her world using the symbolic form of language.

Interestingly, Wells discusses the child's need to go beyond naming and rote recall. We are good at these skills and have trained our children to be experts. This will not help them ultimately, however, as learners and critical thinkers. Notice Wells's use of the words *follow, construct, recognize, anticipate,* and *consider.* These are words that indicate active thinking processes beyond facile rote exercises. In this vision of learning stands a child who is actively making decisions about challenging content.

Numerous studies have been conducted with children at home and in the classroom indicating the value and importance of reading with children. Judith Sostarich (1974) found that sixth-grade children who were avid readers had been read to as young children. Their counterparts could read but did not typically choose to do so. Lifelong habits can be formed through modeling the reading process and sharing the natural enthusiasm that reading good stories provides.

My own experiences with college students show me that frequently those who heard stories read aloud as young children still like to read as adults. They remember teachers who took the time to read good books aloud during class. What I found interesting in my experience with college students is that it is never too late to hook someone on books. I have taught children's literature for 10 years, and I often encounter students who do not like to read. In fact, they recount horror stories of being turned off to reading by doing many of the banal reading activities that we have traditionally made children do both at home and at school. After taking children's literature and being reintroduced to great authors and books and more relaxed reading situations, some of these students turn around and tell me that they don't have time for anything else because they are reading children's literature. As I said, it is never too late to hook someone on a good book.

Cohen's (1968) seminal study took a look at 7-year-old children who had had little or no exposure to literature. She wondered whether a daily read-aloud program would affect their reading ability. After hearing stories for 20 minutes, the children also responded to the books through relaxed activities, which included art and drama. Cullinan et al. (1974) extended the study by including oral language activities after the book sharing. Both studies found that reading aloud had a positive impact on reading test scores in the area of vocabulary and comprehension. More importantly, however, the research designs encouraged teachers to engage children meaningfully with good literature and allowed them to interact on written and oral levels with each other and the books shared. Children are natural meaning makers. We can encourage critical thinking in a variety of formats, one of which includes providing children access to a wide variety of genres and information through reading aloud.

I knew a kindergarten teacher who read to her students constantly, to large groups, small groups, and individuals. She read and reread the same books, depending upon the requests of her students, which included a wide variety of titles and genres as well as a diversity of topics and text difficulty. This was a literate classroom. By the end of the school year many of her students were reading to each other and to themselves. Durkin (1966) and Clark (1976) showed us with their longitudinal studies that children will value education and reading if it is valued in the home. I would expand that to include the classroom as well. If the teacher values a good book, so will her students.

CLASSROOM PROFILE: *THUNDER CAKE*

I recently read *Thunder Cake*, by Patricia Polacco, to a large group of first-grade children. The book tells about a common childhood fear—thunderstorms—from the perspective of a young child and her grandmother. This grandmother has old-world character and knows child psychology. When the girl hides under the bed at the sound of distant thunder, the grandmother calls to her and suggests they make a thunder cake. As they collect the ingredients, the girl proves her valor in small ways, such as climbing a trellis or gathering eggs in a henhouse, which the grandmother points out after the cake is finished and the thunder is upon them. The children, thoroughly engaged with the brilliant pictures so typical of Polacco's style, were enthralled, and they counted with me as the thunder got closer and closer.

The book was excellent. It grabbed their attention even before I began. Thunder cake? What's that? The illustrations pulled them in. The children told me what a thunder cake might be, sharing all they knew from their own thunder experiences. These are the story predictions they offered after hearing the title, all of them logical and indicating a wealth of knowledge about how stories function.

- The cake makes the thunder.
- They could be having a picnic and eating cake and then the thunder.
- Maybe the thunder was the cake.
- The cake would be on the table when they were having a picnic and the lightning struck the pieces and all the pieces fly into their face.
- Maybe they're in the house having a cake because it's someone's birthday and the thunder comes down and the cake starts on fire.

The story was appropriate for their age. They craned their necks to see the young girl under the bed, got quite interested in the actual making of the cake, counted with me as the thunderstorm got closer, and grew silent as the thunder was upon us. Polacco's premise here is that children are afraid of thunder but, like the young child in the story, want to be coaxed out of it, want to learn to bear it. Her topic is on target, and the children related their life experience to the book experience.

We talked. I let them say what was on their minds. I wanted to read this particular story through without too many interruptions because the story builds. They made thunder connections before we started. They predicted what the story might be about on the basis of the book's title and cover. Their interest was piqued.

I read the story in an animated fashion and let them chime in. They were intrigued by the secret ingredient for the cake. An unusual touch. At story's end there was a lot of chatter about thunder cake and storms and flooded streets and a request to make this cake. This group gave the book a two-thumbs-up rating. They loved it and then proceeded to go off for SSR (sustained silent reading) to read their own books. This was a simple experience, stemming from a simple invitation on my part into the pleasure of reading and an acceptance and nurturing of their responses to literature.

Suggestions: Components for Instruction

Reading literature to children on a daily basis includes the following components for classroom instruction:

1. Interaction is a key factor in stimulating response.
2. Variety in oral-language activities is important and includes drama, puppetry, story telling, choral reading, and open-ended questions.
3. Spontaneity and creative expression are a part of response to literature.
4. Children should be encouraged to use their own natural language to express their ideas, feelings, and beliefs about what they are reading.
5. A preoccupation with testing comprehension is not helpful.
6. It is difficult to measure response to literature experiences. Tests do not tend to measure maturity in reading and writing that occur when children are involved with books. How do you measure sensitivity to an issue after a child hears a book like *Sadako and the 1000 Paper Cranes*, *Rose Blanche*, or *The Friendship*?
7. Open-ended questioning extends and encourages critical thinking.
8. Young children need to hear books read again and again. Familiarity helps them learn to read and builds comprehension.
9. Children not exposed to books need much exposure in the classroom.
10. Children become fluent readers when they have time to read silently on a daily basis, what James Britton (1978) terms wide and deep reading.
11. Reading is a social event. Interaction and sharing of good titles foster reading.
12. Let children ask questions about what they are reading and devise their own response activities at times.
13. Encourage writing along with the literature program.
14. Read silently as a parent or teacher during SSR. Children need to hear and see good models. You value it — so will they.
15. Reading aloud takes the child out of self and expands thinking.
16. Be diverse! Historical fiction, poetry, fantasy, realistic fiction, picture books, folktales, myths, information books, biographies, journals, newspapers, magazines . . . Introduce children to genres they might not typically read on their own.
17. Use quality literature in the read-aloud program.
18. Read interactively. And don't neglect the wonderful illustrations.

Comments

A child's sense of theme develops in rich classroom contexts where the child's language and perspectives are valued. Reading books to children is a natural part of that process. I recently spoke to a large group of teachers, and I talked about the value of reading aloud to children of all ages on a regular basis. One man challenged this information. In a disgusted tone of voice, he said that reading aloud and silent reading in the classroom were a waste of time and that a professor in a class he was taking agreed. Children needed, rather, direct instruction in school.

One can challenge the growing body of research, one can dispute test results, but one can't ignore the child's rich response to hearing books read aloud in classrooms and how a community of readers (Hepler, 1982) develops when good books are used and shared in interactive contexts. When the teacher makes a big deal out of reading interesting material, children make a big deal out of reading. Allington (1983) talks about building fluency, and Smith (1988) talks about learning to read by reading, but none of this happens unless children are given chunks of time to do so.

It's been many years since I heard about the principal who saw a class of children reading books and asked the teacher why she was wasting time by doing nothing, and it's been only a few months since I met a man who said he had been vehemently opposed to reading aloud until he tried it for a week. He said with genuine regret, "I wish I had started doing this years ago."

BOOK DISCUSSIONS AND COMPARISON CHARTS

Predictable folktales are effective books to use with young children because of their familiarity, basic story structure, repetitive patterns, and lively illustrations that add a rich balance to the text. (See Appendix A.) Books like these invite children into the reading process. Children can understand and easily identify the plight of the three little pigs because the story cycle repeats itself three times. They expect the third little pig to be successful and are not too surprised that the first two attempts are not successful, regardless of whether the two pigs are eaten or escape. In addition to the rich lessons this teaches about being a risk taker, making solid plans, and following through with them, this story is highly predictable and thus creates a familiar pattern of three, which is typical in folktales.

CLASSROOM PROFILE: *THE THREE LITTLE PIGS*

Children in a first-grade classroom I frequently visit had been exploring versions of *The Three Little Pigs* for 3 weeks. Their teacher, Sandy Debus, had accumulated all the versions she could find. She began by reading Paul Galdone's *Three Little Pigs*, thinking that this would be familiar. She was astonished when the children told her that this was not like the three little pigs they were familiar with! In their version the first two pigs were not eaten and the story ended with the wolf falling into the pot. In Galdone's version the third little pig goes on several adventures and fools the wolf before the final defense with the chimney. The children knew only the Disney rendition, which had not included the two little pigs' being eaten. As she read Galdone's story, the children were tense and extremely agitated because the two little pigs got eaten and there were additional scenes of trickery between the pig and the wolf.

As Deborah Jacques (1990) and Janet Hickman (1979) also observed in their studies, the children made body movements that paralleled the action of the story. In this instance the children tightened up as the story was read, disagreeing with certain episodes through their body movements and by shaking their heads vigorously. This did not fit with their three little pigs schema! They vehemently stated that this was not the right story and constantly interrupted, correcting this author's version of the story!

Comparison Charts

Sandy next read the familiar Disney version of this story. As she read, the children were relieved — this was familiar ground, and no one got eaten. Interestingly, as she read, they kept interrupting to tell her how this version, although familiar, was totally different from Galdone's. One child finally suggested that they needed to make a comparison chart of the two books; the others concurred (Huck, Hepler, & Hickman, 1987). The children then decided what categories they would need to include. As they talked about both stories they looked for interesting words that the authors used. They decided that there were none in the Disney version, but many examples in Galdone's. Quite an indictment on controlled vocabulary from this group of 6-year-old children!

Sandy gave this chart a structure a bit different from that of earlier charts she had done with the children. Sandy and the children came up with the following categories.

1. Books and Author
2. Characters
3. Did the wolf blow the houses in or down?
4. Did the first and second pigs get eaten?
5. The tricks that the wolf made up
6. Did the wolf get eaten?
7. Ending
8. Special words

Sandy had been reading a variety of folktale versions since September, so they were accustomed to making comparison charts both on an oral and a written level. Never before, however, had they independently decided that they needed to make a comparison chart without her direct suggestion. She followed by reading two new versions of *The Three Little Pigs*, a humorous one by James Marshall and a lively Appalachian rendition with a feisty female pig by William Hooks, equally humorous.

The children developed a group comparison chart for the four books, which they added to each day. After the third book, which included quite a bit of trickery on the parts of the third pig and the wolf, the children decided to add another category that included evidence of trickery. The result was that they had to go back over the earlier books to determine what examples they could find of the wolf's trickery. They initially included butter churn as a trick but later decided that the pig had initiated that trick, not the wolf, so it could not be included. What matters is not their answers, but how they got to them. Look at the logic involved just in that one decision about a butter churn.

For each book and each category they used a piece of construction paper to record the compare/contrast information. The children were responsible for recording each bit of information on the pieces of construction paper. Sandy then had them add each category to a large board as it was completed, held on with magnetic strips. The comparison chart finally made it to the hall where it was displayed for all to see. (See Table 5.1.)

I came in a week later and read still another new version as told by A. Wolf to Jon Scieszka, entitled *The True Story of the Three Little Pigs*. Although most of the children missed the rich irony of that rendition, they were intrigued with the wolf's point of view. I, of course, was very interested in their reactions and wanted to see if this savvy group of children would catch the not-so-subtle humor of the wolf's interpretation. The children had a rather concrete response to this story and in an interactive context decided that the wolf of this story was not really guilty of any wrongdoing because he was basically a victim of circum-stance. What a contrast to their initial reaction that Galdone's version was not the real story! They seemed unruffled as the wolf ate the first two little pigs. After all, it was not with intent, and he was merely trying to borrow a cup of sugar.

Children may be naive in their interpretations, but they certainly do take on the perspective of characters when listening to stories. They enjoyed the story but clearly missed the tongue-in-cheek aspect of the telling. Picture books are clearly not just for young children! One must have a repertoire of experiences and a certain level of development to catch the play on situations of a book like this.

Afterwards the children and I brainstormed how this book fit in with the existing categories that were already on the board. They vindi-cated the wolf on the basis of his rather lame excuses for eating the two pigs and decided that he did not belong in jail at the end of the story. Their responses were rich and varied and showed a good bit of abstract reasoning.

I shared this book with the children purposely, to test their con-struction of meaning in interactive contexts. Because it was a tongue-in-cheek spoof and these children had listened to a rich mix of folklore throughout the year, I wanted to see if the humor would be understand-able to them. I read the book in a lively and humorous fashion; they clearly enjoyed it. In fact, they noticed everything from the bunny ears in the wolf's mixing bowl to the pigs' tails that spelled out some of the letters in the text. They laughed at times and openly expressed their reactions as I read. They were observers of all that the wolf did. Yet they missed the subtle spoof that the wolf was rationalizing all of his bad behavior and talking in a conspiratorial fashion to the reader. This is evidenced by their reactions to the story on concrete levels. They bought the wolf's story and decided that in this version he was a victim.

Informal Drama

The children began to reenact *The Three Little Pigs* informally in small groups. Sandy coached them initially by narrating events of the story and assigning parts to different children. The children had to speak when the narrator paused for conversation. In this manner Sandy scaffolded (Bruner, 1983) the event for the children and encouraged them to use oral language in a spontaneous fashion. Each time she narrated the stories changed, depending upon which events were in-cluded from different versions. The children in the audience quickly began to coach Sandy as narrator, telling her which version to follow.

TABLE 5.1. Comparison Chart for Versions of *The Three Little Pigs* by Sandy Debus's First-Grade Class

BOOKS AND AUTHOR	*Three Little Pigs* Paul Galdone	*Three Little Pigs* Milt Banta & Al Dempster	*Three Little Pigs* James Marshall	*Three Little Pigs and the Fox* William Hooks
CHARACTERS	Sow 1 3 little pigs wolf man with straw man with sticks man with bricks	3 little pigs wolf	3 little pigs wolf wolf man with straw man with sticks man with bricks	mama pig rooter oinky hamlet fox
DID THE WOLF BLOW THE HOUSES IN OR DOWN?	in	in	in	neither
DID THE FIRST AND SECOND PIGS GET EATEN?	yes	no	yes	no
THE TRICKS THAT THE WOLF MADE UP	1. turnips 2. apples 3. fair 4. butter churn	1. sheepskin	1. being sweet 2. chimney 3. turnips 4. fair	1. put the sock on the pig 2. apples 3. pretending he was sneezing 4. hiding behind the tree
DID THE WOLF GET EATEN?	yes	no	yes	no
ending	and the little pigs lived happily ever	pigs were singing and dancing	the wolf got gobbled up	they went home to mama to hug and kiss and eat
SPECIAL WORDS	sow	bundle	narrowly	approached, gobbled, runt, fortune, jowls, rutabaga, seek, churn

She then assigned the role of narrator to different children, sometimes in pairs, depending on a child's willingness to take charge and go it alone.

The day I visited the children had already made up some unique versions, including three wolves and three pigs and marriages for six pigs. On this particular day the children decided to include a mother wolf who went on the adventures with her son and ended up in the stew pot with him. There were discussions about whether the pigs would go to gather apples or turnips. In one version all of the pigs got eaten; in another all were spared.

The value of dramatic interpretation of this nature has several facets. First, children are directly involved in using language in meaningful situations. The narrator must remember events and relate them in a sequential fashion. The participants, similarly, respond to story events in an appropriate manner, thereby interpreting events as they unfold. Children are held accountable for listening to the stories that have been read aloud. There is ongoing discussion as to how the events will be related, which will be included, which will be ignored. New versions on the old theme encourage a critical application of narrative structure in which children are reworking a familiar story. At a whole language workshop held at Skidmore College in December 1990, Bruce Amidon suggested that spontaneous drama is an excellent activity to help children organize their thoughts and take a stance toward the story, framing it in a manner that will get them ready for story telling. After dramatizing and writing, Sandy's children began telling their own versions of *The Three Little Pigs.*

Creating Their Own Written Versions

These dramatic interpretations took place in the morning, and in the afternoon the children wrote their own versions. They brainstormed the basic events of the story, and Sandy listed them on the board. With this outline in mind, the children retired to corners of the room to begin creating their own versions of *The Three Little Pigs*. The responses were diverse, and when I visited the following day, several children read their stories aloud. One girl volunteered to read, paused to look at her notes, and said, "I'm not organized enough yet." What a sophisticated response!

Several children had independently decided to work in small groups, creating stories by consensus. The stories followed the format of *The Three Little Pigs*, yet some students went off in their own directions. The composing continued for several days. The sharing continued informally, sometimes with other children, with Sandy, or in front of the large group.

Monica wrote the following story about *The Three Little Ants and the Spider* by herself. It is one of the longer versions that appeared, and rather than have Monica edit and recopy the entire story, Sandy decided to print the story on the word processor, so that Monica could read it and consider the content in an easier format. This would enable Monica to make any structural changes that she noticed in the story itself. Consider the content of her first draft.

Once upon a time there lived three little ants and their mama queen. The first and second and third had to move away. The first little ant met a man with paper.

"Can I have your paper?"

"Why?"

"None of your business," said the ant.

The ant made his house. The second ant met a man with some cardboard. The ant said, "Can I have some cardboard?"

"I don't think you should buy it."

"Shut up, man," said the ant.

The ant took the cardboard and made him a house. The third ant saw a man with some wood.

"Can I have some wood?"

"That is a very good idea."

So the little ant made his house of the wood. Near by the big bad spider was watching. So he went to the first ant's house and knocked on the door.

"Little ant, little ant, let me come in."

"No, no, I'm not letting you in."

"Then I'll huff and I'll puff and I'll blow your house down."

The ant ran to his brother's house. The spider had an idea. He put baby clothes on and rang the doorbell.

"Please let me in. I'm a little baby with no place to sleep."

"No, no, you can't fool us with those baby clothes."

That made the spider mad. So he said,

"Little ants, little ants, let me come in."

"No, no, we are not letting you in."

"Then I'll huff and I'll puff and I'll blow your house down."

So he did. The two little ants ran to their brother's house.

"Hurry up. Let us in. It's the big bad spider."

"Well then, get in."

"Look, here he is, the big bad spider."

Knock. Knock.

"Please let me in."

"No, no, we are not letting you in."

"Then I'll huff and puff and blow your house down."

"Don't blow our house down."

But the bad spider didn't listen. He huffed and puffed but he could not blow the house down.

"Then I'll go down the chimney," said spider.

The three ants said, "Quickly, put some hot water."

Then the spider jumped down the chimney.

The three little ants put the cover on and ate him up for dinner. They lived happily ever after.

Before the children wrote their own versions, Sandy sat down with them and together they brainstormed the main parts of the frame of *The Three Little Pigs*. They decided that the story had the following seven parts.

1. Living together
2. Left to seek fortune
3. Build houses or do something
4. Bad guy attacks — first and second characters
5. Bad guy tries to attack the third character
6. His tricks don't work
7. He gets into third house and bad guy gets it

Monica's version closely follows the basic outline. She has collapsed some portions of the story, which she will have to decide about. Should she make the sections with a parallel structure or leave the episodes as they are and let the reader fill in the gaps? In an individual conference Sandy will ask questions about what happens next in Monica's story. The decision to rewrite or change or flush out information in the story will be Monica's. Sandy will conference about content, but the ultimate decisions are Monica's. In this classroom the teacher does not make decisions of this nature; rather the writers choose how their stories will progress. Other children wrote stories with titles like *The Three Little Kittens and the Big Bad Dog* and *The Three Little Mice and the Big Bad Cat*. On other occasions children might make up their own stories without this kind of outline, but in this particular instance, the familiar structure of *The Three Little Pigs* provided them with a rich backdrop for jumping off into new versions.

CLASSROOM PROFILE: *THE FISHERMAN AND HIS WIFE*

In a similar activity earlier in the year, this same group of first-grade children listened to different versions of *The Fisherman and His Wife*. The result, again, was a class comparison chart, which, in this instance, Sandy recorded on a large grid made on a large piece of newsprint. In this experience the children compared the books with rich oral language and gave less time to the chart itself, which was merely an overview of their class discussions and a sequencing of events in the story based on the fisherman's requests of the flounder.

What differed in this activity was the children's reactions to the rich vocabulary that was used in the different versions. Because Sandy's read-aloud sessions were interactive in nature, she was never quite sure where the children would take her. The day I was in her classroom happened to be one on which the children were listening to a medieval version of the tale. This version was rich with archaic vocabulary and the children, already familiar with the story, focused their attention on the language.

Children are great observers of detail. Monique observed that if you opened the book and looked at the outside, it made one large picture. Sarah noted that the language of this book did not sound like the language in the other one. Ryan observed that a flounder is a magic fish. Sandy then read on the first page that the fisherman went home to his miserable hovel; she asked the children what they supposed a hovel was. Five voices said, "It's a hut!" She then asked them what a miserable hut might be, and Ryan offered that it meant an ugly hut. She countered with, "Well, maybe. What else might it mean besides just ugly?" Lizzie offered "scary," and Ryan tried again, this time with "junky" and "falling apart."

Notice how the children were focused on the story event. They observed illustrations. They offered definitions to each other. They responded freely to Sandy's heuristic line of questioning that asked them to suppose what something might mean — the language of "what ifs." This type of questioning invites participation. Lizzie did not feel afraid to offer "scary" as an interpretation for a miserable hut. In fact, the hut probably was scary in its miserable state. It most certainly was ugly, junky, and falling apart!

As Sandy read further, we found that the flounder was actually an enchanted prince, at which point Tina interrupted to offer that she knew that *enchanted* meant "wishing." Ryan countered with, "handsome prince. It means he's a handsome prince." At this point Eric interjected that "they use old-fashioned words in this book." And Sandy simply stated: "The word *enchanted* means he's under a spell, as if a witch or something has put him under a spell." She added new information to the conversation but did so in such a way that Tina and Ryan and Eric were still able to offer their insights into the story based on their personal perceptions. In this environment children learn because they explore and predict and use context to determine meaning, which fosters their independence not only as readers but as learners. Missy added that the definition for miserable hovel would have to include "dirty." Our time frames for conversations are often different from those of our students.

Sarah continued to make observations during the reading of this story that compared and contrasted information and illustrations from the story that she had heard several days ago. "There's something different than the other poem that they said in the other book." "She's being nicer than she was in the other book. She's not as snotty." "Miss Debus, they never showed the clouds before." "Miss Debus, they're talking different things in that book instead of that book." "In that book they didn't have the houses when she wanted to be something different. [When] she wanted to be something different she losed the house." Sarah did not contribute to the conversations that unfolded about her in a direct fashion; rather, at times, she was on her own wavelength, interjecting information about how the books and characters differed. I have to question how important it is to keep children focused on our tasks and questions at all times. Sarah processed a lot of information and made a lot of astute observations about both versions, which Sandy allowed her to do.

The children got excited about the illustrations, noticing that each time the fisherman returned with a larger and more outrageous request, the seas and clouds roiled and broiled more and more. Their excitement grew, as did the vocabulary that described the emotions of the flounder. "The waves are like a dragon!" Missy offered. The text read: "The ocean smelled putrid." Bryan asked simply, "What's putrid?" to which Eric replied "smelly." The children taught each other because Sandy was willing to sit back and let them discover for themselves. She could be more direct when necessary. The story stated that the wife then wanted to be emperor.

CHILD: What's that?
SANDY: Well, if she's the king, what do you suppose the emperor is?
CHILD: Joker?
CHILD: Queen?

SANDY: Each time she's wished she's wished for something . . .
CHILD: Higher.
SANDY: Higher, better. So if you're the king you rule over a coun-
        try. If you're the emperor you rule over . . .
CHILD: Everything.
CHILD: Sky.
SANDY: Everything. Lots of countries. Lots and lots of countries.

These types of conversations continued as Sandy read. The children were captivated by the old-style language, and when at last the wife wished to be even as God himself, the children's reactions included extreme shock and horror. There were groans of surprise, loud protests that the wife dared such a wish. One child offered, "He's not going to let her." When they saw the turbulent seas and the storm and heard the flounder's final statement returning everything to its original state, there were loud explosions of relief.

At book's end the comments ranged from "greedy" to "she didn't get anything" to "she wanted so much that she didn't think of the only thing she wanted; she should've fought to be God the first time." Dan offered, "She didn't care for anyone else. She just cared for herself. All she asked for was her." Not only their verbalizations but their body movements and their sounds indicated how they processed this book. Having children sit quietly while a teacher reads will not allow or encourage this rich depth of response, which seems to bubble up on many different levels. These children derived meaning from the story and together processed that thematic information.

At this point Sandy asked the children to compare all three books in terms of what the wife had asked for. Three children looked at the books while Sandy recorded responses. The children unanimously chose this book as their favorite version because, as Eric and Dan said: "It was longer. Had more wishes. Had old-fashioned words in it. It's longer and more excitinger."

Notice how the group was involved with interpretation. The children, working together, blended their impressions, pooled their knowledge, and were able to figure out the meanings of words based on a "group analysis." The construction of meaning in this classroom was both an individual and a group effort. Children build on what other children know. Together they often determine meaning, both for new vocabulary and for overarching concepts for stories. They like the challenge and sound of rich vocabulary and the opportunity to discuss what is read. They constantly analyze the actions of characters and assess whether those characters act appropriately in situations.

CLASSROOM PROFILE: *RAPUNZEL*

One fourth-grade class did a study of folktales, with one of the groups producing the following chart based on versions of *Rapunzel*. In this format the children worked in groups of four. They read the stories independently, without the teacher's determining who would read which book. Each child then became a miniexpert on his or her book. The children then decided what categories they would choose for analysis. As they brainstormed categories, the children each contributed the bit of information needed to complete the chart, and the answers were recorded on a large piece of yellow butcher-block paper. The categories chosen by the children included: Illustrator, "Hero," "Bad Guy," Magic Used, and Style of Text and Pictures. (See Table 5.2.) The children decided to decorate their chart and have a tower with a princess as a central motif, again underscoring the importance of including art as a response to literature. An unhappy princess looks out from the tall tower.

The answers and categories they chose were simple. I would expect that a second chart experience with other books would extend the children even further. This is the point at which a teacher can act as an informal guide, suggesting other types of information that might be included in a chart, asking them, for example, what the problem in the story was and how it was resolved. When children work in groups, the teacher is most effective if he or she floats in the classroom. Typically some groups will need more guidance than others. If the teacher has modeled this type of experience prior to letting children work independently, the group work will be a smoother process. The idea is to encourage all of the children in a group to take responsibility for a portion of the information needed so that everyone will contribute. Group work often fails when only a few children dominate. Other teachers have worked more closely with groups first embarking on independent activities of this nature. Be assured that the ultimate goal of such activities is to create independent learners who take charge of their own learning. It doesn't always come easily and may take time and continued exposure to independent work situations. Some children will drag their feet, hoping and expecting the teacher to take over, passing the reins back, saying in essence, "It's easier when you do it for me." Applaud their efforts even when they might not measure up to what your original expectations were. Be willing to let go.

In this activity four basic goals were achieved. The children had to work in concert as they analyzed the stories, because each child was responsible for one book. Second, the children worked independently,

TABLE 5.2.   Comparison Chart for Versions of *Rapunzel* by Fourth-Grade Class

TITLE AUTHOR ILLUSTRATOR	"HERO"	"BAD GUY"	MAGIC USED	STYLE OF TEXT & PICTURES
Petrosinella Giam Battista Basile Diane Stanley	Petrosinella	Ogress	The tower	Pastelles
Rapunzel Grimm Michael Hague	Rapunzel	The Wicked Witch	Her tears	Water colors
Tales Told Again Walter De La Mare Alan Howard	Rapunzel	The Wicked Witch	Her long hair	Drawings
Rapunzel Barbara Rogasky Trina Schart Hyman	Rapunzel	The Witch (Mother Gothal)	Rapunzel's hair	Chalk

making decisions without the teacher. This comparison chart was the first time the children had worked alone in this fashion. Third, the children were exposed to the information in the other books as they listened and shared while the chart was written, an experience that stretched them as listeners and learners. This subsequently led to group members' reading other versions later in the day during free reading time. And fourth, after the activity was completed, the group shared their chart with the whole class. This is a vital part of any activity of this nature: being responsible for conveying information learned to others.

Types of categories that might be included in comparison charts are:

1. Country of origin when using variants of a folktale
2. Protagonist
3. Antagonist
4. Special helpers
5. Magic used
6. Outcomes/endings

7. Journey or tasks undertaken
8. Style of illustrations
9. Style of language used
10. Lessons to be learned
11. Identify good/evil
12. Unique descriptions of characters or incidents

Suggestion: Using Folktales With Older Children

A picture book like *The Three Little Pigs* as told by A. Wolf to Jon Scieszka could be shared effectively with older readers at all reading levels. Older children would enjoy the humor because of their cauldron of stories and experiences with rationalizing and being victims or misunderstood themselves. Older readers who need simpler text should be encouraged to read picture books like these that are written at their developmental levels of understanding and humor. A variety of picture book spoofs exist that would have high appeal for older readers. By fostering the idea that reading picture books is for young children but older children need trade books exclusively, we have created an unfortunate situation that cuts some children off from excellent learning experiences. Folktales benefit children of all ages at all levels of reading ability.

Comments

Children can become competent language users when given time for exploring and responsibility for conveying what they learn. Language is not learned in a vacuum. In classrooms where the teacher is the final arbiter of information, children learn that speaking and teaching are primarily done by the adult. This has the cumulative effect, I believe, of encouraging a spoon-fed mentality that does not disappear even when students reach college age. If lecture is the format from kindergarten through graduate school, the message becomes: You sit, you listen, I talk, you feed back what I tell you, and that is the measure of your learning. When I give college students assignments that are not spelled out in finite terms, some can become extremely threatened and uncomfortable. For example, I recently received a frantic weekend phone call from a student who finally said, "But what do *you* want on this paper?" This attitude was counterbalanced by that of a student who had not taken many risks early in the semester but ended it by writing a paper on C.S. Lewis in the form of a letter to a parent. The parent had expressed shock and anger over a teacher's choice of *The Lion, the*

Witch and the Wardrobe as a reading selection for a fifth-grade class, a censorship issue that we had explored in class a few weeks earlier. Not only was the student's stance extremely clever, the writing was fresh and challenging and presented a clear case for using Lewis's work with this age group. The basic assignment had been open-ended but was to deal with the topic of exploring the roots of fantasy in C.S. Lewis's work.

When you give your students some freedom in determining the path their learning will take, they will frequently surprise you. The hardest task I deal with as a teacher is counteracting the self-imposed parameters my students place on themselves. They are accustomed to restrictions when it comes to learning.

As a teacher, no matter what age your students are, you can give them keys that they can use to open doors. What they find inside can lead them to a rich exploration of their worlds. The problem arises when teachers become preoccupied with their own formats, agendas, rules, and regulations for the classroom — when they hold the floor and won't relinquish it to the learners.

A child experienced in word processing his own novel at home over the course of a year — granted, not a Pulitzer Prize-winning effort — encountered a teacher in an intermediate grade who was so preoccupied with a personal agenda that the child was left out of the picture. The red pen and a system of rules for writing became of paramount importance in this classroom — content was not the main focus. Stern red notes to this child informed him that he did not know how to cross out words properly, that he did not have the right color pen and should know better after 12 weeks that he wrote on the wrong line, that his margins were incorrect, that several of his notebook-paper holes were ripped, and so on. His first oral speech was given a "very good" and was prefaced with half a dozen negative comments — not one positive statement. His was an odyssey of wrong moves and harsh messages from his teacher. His parents received severe notes telling them to sign and return their child's incorrectly margined assignments. They saw few messages of encouragement and no comments that responded to the content the child was occasionally allowed to write. The child lost respect for this teacher and bowed out of the class, although he was there physically day after day.

What message do we send our students when we become rigid conveyors of our own personal agendas? If I've learned anything from my years as a parent, teacher, and researcher, it's that effective teaching often means that I have to step back and learn to listen to my students and allow them to explore new ideas, both in written and oral contexts.

If I am preoccupied with my version of correctness, if my motivation for teaching is that they learn exactly what it is that I know and regurgitate it back appropriately, I have missed an opportunity to grow with my students.

Obviously, the teacher has information that students need, but how is this conveyed? How do children use that information? Who does all the talking? Who is perceived ultimately as right? In an ideal situation, a classroom where the exchange of ideas is real, the teacher need not use the red pen as a weapon nor hold the reins of learning so tightly that a potential "Pulitzer Prize winner" decides to bow out for the year and wait for a teacher with vision.

In contrast to this perhaps extreme example, recall how Sandy's fresh vision for her 6-year-old children helped them. They made a lot of personal discoveries in her classroom. They clamored to analyze books and swap and record information. At a young age these children were already taking much of the responsibility for their own learning. The hand of the teacher was obvious. After all, who chose such challenging books? Who taught the children how to compare and contrast? Who gave them the freedom to explore and construct meaning in interactive situations? Who turned over the responsibility of recording information in a written fashion? And who were the ultimate risk takers?

ASKING THE RIGHT QUESTIONS

Teachers ask questions. Children answer them. If children can't answer adequately they (1) haven't done their work or (2) need additional help. Questions in the old basal readers tested for proficiency at the detail level and even included the right answers for the teacher. Asking good questions is one of the most difficult tasks for emerging teachers to learn. The tendency is to make everything concrete and simple, thereby making comprehension easier to measure and questions easier to design.

The interview questions used in my research were not complex. What they all had in common was that they were open-ended. They invited participation. They asked the reader to tell what he or she knew, thought, supposed, liked, learned — heuristic and imaginative language. They asked the reader to take on the perspective of the authors and consider what the authors thought and why they chose particular events and actions of characters. They were essentially divergent. I did not have a set of right answers that each child was judged against. Teachers mentioned in the previous chapter made a practice of inviting children to share what they knew rather than emphasizing what they didn't know.

Questions can encourage children to take on a variety of perspectives but obviously involve different levels of thought and difficulty. On the basis of an adaptation of Bloom's Taxonomy of Educational Objectives (Huck et al., 1987), we can ask questions in the following sequence of difficulty:

1. *Knowledge:* essentially recall — tell, list, describe, remember
2. *Comprehension:* putting the information into one's own words, describing how one feels about — translate, summarize
3. *Application:* using the information in a new situation — organize, group, classify
4. *Analysis:* breaking information down into parts — take apart, isolate, relate, compare, contrast
5. *Synthesis:* heuristic and imaginative thought — predict, assume, reconstruct, reorganize, alter
6. *Evaluation:* ability to make judgments — judge, criticize, solve, decide, conclude

CLASSROOM PROFILE: *MY FRIEND JACOB*

In an effective classroom teachers talk less and listen more. Their questions are designed to create a response to literature. The children discuss, explore, and define meaning of books read and shared. Detailed questions are not really necessary. As children talk about characters' actions, choices, and dilemmas, a teacher will guide the conversation, but it is the children who will own it.

Consider this discussion in Ruth's third-grade class about the book *My Friend Jacob* by Lucille Clifton. Ruth's students drew heavily on what they already knew, linking life experiences to new experiences in books. Together, her children pooled what they knew and tried to sort out not only what the text meant but what it meant to them in their own lives. Ruth's patience and basic acceptance foster this type of growth.

My Friend Jacob is about a young boy and his older friend. As the text explores their friendship, the reader finds out that Jacob is a lot older than Sam and that Jacob doesn't learn things quickly; he's different somehow. Toward the end of the story, one of the children stopped the reading by voicing an unfinished question at the point where Jacob knocks at the door, just as Sam taught him. "He doesn't seem to . . . " Another student interrupted and explained simply, "He's retarded, Michael."

After reading the story, Ruth invited conversation. "Tell me about Jacob. Maybe something about their friendship." The responses essentially clarified who Jacob was and who Sam was, how old they were, and how they helped each other. Some children didn't understand parts of the story and other students jumped in to explain.

At this point Margie wanted to share something personal. She began by explaining about the story and how Sam's parents might be cautious about letting him play with Jacob and how sometimes people make fun of others who are retarded. She had obviously tangled her personal experience with the book, and Ruth helped her focus on her own experience. "You have known somebody that is slower? Can you explain a little bit more. I didn't know what you meant when you said 'um.'" Here Margie recounted the specific event that had caused her some embarrassment when a friend had pointed at a retarded person at the mall.

Children added to this by talking about a person physically disabled at the school who was in a wheelchair and how they stared and pointed and were essentially uncomfortable, but curious. Margie quickly pointed out that the child was not retarded just because she was in a wheelchair.

What these children are doing is processing the story on one level and relating it to personal knowledge and dilemmas they face in real life. How should they respond? Will their parents let them be friends with a person who is different? Should they point? Is it all right to be curious? What do you do when a friend laughs inappropriately? Is there a difference between a person with mental retardation and a person who is in a wheelchair? Ruth lets her students know that there are no bad or wrong questions. It is OK to want to know. It is OK to ask.

The literature is the jumping-off point. The children take over on the basis of their needs, their questions, and their insights. Ruth connected this story to a chapter book that she had recently read aloud, *Kelly's Creek* by Doris Buchanan Smith, in which the main character has a learning disability and is frustrated because his parents and teacher keep telling him to try harder. He simply can't do what they expect of him. One of Ruth's students, Jake, related that Kelly's mother took away the thing that meant the most to Kelly, thinking it would motivate him to succeed. In the book an understanding adult finally urged Kelly to

share his wealth of knowledge about marsh life verbally with his class-
mates, which one of Ruth's students explained in rich detail. He was
slow in some ways, excelled in others. The book shows how there are
more levels to a person than what might appear on the surface.
Throughout, Ruth helped them to make connections, recapped or summarized what they knew, and prodded them into new directions, help-
ing them make connections to what they already knew.

Throughout the discussion the children continually talked and explained bits of textual information to each other. In fact, specific references in the story acted as catalysts for questions that the children had.
Sometimes they didn't understand a part and made a faulty judgment
based on that perception, but together they talked through events and
clarified information.

Lauren offered that "maybe she (Sam's mother) is not that crazy
about being with a retarded person." This was in direct reference to an
episode in the book where Jacob's mother says that Sam doesn't have to
have Jacob tagging along when he goes to the store. The child had not
identified the "she" correctly and had consequently added her own
experience and perspective to sort out meaning. As they discussed this
episode, that became apparent. Ruth clarified, "It was Jacob's mother,"
and returned directly to the text to reread that portion. Lauren then
understood but offered an unusual rationale. "She was maybe physical
retarded herself?" Ruth's response quite simply was: "Could be. Does
any one else have a different idea on that?" Several responses were then
offered that made inferences based on the text.

JEREMY: Like he doesn't, he might not, his mother might have
          thought he doesn't feel right around retarded people.
JOAN: She was too hard on him ya know, like she, if he did
          something because maybe he's lost his mind he and no-
          body knows what she's gonna do to him.

The children have not sorted out all of their feelings in relation to
the book's characters, Jacob and Kelly, or the girl in the wheelchair at
their school. They are beginning to learn, however, that the girl in the
wheelchair has a different set of special needs than do Jacob and Kelly.
Literature and discussions like these provide the children with a meaningful encounter and give them pause to reflect and share and grow in
their understandings about people. The book experiences stretch them,
but obviously they do not know all there is to know, nor have they sorted
out their own feelings. Their responses are indicative of a process, and
rich literature enhances that process.

CLASSROOM PROFILE: *HOW MUCH IS A MILLION?*

Information books can be used effectively across the curriculum to extend knowledge and to evoke an aesthetic response from students as well. Schwartz's and Kellogg's book does exactly that by posing the heuristic question: How much is a million? It can be answered in a finite manner, but the book takes the reader beyond the concrete by showing the unbelievability of huge numbers in a wide variety of implausible but credible situations. This book makes the abstract concrete. How many goldfish would it take to fill a stadium?

Ruth used this book with her third-grade class, and the immediate response of the children was recognition of Kellogg's style of illustrating. The book also evoked the inevitable "Kellogg's Raisin Bran" and an argument over which book a favorite Kellogg episode was in. Children knew *Paul Bunyan* and *The Day Jimmy's Boa Constrictor Ate the Wash* — both favorites.

"If you wanted to count from one to one million it would take you about 23 days. If a goldfish bowl were big enough for a million goldfish . . . it would be large enough to hold a whale." Children offered a running commentary and possible answers throughout. One child offered 20 as a possible amount of goldfish bowls necessary for a million goldfish.

Counting to a billion would take 95 years. One child picked up on the grave shown in the illustration, and other children made inferences as to whose it was. "Probably was a counter." "Probably the wizard's."

Putting a trillion goldfish in the city harbor evoked five spontaneous responses, ranging from "They'd all die" to "Not all of them" to "That'd be . . . " to "I don't understand." Ruth paused at times and allowed them to wonder aloud, to process information, and then continued reading.

When it was all over, she told the children that several copies would be available in the room. They were immediately reserved. Jeremy wanted to change the title to *Numbers* because it dealt with millions, billions, and trillions. The children imagined how the skies could be filled with millions of stars.

CHILD: There's more than a thousand, more than a million, more than . . .
CHILD: More than a trillion.
CHILD: More than any number you thought you had.
CHILD: It goes on to eternity.
CHILD: It goes on to another galaxy because all the space ships will run out of gas and they won't make it that far.

CHILD: I know the highest number that's known. It's squanto.
CHILD: What about quadrillion?

Facts are solid and comforting. Textbooks teach dates, times, and finite information, rules and formulas. These children are considering infinity. The concept is mind-boggling. Each child adds verbally to the next. This book encourages children to play with ideas and numbers and pushes them into abstract veins of thinking, new ways of looking at their worlds, new ways of thinking about numbers and spatial concepts. How might such a book influence their attempts at writing?

Suggestions: Using Writing to Extend a Child's Understanding of Informational Books

Jumping-off points for these children could include rich contexts offering them a multigenred approach to writing. Graves (1984) has suggested that about 20% of a writer's diet ought to be assigned. He also talks about the importance of modeling new types of writing, and O'Connell (1988) suggests that the focus, as with other types of writing, should be on content rather than editing. We don't usually teach our children to explore the themes of informational books they read and share, nor do we spend much time developing their skills as writers of informational prose. Rothery (1986) has suggested that children's attempts to write about the meaning in texts should be scaffolded (Bruner, 1983) through rich oral language, discussion that includes questions and reactions from the teacher, as well as a joint construction of text.

Working together the teacher and children can write a text exploring a particular base of knowledge, using something other than the traditional narrative structure, what Collerson (1988) calls the factual genres. They include procedures, reports, explanations, exposition, letters, poems, play scripts, posters, advertisements. All of these genres are read and used by children and adults as part of a parcel of lifelong skills that sort out meaning in our daily lives.

What kinds of writing could come out of a factual experience with a book like *How Much Is a Million?* By linking art and writing children could pose their own questions, create their own problems and scenarios, and decide how to seek answers to their questions.

What kinds of writing experiences could evolve from reading *My Friend Jacob* by Lucille Clifton, which is a natural lead-in to informational books about those who are differently abled? Ruth's children wanted to know more. Their discussion of the book clearly showed knowledge gaps and a real interest in learning more about people with special needs. Children have been writing reports for as long as there have been schools, teachers, pens, and papers. How does one teach children to explore the meaning in the books that they hear and read, and how does one extend that knowledge base by encouraging children to write in new genres?

O'Connell (1988) has outlined a series of steps for immersing children in reports about topics for study, which include teacher knowledge, sharing many examples, exploring the characteristics of the particular genre, jointly constructing a text with care and a great deal of negotiation, and finally soloing and conferencing. What impresses me about the emphasis in this kind of informational writing is that children are encouraged to explore the meaning in what they are reading in a logical manner. The teacher must include direct instruction but does so through a process of modeling and scaffolding. Children are meaning makers, but sometimes they need formal and structured guidance to help them acquire new ways of expressing what it is that they know and are learning.

CLASSROOM PROFILE: *THE WHIPPING BOY*

Sandy read *The Whipping Boy* to her students to prepare them for medieval studies, which were to be taken up in three first-grade classrooms. The unit consisted of class projects, readings, and whole-group studies. Children studied heraldry, medieval foods, customs, and famous people like Leonardo da Vinci, who was actually alive in a period of transition as the medieval period became a period of renaissance. This particular novel is set in an imaginary place with castles, kings, princes, and kidnappers, a sort of mini-version of *The Prince and the Pauper*.

Decision Trees

As the children listened to the story, Sandy helped them predict what might happen next by making a group decision tree. (See Figure 5.1.) After Prince Horace and Jemmy ran away from the castle, Sandy asked the children to predict what might happen next. They suggested three plausible tracks for the story: they get lost, tracked down by the king, or killed. Sandy continued reading, and they discovered that the children got caught by robbers. Children then suggested three scenarios. The robbers killed the boys, the robbers took things from the boys, or the boys were ransomed to the king. As you can see from the tree, two of the answers were correct, and the children suggested linking two of the

FIGURE 5.1. In this decision tree first graders explored choices possible for characters in *The Whipping Boy* by Sid Fleischman.

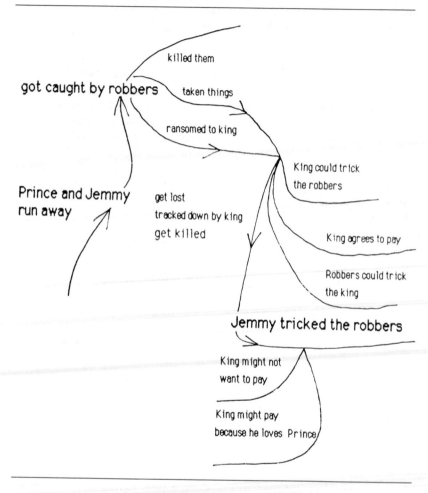

branches and using arrows to show that both events happened. They then predicted that the king could trick the robbers, agree to pay, or the robbers could trick the king. What actually happened is that Jemmy tricked the robbers by trading places with the prince.

At this point Sandy asked what might happen next, and Nickie suggested that the "king might not want to pay because he knows that this son is bad and he never obeys, so if he gets a letter from his son, he might think it's a trick from someone else and he might not agree to pay." Nickie's response shows that he is following the complicated story line and is equally capable of coming up with difficult solutions to intricate problems. His sense of theme is evident when he discusses the prince's shortcomings and the possible responses that his father might have to a boy who does not obey.

A decision tree encourages children to think through dilemmas and to seek solutions to problems. It also encourages them to consider character motivation and choices that characters have. They must put on the perspective of the characters to be able to suggest plausible directions for the course of the book. Had Sandy taken the first prediction to its logical conclusion, the children would have quickly discovered that killing the two main characters early in the book terminated the story. This type of activity obviously encourages critical thinking and gets children actively involved with the type of decision making that authors do all the time.

Character Caricatures

When Sandy had read half the book, she had the children draw giant images of the two main characters, Jemmy and Prince Horace, on poster paper. The children decided that Jemmy required yellow paper because he was so smart and bright. Prince Horace got red paper because he was always getting angry and into trouble. She then asked the children to think about both characters and to think of words that described each character. Table 5.3 shows the words that the children wrote on this giant character collage.

Notice that the children did not like the prince. None of the words are complimentary! Jemmy was described as radical by Ryan because: "He wants to change things. He wants to change the prince from being bad to good." A close look at the words chosen reveals that the children have a basic understanding of the underlying themes of the story as evidenced by the characters. It would be interesting to update this list after the book is read to see how both characters have changed in their estimation. (This idea for exploring character comes from Kathleen Holland in a literature workshop on *Bridge to Terabithia* by Katherine Paterson.)

CLASSROOM PROFILE: RESPONSE JOURNALS

Another third-grade classroom reads novels all year. Pam has guide questions, devised by her, for book sections. The children meet in groups

TABLE 5.3. First-Graders' Words to Describe Characters from *The Whipping Boy*

JEMMY	PRINCE HORACE
polite	miserable
bright	sneaky
gentle	stupid
good	rascal
smart	brat
brave	mean
small	rude
intelligent	spoiled
nice	wicked
radical	selfish

periodically to discuss their reactions to books. Her questions are useful and are discussion starters. She carries this over to daily journal writing as well. On some days the children write specifically about some issue that the book has raised. On other days Pam invites them to respond to one or two questions on a response chart that is taped to the wall. These questions are generic and basically act as catalysts for children who are reading books. The questions merely pull the children into thinking about the books in a variety of ways from a variety of perspectives. Figure 5.2 shows Pam's guide questions.

Notice that the questions are open-ended and encourage diverse response. Pam doesn't have to come up with fresh questions every day to spark a response to literature, nor are the children limited to these questions. Rather they are an invitation to write. Pam responds to the journals regularly and focuses on content rather than editing. They are her peek into the minds of her readers. What do they understand? How do they perceive characters and their actions? Are they comprehending? Are they able to communicate effectively through their writing?

Suggestions: Response Guides

Teacher-made response guides are another way to explore a book on both oral and written levels. Response guides can help children consider a variety of perspectives. Solid questions in guides can ask children to consider the book from a character's perspective, collect interesting vo-

FIGURE 5.2. Questions like these serve as catalysts for journal entries as children read literature.

Choose one or more of these:

1. How did you feel about what you read today?
2. How did you feel about what happened?
3. What would you have done if you had been in the same situation?
4. How do you feel about a certain character?
5. Have you changed your mind about . . . ?
6. What did you learn from what you've read?
7. Did any part of the story surprise you?

Pam Rorick

cabulary, and figure out what the text means by exploring the immediate context. Interesting descriptions can be examined. Children's opinions about why events transpired, why characters made decisions, and what alternatives characters might have missed can be a part of any guide.

Response guides include questions pertaining to:

1. Development
2. Characterization
3. Setting
4. Themes
5. Vocabulary
6. Personal response

At times the questions call on the student to make connections between statements initially made and events that later unfold in a book. The questions act as catalysts for critical thinking and may require some explanation. Response guides encourage children to respond to issues and ideas in books and focus on process rather than product.

Children can be encouraged to use study guides in small groups during book discussions that convene several times a week. Teachers can be participants, observers, or absent. Students can tape-record discussions so that teachers can listen in at a later date. Observations and reactions can be recorded in literary journals by individuals.

Three response guides are provided in Appendix B for *Redwall* by Brian Jacques, an exceptional animal fantasy for upper-grade readers, *Sign of the Beaver* by Elizabeth Speare, a survival story set in the 1700s in a rugged Maine setting, and *Dogsong* by Gary Paulsen, a contemporary survival story set in the northern wilderness, also for upper-grade readers.

CONCLUSION

The questions that we ask are vital. In this chapter we explored discussing books read aloud, writing responses to books read by individuals, and setting up more formal ways for children to respond to literature through the use of response journals, decision trees, brainstorming, response guides, and writing new versions of familiar stories. More importantly, however, is the focus on the child's response, the process, how you get where you want to go.

A student teacher once asked a class of 6-year-olds to think of all the animals that go south for the winter. As the children brainstormed and gave their answers, one child proudly offered that "squirrels fly south for the winter." The teacher barely flinched, heard a few snickers, and asked if there were other animals the children could think of.

The child was pleased but a bit indignant at the laughter and said vehemently: "It's true. My brother saw a squirrel flying out of a tree." There is no doubt in my mind that this child will discover for himself that most squirrels indeed do not fly south for the winter. How profitable would it have been for this teacher to correct the child's mistake, challenge the child's knowledge?

I've pondered that over the past several years and have decided that Cathy handled the situation capably and in the best interests of the child. This child will perhaps continue to be a risk taker, offering his knowledge and sharing what he knows about the world. And don't forget the strong message it sends to the other children, the gigglers, about the freedom to offer what they know in an accepting environment.

We as educators worry that those little mistakes, those bits of misinformation, will somehow destroy the children if we let them pass unchallenged and, worse, uncorrected. I'm not sure that sometimes we don't destroy something more valuable by making sure that all statements are correct or corrected. If Wells's (1986) statement that children are natural meaning makers is true, then the emphasis on process in response to literature will stimulate critical thinking and ultimately create the kind of learners who become independent thinkers. Carol Avery recently suggested at a whole-language conference in Albany, New York, that we must let children set their own agendas rather than imposing ours upon them. I agree with that to the extent that children need a context in which to explore and articulate their thoughts, concerns, and personal responses to the information that they discover in our classrooms.

Remember the range of the children's reactions when I read *The True Story of the 3 Little Pigs* by A. Wolf? Their responses suggested to me that 6-year-old children are not at a developmental level where they understand satire. This is not surprising; however, the event further suggested that my explaining the humor of the piece would be both inappropriate and ineffective. This is not a story I would share with 6-year-old children in the future. Keeping Avery's thought in mind, notice that the children had their own responses, their own concerns, their own unique reactions. They laughed at parts of the story, were fascinated with the rebus-like print, actually enjoyed sympathizing with the wolf, and gave lengthy explanations in his behalf. We need to let go, to not be afraid of losing control of our classrooms. *Empowerment* continues to be a buzzword in education circles. One of the constituencies we must be willing to empower are the learners in our classrooms.

So how do we begin to assist the child in developing a sense of theme, something that my research and that of others have identified as being real and viable in the young child? In the chapters of this book I have made some suggestions and proposals that I hope will be helpful in establishing a learning situation that builds on what the child knows, on what the child is capable of offering in the classroom. My message is hardly unique, but it adds solidly to a growing body of knowledge about young learners in our classrooms. For too long we have worked under faulty assumptions about what children can and cannot do, what children can and cannot think. So much of our traditional learning theory has been based on the behavior of animals in research situations. I agree that one must have a solidly entrenched system of rewards and punishments if the work of the day is banal. How else can you hope to keep learners on task? Much of that approach to learning would be irrelevant if the premises of learning were based on the discovery and exploration of meaningful topics in the classroom — again, hardly new ideas. When well-written books are the substantial fare of the reading program, and questions and activities invite learners to apply skills meaningfully and to engage in thinking and problem solving, children are more likely to sign aboard.

I worry that too many children have opted not to sign on because the price is too low. They perceive at tacit levels that there is no inherent value in expending themselves for the meaningless tasks at hand. I recently watched a 55-minute lesson in which children first took a quiz, then copied an essay assignment off the board, next were given several technical directions as to length and due dates, and then watched the teacher write notes on the board, which they were expected to copy. The remaining 15 minutes were spent in doing any other paperwork chores that the children had not had time to complete earlier in the day.

For homework, the children were actually asked to write an imaginative and lively account of an ecological problem from the viewpoint of a cell, an assignment calling for high-level responses and an expectation of sufficient background knowledge. At first there was some interest; however, as no oral brainstorming occurred and no model was offered, confusion ensued. Boredom quickly followed. The assignment itself, as a culminating study of how cells function and an exploration of the broader question of how they will be able to function in a world of garbage, called for new ways of knowing and picturing the world. Understanding the basic themes studied was a given; however, there was no direct instruction, no group learning or involvement at any level other than of the most technical nature, and no well-written nonfiction books giving solid information. These children were resigned and well trained. They went about their tasks with little complaint, little enthusiasm, and little personal growth. Their response wasn't stifled; it was overlooked. It was irrelevant.

This book has explored the thematic responses of children to realistic fiction and folklore. The example above deals with science and language arts issues. How can I pull in something so obviously off the topic during the final few pages of my book? If one considers response in the context of the classroom, one cannot confine it to one small part of the curriculum. If we assume that teaching is an integrated process where the boundaries of content areas are artificial at best, then response reaches into all aspects of what we do in the classroom. Themes, the verbalization of ideas, are part of a larger process of responding to our world.

I teach a children's literature course for teachers and was recently approached by a teacher who took the course a year ago. She asked if I had developed an "advanced level" yet, to which I replied in the negative. She then told me that she had some ideas for an advanced class that would explore characterization in novels for young children. As I looked at the expression on her face, I realized that what she wanted was a course for her, a course that would stimulate her personally, that would allow and encourage her to explore her world using children's literature as a catalyst. As I began to put those thoughts into words, her expression changed. She beamed. "Exactly. That's the kind of course I mean." This teacher wanted a course that would both give her something practical to take back to her own classroom and stretch her personally by involving her in a learning experience that would value her response to literature.

This is a stunning lesson for me as a teacher. What Judy wanted was the opportunity to be a self-reflective learner. She wanted the opportunity to grow as a professional but also as an individual. For example, *The Devil's Arithmetic* by Jane Yolen may not be a title that Judy can take back to the third-grade classroom; however, understanding why the characters function as they do when the Germans come to the village, say what they say, do what they do, will engage Judy in a personal odyssey with literature that will allow her to explore a grueling historical period through the eyes of a child. Her growth through this process will have an impact on how she discusses books with children, how she frames or poses questions, how she invites them to consider broader issues, and how she deals with those sensitive issues.

I've heard teachers say, "I can't use that in my classroom, so . . . " "If I can't use it in my classroom on Monday morning, I don't want to deal with it." When I share with teachers, I frequently introduce them to a book that I want them to read just for themselves. It is usually a book that has moved me greatly, one that I've had an emotional response to, one that has stretched and challenged my perceptions, a book like *Journey to Jo'Burg* by Beverly Naidoo, a book that has been banned in South Africa. That is my way of getting them to grapple with the larger issues, the wider context, knowing that the literature will evoke a highly personal response. Sharing with teachers is certainly one way that I respond to books and explore authors' themes. Those themes often lead me to other areas, other content, other books and issues. Response is not tidy. I found a Lerner book for children, *A Zulu Family*, which is a photo essay about a Zulu woman in South Africa who was forcibly moved from her village to the tribal homelands. The ideas that I grappled with in Naidoo's book were extended by the reality of this woman's story. I am haunted by her face. I am troubled by her story. She's a real person to me. The power of exploring themes in literature is such that it is not a static experience, nor does it remain in rigidly defined boundaries. It spills over into other parts of the day, as it should.

I would like to suggest that, as we thoughtfully choose our books and questions and watch children leap into new territory, new ways of knowing and structuring their worlds, we be unafraid to grow with them. I really think Judy was onto something important. She was ready to stretch her own sense of theme. I suspect that's what makes her such an effective teacher, for at core Judy is a learner. As we set out to stretch children in their responses to the literature that we share, let's make sure that we have signed on as well.

APPENDIX A

Folktales for Comparison Charts

Little Red Riding Hood

Crawford, E. (1983). *Little red cap* (L. Zwerger, Illus.). New York: Morrow.

Hyman, T. (1983). *Little red riding hood*. New York: Holiday House.

McKissack, P. (1986). *Flossie & the fox* (R. Isadora, Illus.). New York: Dial.

Perrault, C. (1983). *Little red riding hood* (S. Moon, Illus.). Mankato, MN: Creative Education.

Schenk de Regniers, B. (1972). *Red riding hood* (E. Gorey, Illus.). New York: Atheneum.

Young, E. (1989). *Lon Po Po*. New York: Philomel.

Cumulative Tales

Aardema, V. (1981). *Bringing the rain to Kapiti Plain* (B. Vidal, Illus.). New York: Dial Press.

Aardema, V. (1975). *Why mosquitos buzz in people's ears* (L. & D. Dillon, Illus.). New York: Dial Books for Young Readers.

Cauley, L. (1988). *The pancake boy*. New York: Putnam.

Galdone, P. (1975). *The gingerbread boy*. New York: Clarion.

Hogrogian, N. (1971). *One fine day*. New York: Collier.

Kent, J. (1971). *The fat cat*. New York: Scholastic.

Stobbs, W. (1972). *Johnny-cake*. London: Bodley Head.

Native American Tales

Bierhorst, J. (1970). *The ring in the prairie* (L. & D. Dillon, Illus.). New York: Dial Press.

Cohen, C. (1988). *The mud pony* (S. Begay, Illus.). New York: Scholastic.

DePaola, T. (1983). *The legend of the bluebonnet*. New York: Putnam.

Goble, P. (1978). *The girl who loved wild horses*. New York: Bradbury Press.

Goble, P. (1980). *The gift of the sacred dog*. New York: Bradbury Press.

Goble, P. (1984). *Buffalo woman*. New York: Alladin.

McDermott, G. (1977). *Arrow to the sun*. New York: Puffin.

Prusski, J. (1988). *Bring back the deer* (N. Waldman, Illus.). New York: Gulliver.

San Souci, R. (1978). *The legend of Scarface* (D. San Souci, Illus.). New York: Doubleday.

Steptoe, J. (1988). *The Story of Jumping Mouse*. New York: Lothrop, Lee & Shepard.

Hansel and Gretel

Crawford, E. (1979). *Hansel and Gretel* (L. Zwerger, Illus.). New York: Morrow.

Grimm, J. & W. (1975). *Hansel and Gretel* (A. Adams, Illus.). New York: Scribner.

Grimm, J. & W. (1981). *Hansel and Gretel* (A. Browne, Illus.). New York: Knopf.

Grimm, J. & W. (1983). *Hansel and Gretel* (M. Felix, Illus.). Mankato, MN: Creative Education.

Lesser, R. (1984). *Hansel and Gretel* (P. Zelinsky, Illus.). New York: Dodd Mead.

Snow White

Heins, P. (1974). *Snow White* (T. Hyman, Illus.). Boston, MA: Little Brown.

Jarrell, R. (1972). *Snow White and the seven dwarfs* (N. Burkert, Illus.). New York: Farrar, Straus.

Littledale, F. (1980). *Snow White and the seven dwarfs* (S. Jeffers, Illus.). New York: Scholastic.

Rapunzel

Basil, G. (1981). *Petrosinella* (D. Stanley, Illus.). London: Frederick Warne.

Grimm, J. & W. (1984). *Rapunzel* (M. Hague, Illus.). Mankato, MN: Creative Education.

Rogasky, B. (1982). *Rapunzel* (T. Hyman, Illus.). New York: Holiday House.

Jack and the Beanstalk

Francois, A. (1983). *Jack and the beanstalk*. Mankato, MN: Creative Education.

Briggs, R. (1973). *Jim and the beanstalk*. New York: Puffin. (Modern rendition).

Cauley, L. (1983). *Jack and the beanstalk*. New York: Putnam.

Galdone, P. (1974). *The history of Mother Twaddle and the marvelous achievements of her son Jack*. New York: Seabury Press.

Haley, G. (1986). *Jack and the bean tree*. New York: Crown. (Appalachian).

Howe, J. (1989). *Jack and the beanstalk*. Boston, MA: Little Brown. (Retold). (Medieval).

Schenk de Regniers, B. (1985). *Jack and the beanstalk* (A. Wilsdorf, Illus.). New York: Atheneum.

Transformation

Anderson, H. C. (1981). *The wild swans* (S. Jeffers, Illus.). New York: Dial Press.

Clement, C. (1986). *The painter and the wild swans* (F. Clement, Illus.). New York: Dial.

Cooper, S. (1986). *The selkie girl* (W. Hutton, Illus.). New York: McElderry.

Gerstein, M. (1987). *The mountains of Tibet*. New York: Harper & Row.

Ike, J., & Zimmerman, B. (1982). *A Japanese fairy tale* (J. Ike, Illus.). London: Frederick Warne.

Langton, J. (1985). *The hedgehog boy* (I. Plume, Illus.). New York: Harper & Row.

McDermott, G. (1975). *The stonecutter*. New York: Viking Press.

Vagawa, S. (1981). *The crane wife* (S. Akaba, Illus.). New York: Morrow.

Yolen, J. (1977). *The seeing stick* (D. Maraslis, Illus.). New York: Crowell.

Cinderella Versions and Variants

Ai-ling, L. (1982). *Yeh-shen* (E. Young, Illus.). New York: Philomel. (China).

Brown, M. (1954). *Cinderella*. New York: Scribner. (France).

Climo, S. (1981). *The Egyptian Cinderella* (R. Heller, Illus.). New York: Crowell.

Cohen, B. (1980). *Lovely Vasilisa* (A. Ivanov, Illus.). New York: Atheneum. (Russia).

Ehrlich, A. (1985). *Cinderella* (S. Jeffers, Illus.). New York: Dial Books for Young Readers.

Grimm, J. & W. (1981). *Cinderella* (N. Hogrogian, Illus.). New York: Greenwillow. (Germany).

Haviland, V. (1979). *North American legends (The Indian Cinderella)* (A. Strugnell, Illus.). New York: Philomel. (North America).

Hooks, W. (1987). *Moss Gown* (D. Carrick, Illus.). New York: Clarion. (Southern U.S.).

Huck, C. (1989). *Princess Furball* (A. Lobel, Illus.). New York: Greenwillow. (Germany).

Perrault, C. (1972). *Cinderella* (E. Le Cain, Illus.). New York: Puffin. (France).

Perrault, C. (1983). *Cinderella* (R. Innocenti, Illus.). Mankato, MN: Creative Education.

Perrault, C. (1988). *Cinderella* (D. Goode, Illus.). New York: Knopf. (France).

Steel, F. (1976). *Tattercoats* (D. Goode, Illus.). New York: Bradbury Press. (England).

Steptoe, J. (1987). *Mufaro's beautiful daughter*. New York: Lothrop, Lee & Shepard. (Africa).

Vuoing, L. (1982). *The brocaded slipper* (V. Mai, Illus.). New York: Lippincott. (Vietnam).

Whitney, T. (1970). *Vasilisa the beautiful* (N. Hogrogian, Illus.). New York: Macmillan. (Russia).

APPENDIX B

Response Guides

REDWALL BY BRIAN JACQUES

About the Story

Imagine an abbey inhabited by an order of peaceful mice with animals who look to the abbey for leadership and protection. Suddenly rumors reach the abbey that Cluny the Scourge and his band of cutthroats are on the march toward Redwall. Matthias is a young and inexperienced novice, but this threat challenges him to lead the mice and seek the secret of Martin the Warrior, the founder of Redwall. This well-written fantasy is in the tradition of *Watership Down* and has a main character with whom children will want to identify.

This is Jacques's first novel and is the first volume of a trilogy about Redwall Abbey. Although the length of the book may discourage some readers, it is divided into three sections and can be read as three slimmer volumes, which makes it less formidable. Jacques's method of alternating chapters between Cluny's approach and events at the abbey gives the reader a unique perspective on the conflict. Cluny is a rough, nasty character and Jacques shows the reader the twisting callousness of this evil leader as he pits his own soldiers ruthlessly against each other. Oddly, he manages to reveal Cluny as a tormented and pathetic rat who seems caught in a miserable web from which he does not escape. The reader is at times horrified by his actions. Rarely does an author go beyond the stereotypes in fantasy for children when writing about an evil leader. In *Redwall* Jacques does.

Exploring the conventions of fantasy, Jacques does several other things that are of interest. He divides the book into three sections, one of which is "The Quest"; however, this quest is unlike any I've encountered before. Initially, Matthias searches for the sword of Martin the Warrior by going to the upper reaches of the abbey itself. How believable it is for a small mouse to go no further than the rafters of his own abbey, which are inhabited by hostile sparrows who have no great interest in the fight below. The sparrows are so caught up in their own petty squabbles that they have little sympathy for the ground animals and, in fact, hold Matthias prisoner. Matthias finally escapes and must leave the abbey to search for the sword in the caves of Asmodeus, the snake, a character who is dangerous to all of the animals in the book. Jacques has a real gift for making the animals and their adventures believable. And finally, the legend from the past about the sword of Martin the Warrior and a missing piece of an ancient tapestry that hangs in the Great Hall gives *Redwall* a folklore blend that tickles the reader into finding out more.

Initiating Activities

Look at the well-illustrated jacket of *Redwall*. Make some predictions about the two characters, Matthias and Cluny, who appear in boxes. Under what circumstances might they eventually meet? Use the title as a clue.

Thinking Critically

BOOK ONE: THE WALL
Chapters 1–8 (Pages 12–42)
   1. What do you know about Matthias and Cluny? What clues and descriptions of them can you find in the book? What other characters do you meet that you want to tell about? How do they get along with Cluny or Matthias?
   2. What clues or foreshadowings had the author given that something awful is about to happen? What do you think will happen?
   3. What examples can you find of how Cluny uses contemptuous language when he talks to the rats? Why do you think the rats obey a leader like Cluny? What do their names reveal about them?
   4. What do you think Cluny's nightmares mean? Who might the phantom be? Look for other clues as you go on reading.

Chapters 9–14 (Pages 43–76)
   5. On page 47 sister Clemence chides Matthias for not obeying the Abbot. Why is this a turning point for Matthias? After this conversation, how do the other animals begin to treat Matthias differently? How do you think Matthias feels about all of this?
   6. What preparations do Abbot Mortimer, Constance, and Mat-

thias make when they find out that Cluny is coming? Do you think they
have forgotten anything that might be important?

7. Matthias weeps as he stands gazing at the tapestry in the Great
Hall. Why do you think he is ashamed when Cornflower sees him weep-
ing?

8. Cluny feels that the picture of Martin the Warrior is important
to the mice and he wants Shadow to steal it. How do you think this will
help him defeat the mice?

Chapters 15-20 (Pages 77-108)

9. Cluny constantly betrays his own warriors and pits them
against each other. Why should Captain Scragg be worried? What do
you think Cheesethief plans to do? Can you find other examples where
Cluny shows his disregard for his own soldiers?

10. What clues does the author give that make the ending of book
one ominous for both the rats and mice?

BOOK TWO: THE QUEST
Chapters 1-6 (Pages 111-144)

11. How does Matthias feel right now? When Silent Sam leads him
back to the abbey, why is Matthias unsure of his reception?

12. What secrets do Methuselah and Matthias find? What is the
meaning of "I am that is?" Do you think Martin the Warrior can help
the abbey now? How?

13. Old Sela the vixen is a fraud, a double agent. Why does Cluny
put up with her phony magic? What does Sela hope to gain from betray-
ing both Cluny and the mice?

14. You'll have noticed the picture clues that are given at the beginning of each chapter. What do you think the picture clue at the beginning of chapter 8 means? See if you can figure it out before reading this
chapter.

15. Why does Methuselah call Matthias a young scallywag? What
does he mean? Do you think he is angry with Matthias? Support your
answer.

16. Why do you think Martin's sword is so important? How do you
think Matthias will retrieve the sword from the weather vane?

17. What do you think Asmodeus might be up to? How do you
think he might be important later in the story?

Chapters 13-15 (Pages 181-199)

18. How does Matthias win Warbeak's cooperation? Do you think
Matthias should trust the sparrow? Support your answer.

19. What clues does the author give that suggest King Bull Sparra is crazy?

20. Cornflower has a traditional female role in this book. How is her role traditional? Constance has a very different type of role. How is her role different from Cornflower's?

21. What does it mean when the Abbot tells Chickenhound that Cluny is the "spawn of darkness"?

Chapters 16–19 (Pages 200–240)

22. What do you think Basil Stag Hare and Jess have in mind? How do the two animals accomplish this feat alone?

23. Does Matthias successfully complete his quest? When he and the King fall, what do you think will happen?

24. Read the section on pages 236–237. How does Chickenhound get what he deserves for his treachery?

Chapters 20–23 (Pages 241–264)

25. What do you think Matthias's dream means? What do you think might have happened in his dream if he had gone to the end of the long corridor?

26. How does Basil shake Matthias out of his lethargy? What do you think Matthias must now do to complete his quest?

BOOK THREE: THE WARRIOR

Chapters 1–4 (Pages 267–297)

27. How does Silent Sam help thwart the attackers? What ideas do you have for defending the abbey?

28. Why do you think Cheesethief puts on Cluny's tailbarb and the Warlord's cloak and helmet? How does Cluny use Cheesethief's death to his own advantage?

29. How do you think Matthias feels when he finds the entrance to Poisonteeth's cave? What do you think will happen when he enters?

Chapters 5–9 (Pages 298–324)

30. What is the "diversionary assault" that Cluny launched at night? How did Cornflower's soup save the day?

31. What clues do you find that suggest Cluny is behaving oddly? How do you think his soldiers are reacting to his odd behavior? What do you think Cluny's dreams mean?

32. Why do you think Matthias becomes Matthias the Warrior?

Was he able to become a warrior on his own? What kind of help did Matthias have?

Chapters 10–15 (Pages 325–351)

33. How do you feel about Plumpen's act against Redwall? What do you think you would have done?

34. When Matthias appears in the abbey, Cluny is terrified. Why does the sight of this small mouse frighten him?

35. What do the words of the dying Abbot mean: "What a great pity that it took so much bloodshed to unite us all"?

Do It Yourself

1. Silent Sam was an important character, but he didn't speak until a year had passed after Redwall was saved. Try making a journal of some of Sam's thoughts in different parts of the book. For example, what was it like when Matthias was lost and Sam had to lead him to Redwall?

2. What if Cluny had won the battle and Matthias had not found the sword? Life at the abbey and Mossflower Woods would be very different. Write a final chapter one year later and tell about life in Redwall.

3. Some of Cluny's soldiers acted like pretty desperate characters. Imagine that they are wanted by the FBI and you must design the wanted posters.

4. Asmodeus's caves and King Bull Sparra's kingdom in the eaves are just two of the many interesting places described in *Redwall*. Using the descriptions in the book, paint a picture of these places or others like them, for example, Cluny's headquarters. You may want to use tempera paints or watercolors. Mount your picture attractively and display it in your room. At the bottom warn the reader about what he or she must know before entering these places.

5. Methuselah found an ancient riddle that he and Matthias had to solve. Matthias was one part of the answer to the riddle. See if you can compose an ancient riddle that uses your name and some of the history of your family. You'll have to decide if some old family artifact will be the object of this riddle and what type of hidden secrets it might contain.

6. Pretend that you are a newspaper reporter doing a series of articles on the Redwall Abbey and that you arrived just as the Abbot was celebrating his Golden Jubilee at the abbey and Cluny's dreadful

approach was discovered. You decide to stay and do a series of articles on the invasion by Cluny.

Read Some More!

If you enjoyed this adventure you might like to read *Watership Down* by Richard Adams or *Mrs. Frisby and the Rats of NIMH* by Robert O'Brien. Both stories are about animals who must flee from enemies and find new homes instead of protecting their homes from enemies, which make them a little different from *Redwall*. And be looking for Brian Jacques's other books, *Mossflower* and *Mattimeo*.

SIGN OF THE BEAVER BY ELIZABETH SPEARE

About the Story

Sign of the Beaver is set in Maine during the mid-1700s in Colonial America. Speare's book will have high appeal to middle-grade readers. This book can turn even the most reluctant readers on to literature! One of Speare's basic themes explores the relationship between two cultures in conflict. In this book the Indians seem to hold the keys to knowledge, in contrast to traditional books about the Indians.

Matt is left alone in the wilderness to guard the family's cabin and land while his father returns to Connecticut to get the rest of the family. Matt is 12 and makes some initial mistakes that almost cost him his life. He has an encounter with a bear, a trapper who steals his gun, and finally, a beehive that almost kills him. He is found by the Native Americans living in the forest, the Beaver tribe, and is nursed to health. As the weeks go by, he realizes that his parents are late and he does not know what has become of them.

At this point, the story changes and becomes a tale of two young enemies who learn to respect each other and the differences inherent in their cultures. *Sign of the Beaver* is also the story of learning to survive in the wilderness by living with nature rather than fighting it. Attean has many lessons of survival to teach Matt, and middle-grade children will identify strongly with Matt as he learns to fish and set traps. Attean and Matt swap bits of their culture and skills with each other. Each learns to bend and finally to accept the worth of the other. In the end, Matt faces a huge decision. Should he go with the Indians or stay at the cabin in the hope that his parents will eventually join him?

Thinking Critically

Chapters 1–5

1. The book begins: "Matt stood at the edge of the clearing for some time after his father had gone out of sight among the trees." How does Matt feel at this point in time, and how do his feelings change by the end of Chapter 3? How would you feel if you were in his place?

2. Describe a typical day for Matt. Include details that describe where he lives, what tools he uses, the types of chores he must do, and the food he eats.

3. Ben is not trustworthy. What does this mean? How is Ben untrustworthy?

Chapters 6–10

1. Describe the treaty between Saknis and Matt. Why did Saknis want Attean to learn how to read?

2. Why is Attean disdainful toward Matt?

3. Describe some of the outdoor skills that Matt learns from Attean.

4. Why does Attean become angry when Matt reads the chapter where Robinson Crusoe saves Friday's life?

5. How does Matt's attitude toward Attean and his people begin to change?

Chapters 11–22

1. Attean's family does not trust Matt because he is white. What causes them to change their attitudes toward Matt?

2. Movies often depict Indians in stereotyped ways. What is a stereotype? How does this book show what Indians were really like?

3. This book peels away the layers of prejudice that exist between two people. What caused this to happen?

4. New words are encountered in the text, such as *matchlock*. Can you gain meaning from the context? List other unfamiliar words and see how accurately you can predict their meaning by using the book itself. Check yourself with a dictionary.

Chapters 23–25

1. Why does Matt decide to stay alone in the wilderness?

2. Matt is now quite independent. Describe how he has learned to provide for himself.

3. The ending is somewhat bittersweet. How does Matt feel about being with his family and having new neighbors?

4. How did your attitudes about history change by the end of the book?

Writing Activities

1. Write journal entries from Attean's perspective. How did he feel the first time he met Matt? How did his perspective change over time? Describe how he might have told portions of *Robinson Crusoe*.

2. Write about Indian and white attitudes using the book and events today. How have historical events changed attitudes? How have attitudes remained the same?

3. Write an imaginary letter from Matt to Attean one year later. Find someone else who has read the book and have him or her answer your letter as Attean.

DOGSONG BY GARY PAULSEN

About the Story

Gary Paulsen's *Dogsong*, a 1985 Newberry Medal runner-up, is a song of the rhythms of tundra life, a fragile life, almost destroyed by outside technology. Paulsen's book takes place in the northernmost regions of North America in an Eskimo village, a village resting at the edge of the sea — a sea that can give or take life. This is all part of nature's balance, which Russel seeks to discover during his odyssey through the book.

As the book begins, Russel hears the effects of the Outside, as his father coughs up the effects of tobacco. He hears the roar of the snowmobiles that frighten the seals. He sees the tablecloth patterned with the roses his father has never seen growing, but holds so dear nonetheless. Russel prefers the delicate flowers of the tundra. He has learned to ignore the religious pictures cut from magazines, which are taped all over the small government house only because they have somehow helped his father to stop drinking. Both are influences from the Outside.

Russel yearns for something intangible — and it is not until he moves in with the old man, Oogruk, that he knows he misses the old way of life, a way of life unfamiliar to him and yet in his blood. Oogruk can barely remember the old times, yet he lives with the old ways, shunning modern gods, modern electricity, and modern weapons that make too much noise and do not seek the approval of the animals shot. He becomes teacher to Russel.

Russel learns all that he can from Oogruk before he sets out on his own journey, even as Oogruk ends his. Russel's story is one of harmony with the land and harmony with Oogruk's sled team. Whether floating on a piece of ice in the sea with his team or sleeping out a violent snowstorm in the middle of the tundra, Russel knows that he must not fight the land, must learn to become one with his team. Children who are in the midst of learning to fit into their own worlds will be challenged with Russel as he learns to become a part of the tundra and embraces the Eskimo way of life.

While journeying through the north, Russel finds an old stone lamp, worn smooth by centuries of wind, older than any object in the museum back home. It is this lamp that forms the basis of a dream sequence that parallels reality for Russel. Children discussing this dream will be led to question how Russel traveled back in time to become the hunter of the great woolly mammoth. Russel's struggle in the present is with a great polar bear, and it is his knowledge of how he killed the mammoth in his dream that saves his life, as well as the life of a young pregnant girl. Paulsen's use of this dream sequence while Russel journeys to the edge of the tundra makes the line between realistic fiction and fantasy a blurred edge. The reader must decide whether this is a dream or a journey across time.

Dogsong is filled with images that stir the imagination. Invite your children into this song of Russel's run. The following response guide may be used to extend *Dogsong* in the classroom. This richly descriptive book begs to be read aloud, and in doing so, the teacher can make this adventure available to all types of readers.

Activities

These emphasize a comparison of the old ways and the new.

1. To explore concretely one of the major themes of the book, make a comparison chart of the old way of life and the new way of life in the village. Consider dress, shelter, weapons, transportation, food, hunting, preserving food, diseases, customs, beliefs. Are there other areas you can think of to compare and contrast?

2. Russel's new life in Oogruk's house is different from life in his father's house. Make a time line of events that might comprise a typical day for Russel in both houses.

3. Act out selected sequences in the book from different perspectives. Brainstorm and choose favorite scenes. For example, if Russel embraced the new ways and ignored the old ways, how might he enter Oogruk's house for the first time? This would be quite different from what actually happened in the book. Discuss the differences after acting out both sequences. Another scene appropriate for spontaneous drama might be the killing of the polar bear. Find this scene in the book. Lead the children toward a discussion of the kill. Let them explore why Russel killed the bear, why a modern hunter might kill a bear. Are there any differences? What might they be? Encourage the children to act out the hunt scene from different perspectives.

4. Put on the shoes of Russel for a moment. Invite children to walk into their classroom and see that room as Russel might see it for the first time. What are the differences he might notice? What are the similarities? What time of year is it? How does your climate compare with the tundra? Look outside. How is vegetation the same or different from that described in the book? Draw two large parallel murals depicting your world and Russel's world and hang them side by side.

5. There are unfamiliar terms in *Dogsong*, like *ulu*, *uniak*, *muktuk*, and *mukluk*. Find others and make a glossary of terms or phrases. Include sketches.

Writing Ideas

These emphasize how Russel learns to take charge.

1. Ask children to write five journal entries of their thoughts for events before, during, and after the incident on the ice flow in the sea, killing the mammoth in his dream, or leaving the house of his father to life with Oogruk.

2. Russel is proud of his team. He wants to write and tell other Eskimo boys how he readied himself and his team for a dog run across his country. Try writing that letter. What would Russel have to convey to others to make them understand how he had to take charge and become their leader?

3. Tell children that Oogruk appeared to Russel one last time in a dream, after Russel found his song. What did Oogruk say to Russel? In contrast, when Russel returned to the seaside village, what did Russel's father say to his son?

4. Write a final chapter to the book. What became of Russel after he found his song?

5. Write about Russel's dog run as if you were a newspaper reporter. You may choose any perspective from which to write. You might be

an Eskimo or an Outsider. You might be writing as if Russel were lost and had been found. You might wish to emphasize Russel's bravery. Will you include information from an interview with Russel? What might he have to say after finding his song?

Related Reading

Dogsong hums with the rhythms set forth in *Julie of the Wolves* by Jean Craighead George and yet is distinctly different, a companion book. Both books yield a rich description of the lives of two children who live in the rugged country of the North and allow an exploration of character and the theme of survival.

1. A comparison of Julie's way of life with Russel's allows children to concretely explore the lives of two Eskimo children. How is Julie's role as a female different within her culture? What is life like in her village? with her father? What other customs might be found in *Julie of the Wolves* that give a picture of how she lives? Refer back to the chart that compares both the old and new ways.

2. A careful reading of *Julie of the Wolves* allows children to analyze two characters who share common backgrounds and experience a journey on two levels. What conclusions do both characters draw regarding the old ways by the end of the book? What changes do both characters undergo? How do their feelings toward their fathers change? How will they fit into village life after completing their journeys?

3. A comparison of Julie's wild wolves and Russel's sledding team might also lead to some varied observations about the journeys of these two children. Russel becomes one with his team, as leader, even as Julie learns to become one of the pack, as follower. Russel's dogs do not take on individual personalities as do Julie's. Discuss the differences and similarities and how these alter their journeys.

4. A child responding to Julie's journey might be challenged to write her song, even as Russel finally writes his song.

5. Both Russel and Julie are survivors. How do both characters survive? What special qualities must they discover about themselves in order to remain alive? Children will want to talk about these questions and explore what they might have done in similar circumstances.

Read Some More!

Other books by the author include *The Island*, *The Winter Room*, *Hatchet*, *The Voyage of the Frog*, and *Woodsong*.

References

Allington, R. (1983). Fluency: The neglected reading goal. *The Reading Teacher, 36*, 556–561.

Anderson, R., Stevens, K., Shifrin, Z., & Osborn, J. (1977). *Instantiation of word meanings in children* (Tech. Rep. No. 46). Urbana, IL: Center for the Study of Reading.

Anderson, R., Spiro, R., & Anderson, M. (1977). *Schemata as scaffolding for the representation of information in connected discourse* (Tech. Rep. No. 24). Urbana, IL: Center for the Study of Reading.

Applebee, A. (1973). *The spectator role: Theoretical and developmental studies of ideas about and responses to literature, with special reference to four age levels.* Doctoral dissertation, University of London. (ERIC Document Reproduction Service No. ED 114 840)

Applebee, A. (1978). *The child's concept of story: Ages two to seventeen.* Chicago: University of Chicago Press.

Baker, L., & Stein, N. (1981). The development of prose comprehension skills. In C. Santa & B. Hayes (Eds.), *Children's prose comprehension research and practice.* Newark, DE: International Reading Association.

Baumann, J. (1981). *Children's ability to comprehend main ideas after reading expository prose.* Paper presented at 31st Annual Meeting of National Reading Conference, Dallas.

Berndt, T., & Berndt, E. (1975). Children's use of motives and intentionality in person perception and moral judgment. *Child Development, 46*, 904–912.

Bettelheim, B. (1976). *The uses of enchantment: The meaning and importance of fairy tales.* New York: Random House.

Biemiller, A. (1970). The development of the use of graphic and contextual information as children learn to read. *Reading Research Quarterly, 6*, 75–96.

Blachowicz, C. (1977). Semantic constructivity in children's comprehension. *Reading Research Quarterly, 13*, 188–199.

Bleich, D. (1980). Epistemological assumptions in the study of response. In J. Tompkins (Ed.), *Reader response criticism* (pp. 134–163). Baltimore: Johns Hopkins University Press.

Bransford, J., & Johnson, M. (1972). Contextual prerequisites for understanding: Some investigations of comprehension and recall. *Journal of Verbal Learning and Verbal Behavior, 11,* 717–726.

Britton, J. (1978). Response to literature. In M. Meek, A. Warlow, & G. Barton (Eds.), *The cool web.* London: The Bodley Head.

Brown, A., & Smiley, S. (1977). Rating the importance of structural units of prose passages: A problem of metacognitive development. *Child Development, 48,* 1–8.

Brown, A., Smiley, S., Day, J., Townsend, M., & Lawton, S. (1977). *Intrusion of a thematic idea in children's comprehension and retention of stories* (Tech. Rep. No. 13). Urbana, IL: Center for the Study of Reading.

Bruner, J. (1983). *Child's talk: Learning to use language.* New York: W. W. Norton.

Cappa, D. (1957). Sources of appeal in kindergarten books. *Elementary English, 34,* 259.

Cazden, C. (1966). *Some implications of research on language development for preschool education.* Paper prepared for the Social Science Research Council Conference on Preschool Education, Chicago, IL.

Chomsky, C. (1972). Stages in language development and reading exposure. *Harvard Educational Review, 42,* 1–33.

Christie, D., & Schumacher, G. (1975). Developmental trends in the abstraction and recall of relevant versus irrelevant thematic information from connected verbal materials. *Child Development, 46,* 598–602.

Clark, M. (1976). *Young fluent readers.* Portsmouth, NH: Heinemann.

Clay, M. (1979). *What did I write?* Portsmouth, NH: Heinemann.

Cochran-Smith, M. (1984). *The making of a reader.* Norwood, NJ: Ablex.

Cohen, D. (1968). The effects of literature on vocabulary and reading achievement. *Elementary English, 45,* 209–213.

Coles, P., Sigman, M., & Chessel, K. (1977). Scanning strategies of children and adults. In G. Butterworth (Ed.), *The child's representation of the world.* New York: Plenum Press.

Collerson, J. (1988). *Writing for life.* New Rozelle, NSW, Australia: Primary English Teaching Association.

Cox, C., & Many, J. (1989). *Reader stance towards a literary work: Applying the transactional theory to children's responses.* Paper presented at the Annual Meeting of the American Educational Research Association, San Francisco, CA.

Cullinan, B., Harwood, K., & Galda, L. (1983). The reader and the story: Comprehension and response. *Journal of Research and Development in Education, 16,* 29–38.

Cullinan, B., Jaggar, A., & Strickland, D. (1974). Language expansion for black children in the primary grades: A research report. *Young children, 29,* 98–112.

Danner, F. (1976). Children's understanding of intersentence organization in the recall of short descriptive passages. *Journal of Education Psychology, 68*(1), 174–183.

DeFord, D. (1981). Literacy: Reading, writing and other essentials. *Language Arts, 58,* 652–658.

Denburg, S. (1977). The interaction of picture and print in reading instruction. *Reading Research Quarterly, 2,* 176–189.

Donaldson, M. (1978). *Children's minds.* New York: Collins.

Duckworth, E. (1972). The having of wonderful ideas. *Harvard Educational Review, 42,* 217–231.

Dunn, B., Matthews, S., & Bieger, G. (1979). *Individual differences in the recall of lower level textual information* (Tech. Rep. No. 150). Urbana, IL: Center for the Study of Reading. (ERIC Document Reproduction Service No. ED 181 448)

Durkin, D. (1966). *Children who read early.* New York: Teachers College Press.

Favat, A. (1977). *Child and tale: The origins of interest.* Urbana, IL: National Council of Teachers of English.

Fenwick, G. (1975). Junior school pupils' rejection of school library books. *Educational Research, 17,* 143–149.

Fish, S. (1980). Interpreting the variorum. In J. Tompkins (Ed.), *Reader response criticism* (pp. 70–100). Baltimore: Johns Hopkins University Press.

Flavell, J. (1963). *The developmental psychology of Jean Piaget.* New York: Van Nostrand.

Flood, J. (1977). Parental styles in reading episodes with young children. *Reading Teacher, 30,* 864–867.

Goodman, Y., & Burke, C. (1972). Additional guide questions to aid story retelling. Revised for *Reading miscue inventory manual: Procedure for diagnosis and evaluation.* New York: Macmillan.

Goodman, K., Goodman, Y., & Hood, W. (1988). *The whole language evaluation book.* Portsmouth, NH: Heinemann.

Goodman, K., Shannon, P., Freeman, Y., & Murphy, S. (1988). *Report card on basal readers.* Portsmouth, NH: Heinemann.

Graves, D. (1984). *A researcher learns to write: Selected articles and monographs.* Portsmouth, NH: Heinemann.

Halliday, M. K. (1975). *Learning how to mean.* London: Edward Arnold.

Halliday, M. K., & Hasan, R. (1979). *Cohesion in English.* New York: Longman.

Hardy, B. (1977). Narrative as a primary act of mind. In M. Meek (Ed.), *The cool web* (pp. 12–23). London: The Bodley Head.

Harste, J., Burke, C., & Woodward, V. (1979). *Children's language and world: Initial encounters with print.* Unpublished manuscript, Indiana University.

Heath, S. (1983). *Ways with words.* Cambridge, MA: Cambridge University Press.

Hepler, S. (1982). *Patterns of response to literature: A one year study of a fifth and sixth grade classroom.* Unpublished doctoral dissertation, Ohio State University, Columbus.

Hickman, J. (1979). *Response to literature in a school environment, grades K–5.* Unpublished doctoral dissertation, Ohio State University, Columbus.

Hickman, J., & Cullinan, B. (1989). *Children's literature in the classroom: Weaving Charlotte's web*. Needham Heights, MA: Christopher Gordon.

Holland, K., Thompson, D., & Lehr, S. (in preparation). *An investigation of elementary students' reader responses in relation to the reading aloud of information books*. Manuscript.

Holland, K., & Lehr, S. (in press). Children's response to literature: Isn't it about time we said goodbye to book reports and literal oral book discussions? In D. Bloome, K. Holland, & J. Solsken (Eds.), *Alternative perspectives in assessing children's language and literacy*. Norwood, NJ: Ablex.

Huck, C. (1960). *Huck inventory of literary background*. New York: Houghton Mifflin.

Huck, C. (1979). *Children's literature in the elementary school* (3rd ed.). New York: Holt, Rinehart & Winston.

Huck, C., Hepler, S., & Hickman, J. (1987). *Children's literature in the elementary school* (4th ed.). New York: Holt, Rinehart & Winston.

Iser, W. (1980). The reading process: A phenomenological approach. In J. Tompkins (Ed.), *Reader response criticism* (pp. 50–69). Baltimore: Johns Hopkins University Press.

Jacques, D. (1990). *Young children's responses to literature read aloud*. Paper presented at the Annual Conference of the International Reading Association, Atlanta, GA.

Joels, R. (1987). Picture books that bring comprehension to life. *Childhood Education, 63*, 362–365.

Kiefer, B. (1989). Picture books for all the ages. In J. Hickman & B. Cullinan (Eds.), *Children's literature in the classroom: Weaving Charlotte's web*. Needham Heights, MA: Christopher Gordon.

Lehr, S. (1985). *The child's sense of theme*. Unpublished doctoral dissertation, Ohio State University, Columbus.

Lehr, S. (1987). Revised Huck Literature Inventory. In M. White (Ed.), *Instructor's manual for children's literature in the elementary school* (4th ed., pp. 192–197). New York: Holt, Rinehart & Winston.

Lehr, S. (1988a). A child's sense of theme. In C. Anderson (Ed.), *Reading: The abc and beyond* (pp. 124–137). London: Macmillan.

Lehr, S. (1988b). Classroom research explores the child's construction of meaning. *Reading Research Quarterly, 23*, 337–357.

Lehr, S. (1988c). Children & books: A child's developing sense of theme. In J. Kristo (Ed.), *Readings in literacy education* (pp. 36–50). Orono: University of Maine.

Lehr, S. (1989). Understanding the reading process: How does the child construct meaning with literature? In R. Blake (Ed.), *Reading, writing and interpreting literature* (pp. 184–217). Schenectady, NY: New York State English Council. Also available National Council of Teachers of English, 1990.

Lehr, S. (1990, Fall/Winter). Literature and the construction of meaning: The preschool child's developing sense of theme. *Journal of Research in Childhood Education, 5*(1), 37–46.

Levin, J. (1981). On functions of pictures in prose. In F. Pirozzolo & M. Wittrock (Eds.), *Neuropsychological and cognitive processes in reading.* New York: Academic Press.

Liebling, C. (1989). *Insight into literature: Learning to interpret inside view and character plans in fiction.* Paper presented at the Annual Conference of the National Reading Conference, Austin, TX.

Lukens, R. (1982). *A critical handbook of children's literature.* Glenview, IL: Scott, Foresman.

Mandler, J., & Johnson, N. (1977). Remembrance of things parsed: Story structure and recall. *Cognitive Psychology, 9,* 111–151.

Many, J. (1989a). *The effect of reader stance on students' personal understanding of literature.* Unpublished manuscript.

Many, J. (1989b). *The effects of stance and age level on children's literary responses.* Paper presented at the Annual Conference of the National Reading Conference, Austin, TX.

Merton, R. (1968). The Matthew effect in science. *Science,* pp. 56–63.

Meyer, B. (1977). The structure of prose: Effects on learning and memory and implications for educational practice. In R. Anderson, R. Spiro, & W. Montague (Eds.), *Schooling and the acquisition of knowledge* (pp. 179–200). Hillsdale, NJ: Erlbaum.

Nagy, W., & Anderson, R. (1984). How many words are there in printed school English? *Reading Research Quarterly, 19,* 304–330.

New Zealand Department of Education. (1985). *Reading in junior classes with guidelines to the revised ready to read series.* Wellington, New Zealand: Author.

Ninio, A., & Bruner, J. (1978). The achievement and antecedents of labeling. *Journal of Child Language, 5,* 1–15.

O'Connell, E. (1988). Writing reports in year 4. In J. Collerson (Ed.), *Writing for life* (pp. 50–59). Rozelle, NSW, Australia: Primary English Teaching Association.

Otto, W., & Barrett, T. (1968). *Two studies of children's ability to formulate and state a literal main idea in reading.* Report from the Reading Project, Wisconsin Research and Development Center for Cognitive Learning.

Paley, V. (1981). *Wally's stories.* Cambridge, MA: Harvard University Press.

Paris, S. (1975). Integration and inference in children's comprehension and memory. In R. Restle, R. Shiffrin, J. Castellan, H. Linkman, & D. Pisoni (Eds.), *Cognitive theory.* Hillsdale, NJ: Erlbaum.

Pearson, D. (1981). A retrospective reaction to prose comprehension. In C. Santa & B. Hayes (Eds.), *Children's prose comprehension* (pp. 117–132). Newark, DE: International Reading Association.

Piaget, J. (1960). *The language and thought of the child.* London: Routledge & Kegan. (Original work published 1926)

Pichert, J., & Anderson, R. (1976). *Taking different perspectives on a story* (Tech. Rep. No. 14). Urbana, IL: Center for the Study of Reading.

Rohwer, W., & Harris, W. (1975). Media effects on prose learning in two populations of children. *Journal of Educational Psychology, 67,* 651–657.

Rosenblatt, L. (1976). *Literature as exploration.* New York: Noble & Noble. (Original work published 1938)

Rosenblatt, L. (1978). *The reader, the text, the poem: The transactional theory of the literary work.* Carbondale, IL: Southern Illinois University Press.

Rothery, J. (1986). Teaching writing in the primary school: A genre-based approach to the development of writing abilities. In J. Martin & M. Rothery (Eds.), *Writing Project Report No. 4.* Sydney, Australia: University of Sydney.

Rumelhart, D. (1975). Notes on a schema for stories. In D. Bobrow & A. Collins (Eds.), *Representation and understanding: Studies in cognitive science.* New York: Academic Press.

Rumelhart, D. (1980). Schemata: The building blocks of cognition. In R. Spiro, B. Bruce, & W. Brewer (Eds.), *Theoretical issues in reading comprehension* (pp. 33–58). Hillsdale, NJ: Erlbaum.

Schallert, D. (1980). The role of illustrations in reading comprehension. In R. Spiro, B. Bruce, & W. Brewer (Eds.), *Theoretical issues in reading comprehension* (pp. 503–524). Hillsdale, NJ: Erlbaum.

Shuy, R. (1981). A holistic view of language. *Research in the Teaching of English, 15,* 101–111.

Siegel, M. (1983). Toward an understanding of reading as signification. Research Report. (ERIC Document Reproduction Service No. ED 246 388)

Smirnov, A., Mal'tseva, I., & Alova, S. (1971–72, Winter). The development of logical memorization techniques in the preschool and young school child. *Soviet Psychology,* pp. 178–195.

Smith, F. (1988). *Understanding reading,* 4th ed. Hillsdale, NJ: Erlbaum.

Snow, C., & Goldfield, B. (1982). Building stories. In D. Tannen (Ed.), *Analyzing discourse: Text and talk* (pp. 127–141). Washington, DC: Georgetown University Press.

Sostarich, J. (1974). *A study of the reading behavior of sixth graders: Comparisons of active and other readers.* Unpublished doctoral dissertation, Ohio State University, Columbus.

Spiro, R. (1977). Remembering information from text. In R. Anderson, R. Spiro, & W. Montague (Eds.), *Schooling and the acquisition of knowledge* (pp. 137–165). Hillsdale, NJ: Erlbaum.

Stanovich, K. (1980). Toward an interactive-compensatory model of individual differences in the development of reading fluency. *Reading Research Quarterly, 16,* 32–71.

Stanovich, K. (1986). Matthew effects in reading: Some consequences of individual differences in the acquisition of literacy. *Reading Research Quarterly, 21,* 360–406.

Stein, N., & Glenn, C. (1978). An analysis of story comprehension in elementary school children. In R. Freedle (Ed.), *Discourse processing: Multidisciplinary perspectives.* Norwood, NJ: Ablex.

Taylor, B. (1980). Children's memory for expository text after reading. *Reading Research Quarterly, 15,* 399–411.

Taylor, D. (1983). *Family literacy.* Portsmouth, NH: Heinemann.

Thorndyke, P. (1975). Cognitive structures in human story comprehension and memory. Unpublished doctoral dissertation, Stanford University, Stanford, CA.

Thorndyke, P. (1977). Cognitive structures in comprehension and memory of narrative discourse. *Cognitive Psychology, 9,* 77–110.

Tierney, R., Bridge, D., & Cera, M. (1978–1979). The discourse processing operations of children. *Reading Research Quarterly, 14,* 539–573.

Tierney, R., & Pearson, D. (1983). Toward a composing model of reading. *Language Arts, 60,* 568–580.

Trabasso, T., & Nicholas, D. (1977). *Memory and inferences in the comprehension of narratives.* Paper presented at conference on Structure and Process Models in the Study of Dimensionality of Children's Judgements, Kassel, Germany.

Tucker, N. (1976). How children respond to fiction. In G. Fox, G. Hammond, T. Jones, F. Smith, & D. Sterck (Eds.), *Writers, critics and children* (pp. 177–188). London: Agathon Press.

Vygotsky, L. S. (1978). *Mind in society.* Cambridge, MA: Harvard University Press.

Walberg, H., Strykowski, B., Rovai, E., & Hung, S. (1984). Exceptional performance. *Review of Educational Research, 54,* 87–112.

Walberg, H., & Tsai, S. (1983). Matthew effects in education. *American Educational Research Journal, 20,* 359–373.

Waters, H. (1978). Superordinate-subordinate structure in semantic memory. *Journal of Verbal Learning and Verbal Behavior, 17,* 587–597.

Wells, G. (1986). *The meaning makers: Children learning language and using language to learn.* Portsmouth, NH: Heinemann.

Whalen-Levitt, P. (1977, June). *A study of children's strategies for making meaning of visual narrative in Peter Wezel's* The Good Bird. Paper presented at ALA Research Forum on Children's Books.

Whaley, J. (1981). Reader's expectations for story structures. *Reading Research Quarterly, 17,* 90–114.

White, D. (1984). *Books before five.* Portsmouth, NH: Heinemann. (Original work published 1954)

Yendovitskayz, T. (1971). Development of memory. In A. Saparozhets & D. Elkonin (Eds.), *The psychology of preschool children.* Cambridge, MA: MIT Press. (Original work published 1964)

Children's Literature Bibliography

Adams, R. (1974). *Watership down*. New York: Macmillan.

Asch, F. (1982). *Happy birthday, moon*. Englewood Cliffs, NJ: Prentice-Hall.

Bang, M. (1983). *Dawn*. New York: Morrow.

Bang, M. (1980). *The grey lady and the strawberry snatcher*. New York: Four Winds Press.

Blume, J. (1972). *Tales of a fourth grade nothing*. New York: Dutton.

Blume, J. (1980). *Superfudge*. New York: Dutton.

Brown, M. (1972). *The three billy goats gruff*. San Diego, CA: Harcourt Brace Jovanovich.

Brown, R. (1981). *A dark, dark tale*. New York: Dial.

Byars, B. (1973). *The 18th emergency* (R. Grossman, Illus.). New York: Viking Press.

Carle, E. (1979). *The very hungry caterpillar*. Cleveland, OH: Collins.

Christopher, J. (1987). *The white mountains*. New York: Macmillan.

Cleary, B. (1983). *Dear, Mr. Henshaw* (P. O. Zelinsky, Illus.). New York: Morrow.

Clifton, L. (1980). *My friend Jacob* (T. DiGrazia, Illus.). New York: Dutton.

Coerr, E. (1977). *Sadako and the 1000 paper cranes* (R. Himler, Illus.). New York: Dell.

Crowther, R. (1977). *The amazing hide and seek alphabet book*. New York: Viking Press.

Fleischman, S. (1986). *The whipping boy* (P. Sis, Illus.). New York: Greenwillow.

Galdone, P. (1970). *The three little pigs*. Boston, MA: Houghton Mifflin.

Galdone, P. (1975). *The gingerbread boy*. New York: Clarion.

George, J. C. (1972). *Julie of the wolves* (J. Schoenherr, Illus.). New York: Harper & Row.

Hill, E. (1980). *Where's Spot?* New York: Putnam.

Hooks, W. H. (1989). *The three little pigs and the fox* (S. D. Schindler, Illus.). New York: Macmillan.

Hutchins, P. (1971). *Titch*. New York: Macmillan.

Hyman, T. (1974). *Snowwhite* (S. Jeffers, Illus.) (P. Heins, Trans.). Boston, MA: Little Brown.

Hyman, T. (1983). *Little red riding hood*. New York: Holiday.

Ike, J. H., & Zimmerman, B. (1982). *A Japanese fairy tale* (J. H. Ike, Illus.). London: Frederick Warne.

Innocenti, R. (1985). *Rose Blanche*. Mankato, MN: Creative Education.

Jacques, B. (1986). *Redwall*. New York: Philomel.

Jacques, B. (1988). *Mossflower*. New York: Philomel.

Jacques, B. (1990). *Mattimeo*. New York: Philomel.

Johnson, C. (1955). *Harold and the purple crayon*. New York: Harper & Row.

Kennedy, R. (1981). *Song of the horse* (M. Sewell, Illus.). New York: Dutton.

Kraus, R. (1970). *Whose mouse are you?* (J. Aruego, Illus.). New York: Collier.

Krauss, R. (1945). *The carrot seed*. New York: Harper & Row.

LeGuin, U. (1968). *A wizard of Earthsea* (R. Robbins, Illus.). Orleans, MA: Parnassus.

Lewis, C. S. (1950). *The lion, the witch and the wardrobe* (P. Baynes, Illus.). New York: Macmillan.

Lionni, L. (1964). *Tico and the golden wings*. New York: Pinwheel.

McDermott, G. (1975). *The stonecutter*. New York: Viking Press.

McKenna, N. D. (1986). *A Zulu family*. Minneapolis, MN: Lerner.

Naidoo, B. (1985). *Journey to Jo'Burg* (E. Velasquez, Illus.). New York: Lippincott.

O'Brien, R. (1971). *Mrs. Frisby and the rats of NIMH*. New York: Aladdin.

Paterson, K. (1977). *Bridge to Terabithia* (D. Diamond, Illus.). New York: Harper & Row.

Paulsen, G. (1985). *Dogsong*. New York: Bradbury Press.

Paulsen, G. (1987). *Hatchet*. New York: Bradbury Press.

Paulsen, G. (1988). *The island*. New York: Orchard Press.

Paulsen, G. (1989). *The winter room*. New York: Orchard Press.

Pienkowski, J. (1979). *Haunted house*. New York: Dutton.

Polacco, P. (1990). *Thundercake*. New York: Philomel.

Rey, H. (1941). *Curious George*. Boston, MA: Houghton Mifflin.

Rice, E. (1975). *New blue shoes*. New York: Macmillan.

Schwartz, D. M. (1985). *How much is a million?* (S. Kellogg, Illus.). New York: Lothrop, Lee, & Shepard.

Scieszka, J. (1989). *The true story of the 3 little pigs* (L. Smith, Illus.). New York: Viking Press.

Sendak, M. (1963). *Where the wild things are*. New York: Harper & Row.

Sendak, M. (1981). *Outside over there*. New York: Harper & Row.

Silverstein, S. (1974). *Where the sidewalk ends*. New York: Harper & Row.

Speare, E. (1983). *Sign of the beaver*. Boston, MA: Houghton Mifflin.

Steel, F. (1976). *Tattercoats* (D. Goode, Illus.). New York: Bradbury Press.

Steptoe, J. (1969). *Stevie*. New York: Harper & Row.

Taylor, M. (1987). *The friendship* (M. Ginsburg, Illus.). New York: Dial Books for Young Readers.

Turkle, B. (1969). *Thy friend, Obadiah*. New York: Viking Press.

Udry, J. (1961). *Let's be enemies* (M. Sendak, Illus.). New York: Scholastic.

Yolen, J. (1988). *The devil's arithmetic*. New York: Viking Press.

Yolen, J. (1977). *The seeing stick* (R. Charlip & D. Marsalis, Illus.). New York: Crowell.

Zemach, M. (1980). *The fisherman and his wife* (R. Jarell, Trans.). New York: Farrar Straus.

Zolotow, C. (1969). *The hating book* (B. Shector, Illus.). New York: Scholastic.

Index

Active thinkers, encouraging, 134–135
Allington, R., 138
Alova, S., 28
Amazing Hide and Seek Alphabet Book, The (Crowley), 73
Amidon, B., 143
Analysis stage, 24
Anderson, M., 17
Anderson, R., 13, 17, 18, 54, 68
Applebee, A., xii, 5–9, 24, 31, 37, 49, 52, 67, 68
Artwork, 30, 93–132
  children's illustrations of books, 95–96
  constructing meaning through, 97–132
  of fourth-grade students, 95–97, 123–132
  of kindergarten students, 98–114
  reading-aloud sessions and, 40–42
  response to picture book, 96–97
  of second-grade students, 114–121
Asch, F., 73
Avery, C., 164, 165

Baker, L., 6, 28, 61
Bang, M., 39, 61
Banta, M., 142
Barrett, T., 23
Baumann, J., 6, 23, 25, 26, 38
Berndt, E., 21
Berndt, T., 21
Bettelheim, B., 114
Bieger, G., 23
Biemiller, A., 12
Blachowicz, C., 4, 18, 19
Bleich, D., 18

Bloom's Taxonomy of Educational Objectives, xii, 154
Blume, J., 30
Book discussions, 138
Bransford, J., 94
Bridge, D., 23
Bridge to Terabithia (Paterson), 30, 161
Britton, J., 137
Brown, A., 25–27
Brown, M., 39
Brown, R., 73
Bruner, J., 70, 85, 86, 141, 158
Burke, C., 13, 41, 72, 95, 97

Cappa, D., 94
Caricatures, of characters, 161
Carle, E., 73, 83
Carrot Seed, The (Krauss), 7–8, 15, 39, 41, 44, 48, 55, 57, 58, 98–100, 102, 104
Cazden, C., 94
Central meaning, 3. *See also* Theme
Centration, 9
Cera, M., 23
Characters
  as active protagonists, 59–60
  awareness of motivation of, 49–51
  caricatures of, 161
  identification with, 87–89
Chessel, K., 97
Children's Minds (Donaldson), 33
Chomsky, C., 34
Christie, D., 26, 27
Christopher, J., 4–5
Clark, M., 135

Clay, M., 80
Clifton, L., 154, 158
Cochran-Smith, M., 6, 70, 71, 82
Cohen, D., 30, 134
Coles, P., 97
Collerson, J., 158
Comparison charts, 138
    folktales for, 169–172
    for *Rapunzel*, 150–151
    for *Three Little Pigs*, 139–141, 142
Comprehension
    interpretation of main idea and, 23–
        26
    listening to stories and, 134–135
    plot structure and story in, 22–23
    writing and, 158–159
Concepts, 5–10
    schema theory and, 16–20
Concrete operations stage, 7, 24, 38
Constructivism, in reading, 10–16
Context
    as building block of meaning, 17–20
    of children's illustrations, 95–96
    print settings in, 95
    response to picture books and, 96–97
    social situation of book-reading, 93–95
Convergent questioning, 29
Crowley, R., 73
Cullinan, B., 30, 135

Danner, F., 25, 26
Dark Dark Tale, A (Brown), 73
Dawn (Bang), 39, 41, 42, 44, 46, 52, 61–
        66, 128, 132
Day, J., 25
Decision trees, for first-grade students,
        159–161
DeFord, D., 11–12
Dempster, A., 142
Denburg, S., 94
Developmental Formulation of Response
        Categories, 52, 68
Devil's Arithmetic (Yolen), 167
Divergent questioning, 29–31
Dogsong (Paulsen), 164, 180–183
Donaldson, M., 33, 47, 50, 68
Drama, informal, 141–143
Drawing. *See* Artwork
Duckworth, E., 56
Dunn, B., 23–25

Durkin, D., 77, 135
Duvoisin, R., 35

Egocentrism, 3, 8–9
Eighth-grade students, responses to litera-
        ture by, 31
Eleventh-grade students, expectations of
        story structure and, 21
Empowerment, 165
Expectations, of readers, 18, 21, 54, 68

Fables, 34, 35–36
Fairy tales, 34, 35–36
Favat, A., 40, 61
Fear, 9
Fenwick, G., 94
Fifth-grade students, generation of
        themes by, 26–27
First-grade students
    character caricatures by, 161
    comparison charts and, 139–141, 142
    components of instruction for reading
        to, 136–137
    decision trees with, 159–161
    effect of reading on writing of, 12
    Fisherman and His Wife and, 146–148
    informal drama and, 141–143
    phonetic approach and, 10
    retelling of stories by, 20–22
    storytelling by, 20–22, 143–145
    Three Little Pigs and, 139–145, 165
    Thunder Cake and, 135–138
    Whipping Boy and, 159–161
Fish, S., 18
Fisherman and His Wife, The (Zemach),
        66, 132, 146–148
5-year-old children, xi
    negative responses of, to stories, 8–9,
        19–20
    retelling of stories by, 7–8
Flavell, J., 7
Fleischman, S., 160
Flood, J., 70, 92, 94
Folktales, 34, 35–36
    children's responses to, 60–67
    fourth-grade artwork about, 128–132
    kindergarten artwork about, 106–114
    for older students, 151
    rehashing plot of, 61–62
    relevant episodes in, 62–67

second-grade artwork about, 121–123
selection of age-appropriate, 39–41
for use with comparison charts, 169–
    172
Formal operations stage, 24
4-year-old children, 6, 33, 71–92. *See also*
    Kindergarten students
Fourth-grade students, 123–132, xii
    artwork of, 95–97, 123–132
    exposure of, to literature, 35
    folktales for, 128–132
    generation of themes by, 28–29, 30–31
    interpretation of main idea by, 24, 26
    Rapunzel and, 149–151
    realistic fiction for, 39, 41, 123–127
    responses to literature by, 31
    retelling of stories by, 20–22
    study of sense of theme of, 33, 35, 36–
        69
Freckle Juice (Blume), 30
Freeman, Y., 14, 19

Galda, L., 30
Galdone, P., 39, 139, 141, 142
Generalization, 24, 51–52, 68
Gingerbread Boy, The (Galdone), 9, 39,
    44, 45, 47–48, 51, 53, 106, 108–109
Glenn, C., 7, 21, 26, 70
Goldfield, B., 70
Goldilocks and the Three Bears, 76
Goode, D., 61
Goodman, K., 11, 14, 19
Goodman, Y., 11; 41, 72
Graves, D., 158

Halliday, M. K., 16, 19
Happy Birthday Moon (Asch), 73
Hardy, B., 3, 56
Harold and the Purple Crayon (Johnson)
    99, 100, 102
Harris, W., 94
Harste, J., 13, 95, 97
Harwood, K., 30
Hasan, R., 16
Hating Book, The (Zolotow), 39, 41, 44,
    47, 50, 51, 57, 60, 117
Haunted House (Pienkowski), 73–74, 76,
    86
Heath, S., 3, 94
Hepler, S., xiii, 1, 3, 73, 138

Hickman, J., 1, 3, 73, 139
Hildyard, A., 26
Hill, E., 73
Holland, K., 30, 33, 161
Hood, W., 11
Hooks, W., 97, 140, 142
How Much Is a Million? (Schwartz and
    Kellogg), 157–159
Huck, C., 1, 3, 34, 38, 50, 51, 73, 94, 97,
    139, 154
Huck Literature Inventory, 33, 34
    Revised, 34–36, 56, 61, 67, 76
Hung, S., 12
Hutchins, P., 6, 39–40, 58, 72, 74, 95
Hyman, T., 39

Ike, J., 39
Illustrations. *See* Artwork
Informal drama, with first-grade stu-
    dents, 141–143
Interactive-compensatory model, 12
Interpretation
    of main idea, 23–26
    in transactional approach, 15–16
Interviews
    asking the right questions in, 153–154
    with preschool students, 72–74
    See also Questions
Irwin, O. C., 34
Iser, W., 17

Jacques, B., 163, 173–178
Jacques, D., 139
Jaggar, A., 30
Japanese Fairy Tale, A (Ike), 39, 41, 44,
    46, 51, 52, 66, 128, 132
Jeffers, S., 61
Joels, R., 70
Johnson, M., 94
Johnson, N., 20, 21, 26, 50, 68, 70
Journey to Jo'Burg (Naidoo), 167

Kellogg, S., 157
Kelly's Creek (Smith), 155–156
Kiefer, B., 96–97, 98
Kindergarten students, 70–92
    age-specific books for, 39, 41, 73–74
    artwork of, 98–114
    attitudes toward books and reading,
        75–77

Kindergarten students, *continued*
  exposure of, to literature, 35
  folktales for, 39, 41, 106–114
  generation of themes by, 26–27, 78–89
  identification of theme by, 89–91
  negative responses of, to stories, 8–9,
    19–20
  realistic fiction for, 39, 41, 73–74, 98–
    106
  retelling of stories by, 7–8, 82–86
  studies of sense of theme of, 32–33, 36–
    69, 71–92, 98–114
Kohlberg, L., 50
Kraus, R., 74
Krauss, R., 39

Lawton, S., 25
LeGuin, U., 30
Lehr, S., 5, 6, 13, 21, 26, 30, 31, 33, 34,
    42, 67, 68, 70, 89, 94
Let's Be Enemies (Udry), 39, 41, 44, 50,
    51, 57, 60, 114, 117
Levin, J., 94
Lewis, C. S., 151–152
Liebling, C., 29–31
Lifelong readers, encouraging, 134–135
Lion, the Witch and the Wardrobe, The
    (Lewis), 151–152
Lionni, L., 32
Listening, 26. *See also* Reading aloud
Literature as Exploration (Rosenblatt), 9
Little Red Riding Hood, 9
Lukens, R., 2, 3

Main idea, 3, 23–26. *See also* Theme
Mal'tseva, I., 28
Mandler, J., 20, 21, 26, 50, 68, 70
Many, J., 31
Marshall, J., 140, 142
Matthew Effect, in reading, 12
Matthews, S., 23
McDermott, G., 39
Meaning
  building blocks of, 16–20
  child's concept of story and, 5–10
  construction of, through drawing and
    writing, 97–132
  in constructivist view and, 10–16
  context and, 17–20
  negotiation of, 58–59

structure of stories in building, 20–31
  See also Theme *and specific grade lev-
    els*
Memory. *See* Recall
Merton, R., 12
Meyer, B., 22, 26
Moralistic language, 52–53
Mossgown (Hooks), 97
Mother Goose rhymes, 34, 35
Motivation, awareness of character, 49–
    51
Mure, E., 1
Murphy, S., 14, 19
My Friend Jacob (Clifton), 154–156, 158–
    159

Nagy, W., 13
Naidoo, B., 167
Narration stage, 24
Negotiation, of meaning, 58–59
New Blue Shoes (Rice), 39, 41, 43–44,
    98, 99
Nicholas, D., 21
Ninio, A., 70, 85

O'Connell, E., 158, 159
Olson, D. R., 26
Osborn, J., 54, 68
Otto, W., 23

Paley, V., 6, 32, 33, 37, 47, 50, 68, 91
Paris, S., 6
Paterson, K., 30, 161
Paulsen, G., 164, 180–183
Pearson, D., 11, 65, 69, 92
Petunia (Duvoisin), 35
Phonetic approach, 10
Piaget, J., xii, 7, 9, 20, 21, 27, 37
Pichert, J., 18, 54, 68
Pienkowski, J., 74
Plot
  comprehension and, 22–23
  concrete themes based on, 45
  rehashing of folktale, 61–62
Poetry, 34, 35
Polacco, P., 135–136
Preoperational stage of development, 7,
    24
Print settings, 95
Purves-Rippere system, 24

Questions
  convergent, 29
  divergent, 29–31
  importance of asking the right, 153–
      154
  response journals and, 161–164
  See also Interviews

Rapunzel, 149–151
Reading
  constructivist view of, 10–16
  silent, 136
  as transaction, 13–16
  volume of, 12–13
  well-written texts in, 11–12, 23
  theme in. *See* Theme
Reading aloud
  components of instruction for, 136–137
  drawing after, 40–42
  lifelong reading and, 134–135
  listening and, 26
  social situation of, 93–95
Realistic fiction, 34
  active protagonists in, 59–60
  children's responses to, 54–60
  fourth-grade student artwork about,
      123–127
  kindergarten student artwork about,
      98–106
  negotiating meaning and, 58–59
  second-grade student artwork about,
      114–121
  selection of age-appropriate, 39–41,
      73–74
Recall, 6–7, 20–22
  generation of themes in, 26–29
  interpretation of main idea and, 23–26
  plot structure and story in, 22–23
  selectivity of, 5
Redwall (Jacques), 163, 173–178
Reports, written, 159
Response guides, 162–164, 173–183
  for *Dogsong* (Paulsen), 180–183
  for *Redwall* (Jacques), 173–178
  for *Sign of the Beaver* (Speare), 178–
      180
Response journals, 161–164
Revised Huck Literature Inventory
    (RHLI), 34–36, 56, 61, 67, 76
Rice, E., 39

Rohwer, W., 94
Rosenblatt, L., 4, 9, 13–15, 31, 46
Rothery, J., 158
Rovai, E., 12
Rumelhart, D., 16, 17, 20
Rylant, C., 39

Say It (Zolotow), 39, 41
Schallert, D., 94
Schema theory, 4, 16–20, 93
Schumacher, G., 26, 27
Schwartz, 157
Scieszka, J., 140, 151
Second-grade students, 114–123
  artwork of, 114–123
  exposure of, to literature, 35
  folktales for, 39, 41, 121–123
  generation of themes by, 26–27
  happy endings and, 5
  realistic fiction for, 39, 41, 114–121
  study of sense of theme of, 33, 35, 36–
      69
Seeing Stick, The (Yolen), 38
Semiotics, 96
Sendak, M., 114
Seventh-grade students, generation of
    themes by, 27–28
Shannon, P., 14, 19
Shifrin, Z., 54, 68
Shuy, R., 93
Siegel, M., 52, 68, 95–98
Sigman, M., 97
Sign of the Beaver (Speare), 163, 178–180
Silverstein, S., 35
Sixth-grade students
  expectations of story structure and, 21
  generation of themes by, 28–29
  interpretation of main idea by, 24, 25
  responses to literature by, 31
Smiley, S., 25, 26
Smirnov, A., 28, 29
Smith, D. B., 155
Smith, F., 11, 138
Snow, C., 70
Snow White (Hyman), 39, 41, 44, 45, 61,
    62, 122
Sostarich, J., 134
Speare, E., 163, 178–180
Spiro, R., 4, 17, 19, 54, 68
SSR (sustained silent reading), 136

Stanovich, K., 10, 12, 13
Steel, F., 39
Stein, N., 6, 7, 21, 26, 28, 61, 70
Steptoe, J., 39, 51, 40
Stevens, K., 54, 68
Stevie (Steptoe), 39–41, 44, 45, 51, 53, 65, 123–127
Stonecutter, The (McDermott), 39, 41, 42, 44, 46, 48, 53, 62–67, 128
Story grammar, 20, 21
Storytelling, by first-grade students, 143–145
Strickland, D., 30
Strykowski, B., 12
Summarizing, 24, 48–49
Swineherd, The (Zwerger), 5, 14, 39, 44, 46, 50, 52, 54, 61, 122
Symbolic representation, 7
Symbols
    linking pictorial and written, 96
    recognition of, 95

Tattercoats (Steel), 39, 41, 44, 45, 61, 62, 122
Taylor, B., 22, 23, 25
Taylor, D., 71, 91
Theme
    abstract statements of, 45–46
    books matched by, 41–46
    characteristics of child's developing sense of, 46–54
    in child's concept of story, 5–10
    of children vs. adults, 47–48
    concept of, 2–5
    concrete statements of, 43–45, 87
    exploration of, through art, 98–132
    generation of, 26–31, 78–89
    identification of, 89–91
    interpretation of, 23–26
    manipulation of, 22–23
    See also Meaning *and specific grade levels*
Third-grade students, xiii, 33
    expectations of story structure and, 21
    How Much Is a Million? and, 157–159
    interpretation of main idea by, 25
    My Friend Jacob and, 154–156
    quality of text and recall by, 29–30
    response journals and, 161–164
    writing by, 158–159

Thompson, D., 33
Thorndyke, P., 22, 23, 26
Three Bears, The, 1-2, 3, 9, 14, 17, 75, 76
Three Billy Goats Gruff, The (Brown), 39, 41, 44, 45, 47–48, 50–51, 106, 108
Three Little Pigs, The, 9, 106, 108–109, 139–145, 165
Three Little Pigs, The (Galdone), 39, 41, 44, 45, 51, 139, 141, 142
Three Little Pigs, The (Hooks), 140, 142
Three Little Pigs, The (Marshall), 140, 142
3-year-old children, xi, 3
Thunder Cake (Polacco), 135–138
Thy Friend, Obadiah (Turkle), 39, 41, 44, 45, 51, 53, 123, 125, 127
Tico and the Golden Wings (Lionni), 32–33
Tierney, R., 11, 23, 25
Titch (Hutchins), 6–8, 39, 41, 43–44, 45, 47–51, 53, 55, 57–59, 74–76, 78–82, 85–92, 95, 98–100, 104
Townsend, M., 25
Trabasso, T., 21
Transaction, reading as, 13–16
True Story of the Three Little Pigs, The (Scieszka), 140–141, 142, 151, 165
Tsai, S., 12
Tucker, N., 40
Turkle, B., 39

Udry, J., 39

Very Hungry Caterpillar, The (Carle), 73–75, 82–86, 88
Vygotsky, L., 6

Walberg, H., 12
Wally's Stories (Paley), 32–33
Warren, R. E., 17
Waters, H., 22, 26
Wells, G., xi, 33, 133–134, 164
Whalen-Levitt, P., 82
Whaley, J., 21, 22, 26, 70
When I was Young in the Mountains (Rylant), 39
Where's Spot? (Hill), 73

Where the Sidewalk Ends (Silverstein),
    35
Where the Wild Things Are (Sendak), 114
Whipping Boy, The (Fleischman), 159–
    161
White, D., 6, 56, 78, 97
White Mountains, The (Christopher), 4–
    5, 23
Whose Mouse are You? (Kraus), 74
Wizard of Earthsea (LeGuin), 30
Woodward, V., 13, 95, 97

Writing, 38
    construction of meaning through, 97–
        132
    effect of reading on, 12
    to extend understanding, 158-159

Yendovitskayz, T., 26
Yolen, J., 38, 167

Zolotow, C., 39
Zwerger, L., 5, 39, 54, 61

About the Author

Susan Lehr is an associate professor of reading and children's literature at Skidmore College, Saratoga Springs, New York. She received her Ph.D. at Ohio State University. She has published more than 20 articles and book chapters, writes the Professional Books column for NCTE's *The Bulletin*, a journal of the Children's Literature Assembly. She has taught in the elementary classroom and her research continues to be conducted in classroom contexts. She chaired the committee responsible for developing The Charlotte Award for the New York State Reading Association, first awarded in 1990 to Jane Yolen, Jane Dyer, Joanna Cole, Bruce Degen, and David Macaulay. Her commitment to the use of quality children's literature in the elementary classroom as well as furthering our understanding of response to literature are areas in which she will continue to research.